The New Iraq

The New Iraq

Rebuilding the Country
for Its People,
the Middle East,
and the World

JOSEPH BRAUDE

BASIC
BOOKS

A Member of The Perseus Books Group

Designed by Bookcomp, Inc.

Library of Congress Cataloging-in-Publication Data

Braude, Joseph.
  The new Iraq : rebuilding the country for its people, the Middle East,
and the world / Joseph Braude.
     p. cm.
  Includes bibliographical references and index.
  ISBN 0-465-00788-0
  1. Iraq—History—1991– I. Title.

DS79.5.B73 2003
956.7044—dc21   2003001657

      03 04 05 / 10 9 8 7 6 5 4 3

To
Daniel Pearl, of Blessed Memory
My Beloved Family
All Iraqis Everywhere

Contents

IV TRUTH

Prologue

A Time to Engage

I happen to be doing a cultural center for the place where civilization was invented—that is Iraq. Before [Baghdad] was destroyed it was a beautiful circular city. . . . Now what is left of the city has struck oil and they have immense sums of money. They can bring back the city of Harun al Rashid today. They are not likely to do it because a lot of Western architects are in there already building skyscrapers. . . . So it seems to me vital over there to try and make them see how foolish it is to join that Western procession.

—FRANK LLOYD WRIGHT, 1957[1]

The cultured people of Iraq have been inspired through their hard work to serve as the heirs to Iraq's grand civilization. They are striving to perpetuate that civilization's potential and accomplishments through renewed participation in . . . an era of deep flourishing, stability, and civilization building in the new Iraq.

—NAJI SABRI, 1988[2]

During the current American campaign for regime change in Iraq, it is the people of Iraq, the vast majority of whom have paid a terrible price in poverty, malnutrition and illness as a result of 10 years of sanctions, who have dropped out of sight.

—EDWARD SAID, 2002[3]

This book is not about Saddam Hussein.

Media attention to Iraq in the past decade has largely focused on the strongman who has run the country for 23 years. The effect has been to play into the personality cult Saddam has constructed around himself, reinforced by American political leaders, who have turned his name into a household word. To be sure,

Saddam looms large in the landscape of Iraq. He has ruled his people with a brutal police state and launched military ventures against most of his neighbors, in one case with the support of the United States. But there is an Iraq beyond Saddam Hussein, an Iraq that preceded him and that will remain long after he has been relegated to the margins of history. This book is about that Iraq—the Iraq that endures and today stands in a state of flux.

This book is also about you. You may not know it yet, but an essential Iraq, with its roots stretching back to the dawn of human civilization, has indelibly shaped your social reality. It bequeathed the bridges you drive on and the tunnels you drive through, the principles of law you adhere to, and many of the religious values and traditions that underlie your beliefs about God. At the dawn of the twenty-first century, much of the world is on a course to reengage Iraq's economy, societies, and peoples, and the transformation will be mutual.

The pioneering American architect Frank Lloyd Wright understood this. From childhood, he was fascinated by Iraq, even titling one chapter of his autobiography "Aladdin," after the well-known story from *1,001 Nights*.[4] He felt compelled to give back to Iraq for the great civilizational legacy it had provided him, and was honored late in life to be commissioned by the Iraqi government to build the country's first opera house. (Iraq's government changed hands a few months later in the first of several republican coups, and Wright never carried out the project.) Wright felt that his design should weave organically into what remained of the city's historic landscape, unlike the Western skyscrapers cropping up along the Tigris River in Baghdad. His design evoked memories of ancient Tower of Babel-esque ziggurats and medieval palaces from the city's Islamic period—a cutting-edge cultural center for modern Iraq grounded in the country's past.

Wright's impulse was not merely that of an Orientalist romanticizing the exotic Middle East. It is shared today by Iraqis themselves, many of whom frequently evoke their country's claim to have been the "cradle of civilization" while imagining that they are constructing "The New Iraq." Naji Sabri, a journalist and editor who like many Iraqi media men in recent years would go on to a career in politics, evoked both as editor of the

1988 Iraqi government yearbook. As his country emerged from a bruising eight-year war with Iran, Sabri described his fellow citizens as "heirs to Iraq's grand civilization" who were building "The New Iraq" (*al-Iraq al-Jadid*). Sabri enjoyed a meteoric career in the years that followed, and went on to serve as Saddam's foreign minister during the tense 2003 showdown over Iraq's disarmament.

But his vision of a new Iraq ran into a brick wall just three years after he penned those words, as Saddam's invasion of Kuwait turned the international community against the country and led to a sanctions regime that would cripple Iraq for over a decade. The new Iraq that emerged was a stunted society, beset as before by Saddam's iron rule but now additionally by the crippling impact of sanctions. And yet, we know very little about what this new Iraq looks like. As Edward Said has noted, Americans are profoundly unaware of the society that has persisted beneath Saddam's vast shadow. Iraq's social and political institutions, economy and industries, and arts and media have in some ways transformed but in other ways manifested resilient continuities from a more distant past. All these institutions, such as they are, form the starting point for Iraq's reconstruction and the basis for its reintegration in the global economy.

This book aims to cast a light on that elusive world.

Understanding the Iraq of today is a necessary first step in planning to reengage the country in an effort at state-building. The project will consume formidable resources from many countries, beginning with the United States, and in this sense it concerns all of us, not just Middle East experts and policy makers. The atomization of Western societies raises concerns that only a few "Iraq specialists" will be on hand to assist foreign diplomats and soldiers as they engage Iraq in the years ahead. This book aims to help broaden the cast of characters, by attracting professionals, entrepreneurs, a wide variety of nongovernmental organizations (NGOs), and artists to engage their Iraqi counterparts.

A country that has been denied access to the global economic resources that exploded in the 1990s will welcome entrepreneurs of all kinds—not just major industries, from oil and gas to telecommunications and IT to heavy industries and agriculture to movies and music, but small and medium-size companies as well. The country has the resources to fund aspects of its own renewal, as well as a receptive international donor community favorably disposed to offering grants and loans, including familiar granteurs like the World Bank and the International Monetary Fund (IMF) as well as affluent members of Iraq's diaspora communities. Although the country is geographically remote, its likely commitment to joining the World Trade Organization means that familiar business practices and a process of economic liberalization will be very much in play. Baghdad is also poised to reclaim its traditional role as a hub of Middle Eastern commerce. The country may soon begin exporting manufactured goods to the region as well as serve as a gateway to other emerging markets, from vast neighboring consumer markets like Iran to more distant places east of the Oxus.

NGO workers new to the scene will find Iraq a stimulating environment in which to work. Because its political system is in a state of transformation, new initiatives will be more likely to have an impact here than elsewhere in the region, where systems are stratified and frustrating for idealists. Iraq presents a rare opportunity to take part in a work in progress.

Does rebuilding Iraq stand to transform the Middle East? Yes. A viable Iraqi economy will reinvigorate intellectual activity throughout the Arab world by vastly increasing the demand market for Arabic-language books. (Iraqis are considered to be among the region's most voracious readers, and their recent impoverishment has been devastating to publishers.) A viable Iraqi economy will alter the region's business ecosystem by resuscitating a battered but formidable consumer market. It will also facilitate the creation of a new industrial base that exports to other countries, as well as the revival of a commercial base of historic importance to its neighbors. Creating a space for the emergence of a religious establishment that fosters ecumenicism will promote ideals of coexistence and tolerance in countries that badly need them. By transforming its military from a force that threatens neighboring states into a twenty-first-century army of nation-building and defense, Iraq can provide a model that strengthens security in the region and reduces bloated military budgets that divert public funds from investment in education, health, and industry. A viable Arab government spending less on defense and more on its people will raise expectations among societies vis-à-vis their governments region-wide.

This book is a bridge between many audiences. Policy makers need a panoramic view of the social, political, and economic challenges Iraq faces; this book is intended to advance that discussion. For readers in the Arab world, this book reflects one Iraqi American's point of view on new directions for bridging cultural and commercial gaps. For the private sector, this book lays out the major business opportunities Iraq offers, as well as challenges unique to the Iraqi environment. Moreover, the book will demonstrate that effective engagement will mean giving back to Iraqi society at every step of business development. For NGOs, the book explains some of the country's many needs, from educational to legal systems, to labor organizing and the development of robust nonprofit social services. Social activists dare not sit out the new Iraq. Their insight and concerns are the best check on the excesses of business and government, and the only hope for the human crises of health, sanitation, and hunger that profit motive and geopolitical calculations alone will be disinclined to meet.

Finally, this book is addressed to the people of Iraq, from its 4 million-strong diaspora communities in Iran, Jordan, Europe, and North America to the 24 million Iraqis who inhabit the country today. It offers Iraqis on the inside a sense of how the world around them—from which they have been cut off for over a decade—can be an enormous source of support in the rebuilding of their country. And Iraqis who are now pondering whether to return from years, even decades, of exile will learn from this book how important a role they have to play.

The first section, "Memory," examines how Iraqis remember a 5,500-year past, a history that looms large in Iraqi popular culture and the way Iraqis perceive themselves. They remember a land constantly struggling to make order out of chaos, from Sumerians taming the floodwaters on Mesopotamia's fertile plains to crackdowns on dissidents and deviants by Assyrian emperors, Baghdadi caliphs, and the man this book is not about. The fact that today Iraq is the most ethnically diverse country in the Arab world reflects the extent to which its historical transformations have stemmed in part from conflict and contact with newcomers—invaders, itinerant preachers, traders, and refugees—who each in their own way left their mark and became integrated into Iraq's diverse social fabric. Recognizing these historical memories challenges us to make the present encounter with Iraq as constructive, respectful, and innovative as possible.

The next section of the book delves into the condition of "Power"—the process of transition and transformation from the rule of a single party to a pluralism of voices, and legacies of Islamic spiritual and political leadership and their potential impact on the country's future. The section also includes a plan to reengineer Iraq's army to an institution of nation-building and defense.

"Power" is followed by a section on "Money," which details the state of Iraq's physical infrastructure, industries, and human and natural resources and imagines their reintegration in an economy of reconstruction. The final section, "Truth," explains the state of the country's enterprises of criticism and reflection—film and entertainment, journalism and media—as well as its legal and educational systems. The section demonstrates that Iraqis will encounter truth when they reclaim the freedom to build their own memories, a freedom that has in some ways been hijacked in recent years.

The difficult questions hanging over the new Iraq will induce a healthy skepticism about prospects for a renaissance in the short term. What happens when Europeans, Saudis, Americans, and Iranians rub shoulders and compete for influence in a wobbly emerging state remains to be seen. Some well-meaning outsiders who wish to engage the country may find themselves aping the imperialists of the past two centuries, to say nothing of those who bluntly set out to do so. Whether the United States and its allies have the focus and commitment to the long haul that Iraq's reconstruction requires is unclear. Nor would an imposing Western presence in the country serve to reduce anti-Western sentiments that now pervade the region. Can Iraq really be rebuilt, and can that rebuilding be profitable? The country has been devastated, is filled with ethnic and religious tension, has seen its middle and professional classes disintegrate, and has come to know the rule of fear and brutality as commonplace.

Nevertheless, memories Iraqis share about their history offer reasons to be optimistic. There is a recurring theme in the country's storytelling traditions of joy emerging after periods of the darkest trauma. Iraq's ancient literature more than two thousand years before the Common Era chronicled the aftermath of a great flood that engulfed the world, only to leave a better world in its wake. A prolific tenth-century Baghdadi judge wrote volumes of stories united by a theme he called "Relief after Distress" (*al-Faraj Ba'd al-Shidda*), near-tragedies overcome at the last moment by a happy ending. Do these stories offer hope for the future out of the past, and if they do, how will the story of the new Iraq be written?

In a great Iraqi tradition, the answer begins with a story.

The Islamic Abbasid Empire, which ruled from Baghdad and its environs for five centuries beginning in the year 750, had at its helm a political leader known as the caliph. The ninth-century caliph Abu Ja'far al-Mansur once said, "There are four people I need by my side. They are the pillars of my state, as indispensable as the four legs of a couch: the chief judge, the chief of police, the chief of taxation, and the postmaster who keeps tabs on the first three and writes me reliable reports about them."[5]

Communicating over great stretches of desert has always been a challenge in the Middle East. The call of Islam made its way across the Arabian Peninsula 1,400 years ago through the movement of bedouin armies and via messages carried on camels' backs and in pigeons' beaks. These days, business consultants like me reach the Gulf on Saudi jumbo jets to advise the region's telecommunications operators on overhaul strategies for their mobile phone networks and Internet ventures. But the challenges of effective information flow remain, hampered by security concerns and cultures of secrecy.

The Abbasid caliph al-Mansur required a steady stream of information on politics and economics from every corner of his empire and beyond. He routed his information network through one central address: the Round City, Baghdad. He maintained his authority through military might and political tact, but relied at all times on a formidable intelligence service with eyes and ears spanning the empire, under the leadership of one man called the postmaster.

Beginning in the eighth century C.E., the Abbasid postmaster built and maintained a vast physical infrastructure exclusively for the collection and dissemination of political and economic intelligence on every province the caliph ruled, a land mass spanning from Tunisia to Pakistan on the political map of today. The postmaster had a fleet of horses, camels, mules, and carrier pigeons to carry written messages. Roads connected remote locales across deserts and rugged mountains, and featured resting places every few miles for horses and riders. A man could gallop at full speed through the harshest terrain from one rest area and exchange his exhausted steed for a fresh one at the next. As a graduate student poring over medieval Arabic manuscripts and maps in Princeton's Firestone Library, I used to imagine that this extraordinary network viewed from space might have looked something like a diagram of the World Wide Web, with nodes and ports linking distant places.

Lugging prose across great distances was only half the postmaster's task. He had to find the information. To do so, he recruited spies and informants in every town and province, fluent in local languages and familiar with the cultural challenges of extracting information in different places. They monitored the political situation around the empire, watching for underground movements and popular revolts. They gathered economic data like the price changes of basic commodities. And they reported on the workings of the government itself, keeping abreast of corruption and infighting. Spies sat in cafés and eavesdropped on conversations, walked the fields and counted rows of corn, debriefed dervishes and prostitutes, and closely monitored the court gossip. Each day a spy wrote up his findings and dispatched the report with a rider to Baghdad. The postmaster read and weighed every word. Then, each night, he walked to the round palace of Baghdad for an appointment with the caliph. In a short meeting, he told the ruler everything he needed to know about the day that had passed.[6]

Of course, the system has been out of commission for a very long time. But the graduate student-turned-entrepreneur finds continuities in the most unlikely places. So on a weekend off during a consulting visit to Saudi Arabia, I rented a Lincoln Town Car and drove 750 km north out of Riyadh, down a narrow desert road to the Iraqi border. I marveled at the fact that a road spanning this distance a thousand years ago served as an information lifeline for the Abbasid postmaster. It was the main artery for riders connecting Baghdad to one of the empire's major listening posts, the holy city of Mecca, where Muslims came from far and wide to pray and chat.

As the bright lights of Riyadh faded away, the black tar stood in stark contrast to the parched desert land around it. The temperature gradually rose; the land was baking. The names of the occasional bedouin encampments on signposts along the way testified to their isolation. I passed "Mother of Skulls" (*Um al-Jamajim*) and stopped for gas and a snack in a village called "Dig of the Depths" (*Hafr al-Batin*). The road still continued on to Baghdad, but these days, it is cut off by a military garrison at the border of modern Iraq. The last town on the Saudi side is called Rafha.

Rafha is a physical representation of the area's recent history. When the United States launched its ground invasion of Iraq in 1991, the tanks rolled out of Rafha. A few weeks later, when Saddam's army was on the run and President Bush encouraged Iraqis to overthrow their leader, Rafha was poised to become a vital meeting point between these two modern nations. But the uprising was crushed, Saddam's regime survived, and many Iraqis fled. Some crossed over the eastern border into Iran. Others went north into Turkey. Thirty-three thousand of them took the old road south toward Mecca, and ended up here in Rafha.

The Saudis had never absorbed refugees before. The military built a camp about 20 miles outside of town and surrounded it with barbed wire. Iraqis were forced to stay inside the 6 km enclosure. Over the next few years, most of the camp's residents were resettled in other countries. By the time I reached Rafha, eight hours after leaving Riyadh and 11 years after the end of the 1991 war, 5,000 Iraqis remained.

The Rafha camp is an extraordinary sociocultural creation, a group of urban Iraqis living in the middle of the desert, the only fully constituted Iraqi Arab community outside of Saddam's grip. Although there are 4 million Iraqis living all over the world, with the largest concentrations in Jordan and Iran, all these people are working either to find a place for themselves within the culture of their host country or to move on to someplace else. For the refugees of Rafha, for better and worse, the only full-time job is to be Iraqi.

The Rafha camp offers a vision of what an Iraqi community looks like without Saddam Hussein. Its residents do not enjoy complete freedom, but they are free of the brutality of Saddam's regime. In this sense, Rafha is a petri dish of the new Iraq. It does not look like the television images of a refugee camp. The streets are clean. People generally dress well. On the afternoon I arrived, the town was bustling. Children headed home from school. Vendors sold food and spices in an open-air market. Next to one vendor, a man in his 70s played the Oud—the fretless, 13-string precursor of the European lute, strummed with a feather. He sang a mournful, drawn out Iraqi *mawwal*—a poem set to music without rhythm.

And in that petri dish, to my surprise, I met the person who inspired me to write this book.

"Dhiya" is a short man in his early 60s with high cheekbones and a full head of gray hair. We met by chance at the outdoor market. He took an interest in me, he later said, because few outsiders ever make their way into this camp. (A friendly Saudi officer was kind enough to let me in.) When they do they are usually looking for something, and Dhiya usually knows where to find it. That is more or less what keeps him occupied most of the time.

When the Saudi military found themselves running a camp of thousands of urbane Iraqis—most of whom had played some role in the violent uprising that immediately followed the 1991 war—they needed to build a makeshift intelligence system to keep tabs on suspicious persons and rein in political activity by the refugees. They broke the camp into 13 sections and appointed 13 information chiefs from among the refugees, each to report on goings-on within his section. These chiefs won a comfortable living but bore the responsibility of stifling constituents by informing on them. Dhiya was one of the 13, but as I later learned, he used his remarkable talent and experience at manipulating information informally to carve out an even more important position.

He invited me to his home for lunch. His wife and son served us *chai Iraqi,* a reddish-brown tea poured into elegant small teacups. The dark, cool room was a pleasant contrast to the sweltering heat outside. We sat on the floor, on an old, thick Iraqi carpet. The cushions supporting us looked newer, perhaps a recent acquisition from a shopping mall in Riyadh.

"In Basra where I'm from," Dhiya said, "I was trained as an engineer but worked for many years as a high school math and science teacher. This, plus my government responsibilities." Like roughly 20 percent of adult Iraqi males, Dhiya was a source for Saddam's intelligence apparatus. He reported on the political sympathies of his students' parents, information he divined through youngsters' offhand remarks over the course of a school year.

"I resented this work," he said. "I didn't want to turn in my neighbors for opposing Saddam. So I did what I could to protect people. If a child told me his father attended a meeting, I overlooked it. But sometimes, people were too obvious. If I didn't turn some people in, my superiors would hear about it from someone else and start asking questions about me. I had to make choices and, of course, I informed on a number of people."[7]

When the uprising came, Dhiya supported the rebels by offering advice based on his extensive network of acquaintances. He knew who the likely government informants were, as well as who might help work out the logistics of the uprising. He identified key army personnel willing to defect and help raid weapons silos to arm the insurgents.

Saddam managed to put down the uprising with brute force over a few days. Dhiya joined thousands of other survivors fleeing to Rafha.

"Why did the Saudis choose you to be one of the camp's information chiefs?" I asked.

"Many of us in the camp were in demand in the early years, right after the war," he said. "American intelligence, the Saudis, the British came in here looking for information about what's going on inside Iraq. I knew so many people in Basra that I had answers to many of their questions. And that's how the Saudis got to know me and I won their confidence, if not their trust. Of course, eventually my information about Iraq became old. I ceased to be an expert on Iraq and came to be an expert on this camp."

Conditions in the camp had been harsh. Fresh fruits and vegetables rarely arrived. The tents in which residents lived did little to shield them from the harsh desert climate. They were given school textbooks that were either outdated or politically loaded, advocating the Sunni Wahhabi ideology that dominates Saudi Arabia to an overwhelmingly secular Shi'i refugee community. Some refugees began plotting to escape, while others organized night attacks on guards. The Saudis needed to know about planned disturbances. Dhiya was among their chief sources.

"How do you find out about things like this before they happen, when everybody knows you're an informant?" I asked.

"I use information the way a businessman uses money," he said. "It strengthens my relationship with all the families in my camp district and beyond. And believe it or not, I even use information to strengthen our hand with the Saudis."

Within the refugee community, Dhiya has functioned as a go-between and mediator to resolve rifts between families and even match up Iraqi singles for marriage. This expenditure of emotional capital, he explained, also kept flowing the sort of brass tacks information his Saudi employers required.

"At a certain point," he said, "I realized that we could leverage our usefulness to ask for things from the military. Some of the Saudis' other sources began to pool their information with me." If, for example, a foreign intelligence agent entered the camp looking for information, the request would come to Dhiya's attention. He maintained a list of demands for the

Saudis, and negotiated to exchange information for material improvements. He takes credit for winning a Saudi commitment to replace some of the ramshackle tents with cement houses. The Rafha refugees were also granted occasional shopping trips into town and sometimes to Riyadh. The quality of food in the camp improved. Dhiya had even procured the Oud for the musician I had heard playing earlier. Through his shrewd management of knowledge in his community, Dhiya helped transform the woebegone refugee camp into something resembling a modest Iraqi town. At least, that is how he explains it.

Of course, Dhiya's career as information chief had necessitated numerous moral sacrifices. To maintain his position, he had to support the Saudis' quest for recalcitrants to lock up and question. Despite his charm and cheerful demeanor, no one—neither his Saudi bosses nor the community he serves—entirely trusts him. "I try to explain to people what I am doing and why," he said. "Sometimes they see that. But most of all, I try to remind them that it is a much better situation than if we were in Iraq." Such is the precarious role of the postmaster of Rafha.

If Dhiya lived in a functioning state instead of a refugee camp, his skills at manipulating information in the private sector could be channeled to ruthless competition and revenue growth. How long before Dhiya lands his dream job? How long before Baghdad starts hiring?

My drive to the edge of Iraq was also a journey to a border of ideas and influence that Americans have been barred from crossing for years. On the other side lived millions of Iraqis under a regime that restricted information flow as brutally as it blocked people flow—a refugee camp the size of a country. Their isolation, together with the adversity they have faced for decades, has preserved and reinforced elements of a traditional culture with attitudes and skill sets that other societies in the region would be hard pressed to match.

I imagined Dhiya making the trip back with me, 750 km south to the Saudi capital of Riyadh. In a city where American ideas mesh uneasily with bedouin and Islamic sensibilities and a hodgepodge of ethnic groups are left to duke it out in the private sector, Dhiya would find a unique niche for himself. A Western CEO might be happy to hire him as the company's knowledge manager. But it would also be tempting to push him across that northern border, deep into the interior of Iraq.

Iraq's renewal rests on the energy and imagination of its people. Newcomers from nearby and far away will introduce themselves to the Iraqi interior. In the public sector, foreign powers will try to foster a smooth transition to a benign new government. In the private sector, entrepreneurs and investors will work to rebuild the country's infrastructure and industries. But Iraqis will process and react to these new advances from their own unique perspective, informed by recent decades of hardship and distant centuries of greatness. The recipe for a prosperous new Iraq will marry the external demands of the global marketplace with an internal reappropriation of the unique attributes of Iraqi civilization.

For 500 years, the postmaster of Baghdad helped caliphs control their empire by bringing word of rebels, corrupt governors, and economic crises. Without aspiring to build a new landed empire, Iraqis like Dhiya can use their superior information management skills to resurrect the Abbasid post in a form that resolves intelligence gaps in the Arab corporate world and reestablishes Baghdad as a regional center of commerce and information.

The path to the new Iraq is not without its roadblocks. For a few years, the skills Dhiya says he used to improve Rafha may be directly applicable in a transitional Iraq struggling to establish order and security without a brutal central government. But once Iraqis stabilize and liberate their own capacities and infrastructure, they will turn outward. Then the modern standard-bearers of the world's oldest civilization will use their extraordinary talents as entrepreneurs and facilitators to shine light on knowledge and information gaps all over the Middle East and beyond.

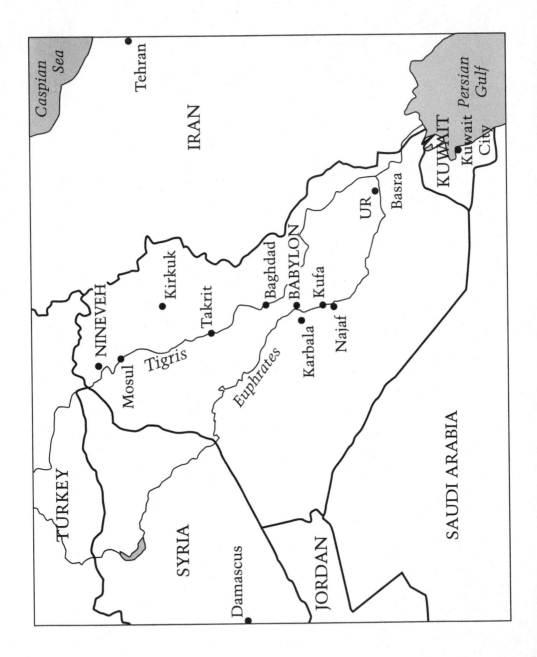

Part 1
MEMORY

One

The Legacy of Ancient Iraq

In the movie *Memento*, a man with a neurological problem that prevents him from forming new memories finds constructive ways to manipulate the little he does remember of his distant past. He leads a rough and violent life, but manages to build a myth that sustains him with a sense of purpose. Modern nation-states blazed out of war and imperialism sometimes do the same thing: although a historic morass of intrigue and violence might lie behind the birth of a nation, ideologues instead weave together a clean national history designed to instill patriotism in young people. Witness Iraq, a country formed by British politicians after World War I out of disparate provinces of the former Ottoman Empire. Though the new country as such had no political history of its own, the lands it comprised used to host some of the most innovative empires and civilizations of human history. The narration of an essential Iraq through time has been an ongoing project for Iraqi political ideologues. It has involved the selection of certain memories and the omission of others. Rulers in twentieth-century Iraq justified militaristic policies by emphasizing warrior icons from the country's past. Proponents of humanism in Iraq have meanwhile drawn inspiration from the great thinkers of local medieval and ancient history. The engineering of memory is poised to begin again as a new Iraqi government takes shape and its people attempt to renarrate their past.

An Iraqi diplomat I met in Iran a few years back provides a case in point. Hearing him recount Iraqi history was as interesting for what he chose to include as it was for what he left out.

Abu Abdullah was a classmate of mine at a Persian-language institute in Tehran in the summer of 1998. He worked for the Iraqi embassy as its cultural attaché, the job description for which presumably stipulated that he should miss no opportunity to expound on Iraq's heritage to all who cared to listen. But as diplomatic affairs buffs know, the post of "cultural attaché" is oftentimes reserved for the embassy spymaster, who only dabbles in cultural dialogue while actually eavesdropping on his host country's leadership, particularly in the case of an Iraqi diplomat dispatched to Iran in the 1990s, not 10 years after a decade of war between the two neighboring countries.

Abu Abdullah lived in an apartment on an unassuming street, apart from the compound where most of the diplomats lived. He invited me over one evening and began asking questions immediately. Where were the other Americans from? Why were they here? Where were they living? Did we know of any Iraqi students in the dorms, and were they politically active?

I was part of a cultural exchange program with a dozen or so other Americans, but most of our other classmates were European embassy personnel. As cultural attaché he collected information on the program; as a proud Iraqi, it would seem, he could not help but bristle at the détente that seemed to be blossoming between Iran and the world amid the continued international isolation of Iraq. On the table between us was an Iraqi dish called *pacheh*, made of boiled sheep's head and feet.

"You must know that Iraq is the cradle of civilization," he said. "The wheel, the technology of writing, the world's great religions, they began there. When I say Babylon, what do you think of?" Before I had a chance to answer, he said, "You must come to Iraq. It is paradise. It is where the Garden of Eden was."[1]

He might be right. The Tigris and Euphrates, the two rivers that form the heart of modern Iraq and nursed the earliest civilizations, are according to legend two of the four rivers that flowed through Eden. Furthermore, many scholars in Iraq and elsewhere contend that the country's history has been in part determined by its geographical position as "the valley between two rivers" (*Wadi 'l-Rafidayn*).[2] That term is similar in meaning to the Greek word "Mesopotamia," which until the early twentieth century was the name most frequently used to denote the lands of Iraq. Over millennia, Mesopotamia has swung like a pendulum between the glory of conquest and the shame of colonization by foreigners. When a strong enough ruler emerged in the "valley," it became the center of a great empire. Without strong central government, the river valley's plains were easily overrun by invaders. But how does present-day Iraq fit into this historic paradigm, and how did Eden become the pariah of Saddam's regime?

Abu Abdullah was just a foot soldier in the legions of the Ba'th party, whose ideology was quintessentially modern, a fusion of socialism and Arab nationalism. But he nonetheless saw himself as heir to an ancient history stretching from the Sumerian pioneers of the fourth millennium B.C.E. to the present day. Therein lies a paradox of Iraqi political memory: while constituted of sharp contrasts and rupturous deviations, with empires that have come and gone, civilizations that have vanished, and an ever-changing landscape of religions, ethnicities, and cultures, it also represents a continuous history remembered in the consciousness of Iraqis today as a tale of glory and achievement. This history includes stories of outsiders who shape the landscape even as they are shaped by it. As a result, there is an exchange between settler and land that creates a hybrid political culture upon which each successive conquest builds. Each ruler of "Iraq" has brought to the country a modernizing ideology of his own. From the Sumerian attempt to tame the floodplains, to Hammurabi's bid to rein in human nature with his code of laws, to Assyria's effort to unify all under its powerful empire, to Abraham's and Muhammad's attempts to stitch together all mankind under one God, most of the major political trends of ancient history found expression in the lands of Iraq. Many Iraqis, including Abu Abdullah, narrate these memories as a continuum to which Iraq and much of modern civilization is heir.

Abu Abdullah's first point deserves some clarification, however. Though the lands of Iraq are the cradle of civilization, the Sumerians who first nursed this cradle might easily have hailed from somewhere else. Little is known about the origins of the

Sumerians. Their language remains anomalous, failing to fit into any of the language families known to modern linguists. We do not know what brought them to Iraq, but we do know a great deal about what they did once they got there.[3]

Today's southern Iraq, which formed the heart of the Sumerian Empire, is at once a likely and an unlikely land for the birthplace of civilization. The land is flat. With a good pair of binoculars, one could peer through the occasional palm groves and long patches of reeds and marshlands and see clear across the country. Throughout history, the plains of Mesopotamia proved highly conducive to civilization and warfare. Cities could be easily built and more easily sacked by marauders descending on the lowlands from surrounding hill-country.

The Tigris and Euphrates rivers that nourish these plains also threaten all living things in their path. Though more conducive to life than the desert that surrounds them, the marshy floodplains have managed to disrupt even the best-laid plans. The rivers carry vast quantities of silt, which when deposited along the river create banks higher than the plains below. This means that the slightest crack in the river banks can create anything from a tiny stream to a deluge large enough to leave an entire city six feet underwater.

This threatening environment forced man to organize. The rivers imposed the need for irrigation projects, which in turn required cooperation and compulsion. And with that, some historians say, civilization was born. To construct, finance, and maintain the irrigation system, ancient Sumerians needed a civilizational apparatus that allowed for joint labor efforts, taxation, and record-keeping. And with those functional aspects of civilization inevitably came the loftier elements, religion, art, and culture more generally.[4] In Mesopotamia, politics and culture emerge as twins in the cradle of civilization.

Abu Abdullah took pride in pointing out that Sumer is a civilization of firsts. Samuel Noah Kramer, the noted scholar of ancient Sumer, proclaims the same in his book, *History Begins at Sumer*. His book counts 27 firsts, but a more recent edition grows the list to 39. Among them are the first schools, the first law code, the first proverbs, and more frivolous firsts such as the first case of "kissing-up" to a teacher and the first tax cut in history.[5]

Sumer was also the first civilization to go to war. Much like the later Greek civilization, Sumerian civilization included a loose federation of city-states that often jockeyed with one another for positions of influence, power, and wealth. Traditionally, the city of Kish led the Sumerian federation, serving as its cultural and religious center. But around the year 3000 B.C.E., the city of Erech found itself on the ascent.[6] Its increased wealth brought with it increased stature, and the increased envy of Kish. Agga, the ruler of Kish, laid siege to Erech and demanded the submission of Erech and its ruler Gilgamesh. In response, Gilgamesh convened what has been called the first bicameral congress in history. The people of Erech met, divided between a council of elders and a "lower house" composed of the city's arms-bearing men. Gilgamesh requested their advice: should we submit or should we fight? The elders, cautious and perhaps weary of war, voted to submit. Gilgamesh vetoed their proposal and went before the lower house. There he posed the question again: should we submit or should we fight? "Do not submit to the house of Kish, let us smite it with weapons."[7] How the story ends we do not know. The sands of time have worn away the record of the event, which in any case we have only as written centuries later. But in Sumer, amid the swamps of the floodplains and the heat of the desert, we find the first meeting of a legislature, a cross between protodemocracy and traditional tribal council, all preserved for us through the Sumerian invention of writing. That unlikely place for the birth of civilization has produced an equally unlikely phenomenon: quasi-democratic deliberation in the face of military assault.

The Sumerian city-states, having bequeathed so many "firsts" to civilization, soon gave way to the first empire. Not surprisingly, that empire was founded by an outsider named Sargon, an Akkadian in the Sumerian city of Kish, who was a gardener in the royal court. He lived in Kish but spoke Akkadian, a Semitic language akin to Arabic and Hebrew. He was a cultural outsider and a social climber in a world defined by religious and social hierarchy. He managed to build the world's first empire through a clever mix of military expansion, cultural co-option, and practical know-how.

As gardener in the royal court of Kish, Sargon was no mere landscape artist.[8] The very task that drove the development of Sumerian civilization—the need to tame the flood-prone rivers through an irrigation system—fell into his hands. As such he commanded thousands of men and wielded a great deal of power. Sargon led a successful palace revolt, became king of Kish, and soon ruled an empire.

But the Iraqi landscape has a tendency to shape those who trample it as much as they shape it. Or so many Iraqis remember. As an Arabic proverb puts it, "The desert is the cradle of the Arab, and Iraq is his grave."[9] To rule his sprawling empire successfully, Sargon had to embrace Sumerian culture. He married off his daughter the priestess to the Sumerian moon-god Nanna, a clever twist on the ancient custom of using marriage as a tool of geopolitics.[10] Sargon the Akkadian quickly out-"Sumerianed" the Sumerians, assimilating into their urban culture and transforming himself from a threatening outsider to a consummate insider. The wily outsider proved to be the boldest and most adept leader. He ruled for 52 years; his son and grandson in turn succeeded him.

But the Akkadian Empire was short-lived. City-states of Mesopotamia were loath to cede their independence to the Akkadian ruler and his descendants. Revolts sprang up throughout the region, and the empire disintegrated. Despite its brevity, Akkadian rule coincided with a key moment of cultural flowering. Ironically, Sumerian art and literature thrived under Akkadian rule, a catalyst that proved an unexpected driving force behind the empire's cultural and political growth and renewal.

The fall of Sargon's empire leads to another moment in history that launched an effusive bout of Iraqi pride in Abu Abdullah: the rise of Babylonia. The city-state of Babylon had during the period of Sargon's rule risen to greater prominence, and was by the second millennium B.C.E. the dominant city in Mesopotamia, becoming the capital city of one of the most widely remembered empires in history. Babylon is known to readers of the Bible as a den of iniquity. It is the site of the construction of the Tower of Babel, humankind's first attempt at self-deification and an eternal reminder of the danger of overambition and pride. Babylon is also the stand-in for Rome as the model of decadence in the New Testament,[11] and home to the lush if overindulgent hanging gardens, one of the seven wonders of the ancient world. It is the empire to which the ruler Nebuchadnezzar transferred many of the Jews from Judea after he destroyed the Temple of Solomon in Jerusalem in 586 B.C.E.—the mass transfer that created the oldest continuous diaspora community in Jewish history.

Iraqis today remember Babylon as home to one of history's first law codes, an early attempt by humankind to replace the capricious rule of man with the just rule of law. It is also the birthplace of Abraham, who rejected the idol-worship of his father's home and opened humanity's eyes to the oneness of God. All the while, Babylon is the ancient world's center of trade and commerce. Bringing brightly colored cloths from the east, pottery from the west, fine wool from the north, and pearls from the south, traders populated Babylon's marketplace, making it one of the first "globalized" cities in the ancient world.

Babylon is a land of contradictions, beginning with the complex personality of its first and greatest ruler, Hammurabi. Known to all as the author of Hammurabi's code, this skilled ruler transformed Babylon from a modest city-state into the center of a great empire through a paradoxical mix of his impersonal legal code and his towering personality cult and uncompromising micromanagement. Small wonder that Saddam Hussein appropriated Hammurabi's image in a variety of contexts. He named one Iraqi army brigade after Hammurabi, and another after Nebuchadnezzar.

Hammurabi's law code opens with a description of how the gods had appointed him, "Hammurabi, the reverent god-fearing prince, to make justice appear in the land, to destroy the evil and the wicked so the strong might not oppress the weak . . . to give light to the land . . . set forth truth and justice throughout the lands and prospered the people."[12] Despite his highly formalized legal code, Hammurabi was anything but dispensable. Hammurabi was a workaholic. Modern-day management consultants

would be horrified by Hammurabi's inability—or unwillingness—to delegate responsibility. He met personally with all vis-
iting heads of state, managed the canal and irrigation projects,
inspected his troops and dictated their movements, and settled
minute questions of administrative justice and land distribution.[13] Hammurabi's rule was an odd mix of impersonal justice
and personality cult, something not unfamiliar in modern times.
It is perhaps no surprise that shortly after his reign, Abraham
would emerge from the Babylonian city of Ur, using a similar
mix of personality and legal justice to spread his message of
monotheism, a message that would in the course of the next two
millennia spread throughout the Near East and the entire Western world, transforming Iraq and the West in the process.

Hammurabi was also known in his time for his bold-faced
military strategies. It was not unheard of for Hammurabi to
divert an entire river to crush an enemy.[14] But his brutality
proved no match for the Assyrians that rose to power in the
region in the tenth century B.C.E. Based in the northern city of
Nineveh, the Assyrians reinvented the empire through a mix-
ture of bureaucratic obsessiveness and military brutality.

Perhaps more than at any other moment in history, it was
through this historical mirror that Abu Abdullah saw himself
and the Ba'th party's rule in modern Iraq. For Abu Abdullah, the
Assyrians are a model of the strong Iraqi, the state-builders and
powerful rulers not afraid to flex some muscle to maintain control. Assyria was the first totalitarian state, using the fetish of
violence and the power of bureaucracy to rule people through
terror rather than acculturation and accommodation. Assyrians
practiced population transfer to minimize internal rebellions
and invented the internal passport to keep tabs on the movement of people across the empire.[15] In their victory art, they
showed the vanquished enemy trampled underneath passing
chariots and the horses lined above the carcasses of the dead, to
celebrate killing and to send a powerful warning to potential
enemies and rebels.[16] This imagery resurfaced again in the twentieth century, but with a tragically ironic twist. In 1933, when
Colonel Bakr Sidqi directed a massacre in northern Iraq of Assyrian Christians, a Syriac-speaking people who claim descent from

the ancient Assyrians, there was so much popular enthusiasm that in the city of Mosul, triumphal arches were set up, "decorated with melons stained with blood and daggers stuck into them."[17] With the Assyrian massacre of 1933, it seems, history and memory came full circle.

To modern readers, this odd mix of raw power and calculated administration seems all too common. But the ancients may have been less cynical. The biblical tale of Jonah captures well the paradox of Assyria's violence and administrative achievements. Jonah is commanded by God to go to the Assyrian capital of Nineveh and warn the people to repent or be destroyed by the hand of God. Jonah refuses the mission, fearing that God will too readily forgive the sins of the Assyrians. After a brief interlude in the belly of a giant fish, Jonah reluctantly delivers his message to the people of Nineveh, who promptly repent and are spared God's wrath.

Translated into secular terms, the sin and repentance of the Assyrians is simply a turn from military destruction to administrative construction. Assyria was a corrupt society, indulgent and abusive of power. But the Assyrians readily repented, embracing the other side of the imperial coin—a well-organized and sophisticated bureaucracy. The Assyrians achieved, in ancient form, what Kafka later portrayed in his modern, anxiety-ridden literature. Assyria was not the first empire in Iraq, but of all its fellow ancient empires it can be said to have the most modern students.

The fall of Nineveh in 612 and the subsequent fall of the Babylonian Empire in 539 B.C.E. brought to Iraq a new outside influence. Cyrus, ruler of the Persian Empire, invaded Mesopotamia in 539 on his way to constructing the largest empire the world had ever seen.

With tea and figs on the table, the Iraqi diplomat Abu Abdullah and I finally reached this late date in history. As he deftly moved from Babylonian rule to the conquest of Alexander, I stopped him, politely reminding him that he had accidentally skipped Persian rule in Iraq. But it was no accident, much as it was no accident that the history of Iraq on the official Iraqi government Web site made no mention of Persian rule.[18] A brutal decade-long war in the 1980s that left nearly a million dead can cause a great deal of historical amnesia. As if bristling at my reminder, Abu Abdullah paused, collected his thoughts, and conceded that Cyrus, praised in the Bible for allowing the Jews to rebuild their temple in Jerusalem, was a benevolent ruler, a much-needed rebuilder, and a pleasant alternative to the heavy-handed rule of the Assyrians.

Cyrus ruled by granting autonomy and religious freedom to the Jews, Zoroastrians, and countless other religious and cultic groups of the ancient Near East. He built an empire that adopted a posture of tolerance in the face of a complex ethnic and religious environment that since the dawn of time had been plagued by warfare and conflict. Babylonians and Assyrians had played a zero-sum game of imperial politics; one state's gain was another's loss. But Cyrus ruled through preserving the cultural autonomy of his subject peoples whereas Sargon had ruled through cultural co-optation and Assyria through terror and forced assimilation. The new Iraq might be well served by the resurrection of the memory of Cyrus, a realist and an idealist rolled into one.

Nearly two centuries later, the Persian conquest from the east gave way to a new conquest from the west. In 331 B.C.E., Alexander and his armies seized the city of Babylon, reaching a new milestone in the first Western imperialist venture into Iraq. Alexander was determined to return Babylon to its former glory, perhaps even to transform it into the capital of a world empire that he was unable to maintain. The residents of Babylon were pleased to have this seemingly benevolent ruler return Babylon to its much deserved place at the center of the civilized world. Alexander just needed to complete one rite of passage. For centuries, at the beginning of each new year, the ruler of Babylon would play the central role in the Akitu festival. The Babylonians believed that the performance of this ancient rite by the king was necessary in order to defeat the forces of sterility and chaos, both real and supernatural, which annually threatened the extinction of society.[19] Alexander failed to participate in this festival and a local played the role of king instead.[20] Alexander later discovered his cultural faux pas, but the damage had been done. The conqueror had shown himself to be an outsider with a cultural tin ear.

With the death of Alexander came the division of his mighty empire. Iraq fell into the realm of the Seleucid Empire. The Greek rulers built a new capital, Seleuceia-on-Tigris, a few miles away from Babylon. The new city used the ruins of ancient Babylon to construct a metropolis whose population quickly grew to 500,000, a melting pot of Babylonians, Greeks, and dozens of ethnic and religious peoples from across the Near East.[21] Babylon became a ghost town. Resentment against Greek rule increased. As the Seleucids turned Babylon into a Greek polis, the local population began pushing back, launching a revolt in 168 aimed at reestablishing Babylonian rule in Babylon.[22] The revolt failed, but soon thereafter so did the Seleucid Empire.

The Seleucid Empire collapsed, eroded by a combination of internal dissent, advancing forces of Rome in the west, and the encroachment of the Parthians from the east. After the Seleucid fall, the Parthians quickly filled the vacuum, once again absorbing the lands of Iraq into a Persian Empire. Under the Parthians and later the Sassanians, Iraq reached a peak in its religious and ethnic diversity. Near Eastern religions gave way to a mix of syncretic Hellenistic beliefs and oriental mystery cults. Zoroastrianism, Manichaeanism, and Mazdaism all grew in popularity, each enjoying general tolerance while enduring sporadic moments of suppression and persecution. The Jewish community of Iraq thrived, establishing academies that served as the capital and trendsetter of the global Jewish diaspora for centuries to come, and producing the Talmud, which shapes Jewish identity to this day.[23] Christianity also emerged, beginning in Palestine and spreading across the Near East. The land from which Abraham went forth now reaped the fruits of his labor as Christian monotheism came to dominate the religious landscape. On the eve of the Islamic conquest of Iraq, the area's inhabitants had been exposed to the concept of monotheism and the Bible that bore its message and were therefore somewhat prepared for the new message of Islam that bedouin armies would bring.

By the time antiquity drew to a close, nearly every major empire, religion, and ethnic group had traveled through the streets and markets of the lands of Iraq en route to ephemeral greatness, each leaving a unique legacy along the way. Imperialism came to Iraq long before the ideology received its name in modern times. And along with it came all the peoples and beliefs that constitute the mosaic that is Iraq to this day. Legacies of ancient history can still be seen in the faces of Iraq's peoples, in the ruined clay and bricks of ancient cities' archeological ruins, and in the words and deeds of leaders who boldly harken back to the glory of "historic Iraq." Iraqis today remember their country as the birthplace of writing and pedagogy, democracy and terror, monotheism and the rule of law, warfare and organized violence. Those who set out to revise memory in the new Iraq have a legacy of symbols and models to choose from as variegated as human history. The legacy of ancient Iraq is the legacy of civilization itself.

A Genealogy of the Prophet Mohammad

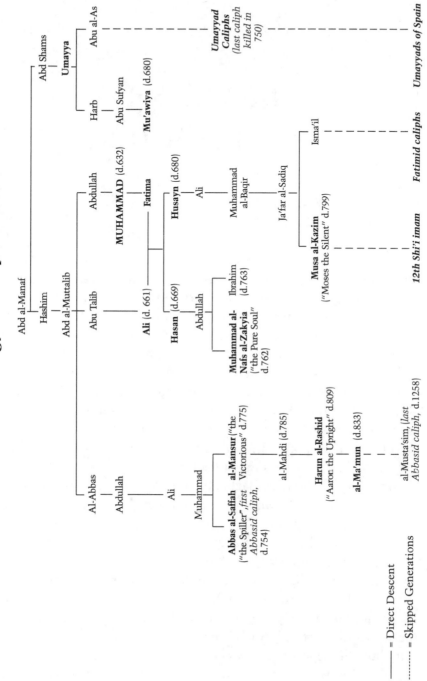

——— = Direct Descent
-------- = Skipped Generations

Two

The Struggle for Islamic Iraq

⁓

Iraqi memories of an ancient past conjure up images of ziggurats and hanging gardens, ancient courts and primordial battles. Yet the archeological ruins that testify to these memories are scattered in parts of modern Iraq where few people live. Medieval memories, by contrast, have a few physical vestiges in the Islamic shrines that dot the cityscapes of the country's biggest cities. If you stand on the A'imma Bridge over the Tigris River facing south on a Friday afternoon, Baghdad sprawls out before you. Throngs of people traverse the bridge en route to the weekly Jum'ah prayer in two of the city's main mosques. Children, jostled in the commuter crowd, grip their grandparents' hands. To your left, in Baghdad's old Adhamiya neighborhood, Sunnis flock to the tomb of revered eighth-century jurist Abu Hanifa. To your right, Shi'is shuffle toward the old Kazimiya quarter, named after the ornate domed mausoleum of Musa Kazim, a contemporary of Abu Hanifa and the seventh Shi'i imam. Their tombs separated by the Tigris, these legendary figures mark the flow of people traffic in twenty-first-century Baghdad, just as they helped shape intellectual life in Baghdad's earliest days, articulating competing ideas about Islam from a city built in 758 as the new center of the Muslim world.

Baghdad was the medieval capital of something many times larger than modern Iraq. The ancient meaning of the word "Iraq" is not entirely clear. It may mean, "sunny land," "coastline," or "flat plains," among other possibilities. The word came to be used in the Islamic period by geographers to denote a stretch of land, although the land still had no political identity of its own. "Arab Iraq" (al-Iraq al-Arabi) referred to a region in the southwest of the modern country that came to be associated with Arabic-speaking inhabitants from the Arabo-Syrian desert tableland stretching toward the Tigris and the Euphrates. "Persian Iraq" (al-Iraq al-Ajami) meant the lands to the northeast approaching the mountain chains of western Asia and what is now Iran. Though these two areas did not form a state, their most populous medieval city, Baghdad, was capital of the Islamic Abbasid Empire, one of the largest landed empires in the history of the world, which survived for centuries.[1]

Abu Hanifa, the man interred in the Sunni shrine who died just eight years after Baghdad's birth, fathered one of four schools of Sunni religious law and also served the empire as official brick measurer during the construction of the city. Musa Kazim, buried in the Shi'i shrine across the river, died a few decades later while imprisoned by Baghdad's legendary ruler, Harun al-Rashid. Though his name al-Kazim ("the Restrained" or "the Silent") does not sound like the name of a revolutionary, Kazim nonetheless represented a dissident strand of Islam that continually challenged the authority of the Abbasid Empire. Premodern historians contend that Kazim was poisoned in prison.[2]

It was in Baghdad that both contributed to the legal codification of Islam's Sunni and Shi'i traditions respectively. And it was in the medieval lands of Iraq that a cloak-and-dagger struggle for the soul and reins of Islamic politics played out in ways that would define the contours of modern Iraq over a millennium later.

Against the backdrop of epic religious and political drama, Islamic Iraq emerged as a torchbearer of civilization as the "dark ages" descended on Europe. Sparks extinguished in the West, most notably ancient Greek philosophy, were preserved and elaborated in Iraq, parallel to the codification of Muslim political, religious, and intellectual culture. Memories of the sensibilities forged during this period are very much alive today in Iraq, from the shrines in Baghdad, to Sunni/Shi'i tensions, to the question of who has the right to succeed Saddam Hussein in power.

The House of Ali

A two-hour drive south of Baghdad lies Najaf, possibly the city with the most graves per capita in the world.[3] The city proper is surrounded by a semicircle of sepulchers, known as the City of the Dead. You can drive through its streets, stopping off inside the *Wadi 'l-Salam"* ("Valley of Peace") Cemetery to explore the variety of tombs. Small brick and cement structures are interspersed with larger mosque-shrines, many displaying photographs of the dead, who stare back at the living. Nearly all are Shi'is.

Shi'is from around the world bury their dead in Najaf, part of a mystical tradition of ending life as a "neighbor" of Imam Ali, the cousin and son-in-law of the prophet Muhammad whose adoration pervades Shi'i memory and identity and whose ornate domed shrine stands in the center of Najaf. But the politics of Saddam's Iraq have prevented many Shi'i dissidents from returning to bury their relatives. Thousands of Shi'is are interred temporarily outside Iraq (many in Syria and Iran), waiting to be reburied in Najaf.[4]

The profound significance of Ali to Muslims stems from the importance of his cousin, the prophet Muhammad, who pioneered the venture of Islam a few hundred miles south of Iraq in the Arabian Peninsula. Many of the ancient empires that colonized Iraq had limited influence on Arabia. The vast empire of Alexander, for example, snaked around the Arabian Peninsula, stretching through Palestine into Egypt. In the seventh century, the peninsula hosted diverse tribes, pagan traditions, and Jewish and Christian proselytizers. Muhammad invoked the monotheistic call of Islam to rally together Arabia's tribes in an army of conquest. Over successive decades, Muslim armies expanded their rule beyond Arabia: west through Egypt and into North

Africa, northwest through Jerusalem into Syria, and north through Iraq into Iran. In 637, four years after Muhammad's death, his general Khalid bin al-Walid (nicknamed the "Sword of Islam") led a campaign along the Euphrates River challenging Persian rule in Iraq. The next year, at a decisive battle near Najaf at the village of Qadisiyya, powerful Persian forces—equipped with 33 elephants bearing archers—engaged Arab commando units, who sliced the elephants' stomachs and pierced their eyes with spears. When the dust cleared four days later, the Arabs had routed the Persians and found Iraq theirs for the taking.[5]

The debate over who should succeed Muhammad in the leadership of the Muslim *umma* (nation) still defines the split between Shi'is and Sunnis. The latter hold that the heir to Muhammad's rule should be chosen by consensus, citing a tradition of the prophet Muhammad: "My people will not unite on an error." The followers of Ali, by contrast, view the rightful political leadership of the Islamic project as a dynasty, with rulers culled from the direct line of Muhammad, via Ali and Fatima's progeny.

Ali, the prophet's cousin, married the Prophet's daughter Fatima, and their line of offspring came to be seen by many Muslims as the Prophet's anointed successors. Indeed, Muhammad's death in 632 touched off a heated battle for who would be *khalifat rasul allah*—the successor to the Prophet, or caliph. Muhammad's father-in-law Abu Bakr became caliph, but Ali's faction—the *Shi'at Ali* ("party of Ali"), or Shi'a—held firm in the belief that Ali was the rightful successor.

Abu Bakr's successor, the caliph Umar, instructed his followers from Arabia to build military bases in the new Iraqi garrison towns of Basra and Kufa. But Umar was assassinated seven years later, and the caliph Uthman met a similar fate 12 years later. So in 656, Ali at last assumed the mantle of caliph—during a time of civil war, as Uthman's clan challenged his election. Ali moved the seat of Islamic power out of Arabia to Kufa, the new southern Iraqi garrison town, from which he tried to consolidate his rule. The opposition moved to Basra.

Mu'awiya, the Muslim governor of Damascus and a relative of Uthman, refused to accept Ali's rule as caliph. The rivals met for battle outside Damascus. Mu'awiya's forces appeared with copies of the Qur'an attached to their lances, a signal that Ali should settle the dispute through arbitration. Ali agreed, and promptly lost out. Returning to Kufa, he faced opposition from a faction of disaffected followers, disappointed that he had agreed to arbitration. One morning in 661, as Ali came out to wake the people of Kufa for dawn prayers, one of the disaffected suddenly lunged at Ali and struck him in the head with a poison-tipped sword.[6]

For Shi'is, Ali's murder marks the beginning of an enduring tradition of mourning. Ali's followers were fractured, and the imam's martyrdom would soon be repeated by his sons. In the meantime, Mu'awiya declared himself caliph, shifting the caliphate to Damascus and building his Umayyad Empire (named after the patriarch Umayya, the brother of Muhammad's great-grandfather), on the backbone of the Byzantine Empire's bureaucracy.[7]

The lands of Iraq came under the rule of an Umayyad governor named Hajjaj, who massacred thousands in an attempt to subdue the restive native population. Hajjaj's iron-fisted rule looms large in the Iraqi imagination, even with Saddam's nationalist Ba'th party, which used Hajjaj to reinforce the idea of the state's absolute power. Up through 2002, all Iraqi ninth graders had to memorize Hajjaj's bloody admonition: "I see heads that are ripe, and I am the one to pluck them. . . . O people of Iraq, people of discord and deceit . . . I will bind you like a bundle of twigs. I will beat you like stray camels."[8]

Nineteen years after the martyrdom of Ali, Shi'ism remained a powerful force throughout the empire and especially in Iraq. When Mu'awiya decided to appoint his son caliph, he realized that Ali's sons Hasan and Husayn (who were also Muhammad's grandsons) posed a threat, and promptly had Hasan poisoned. In 680, opposition forces in Kufa urged Husayn to return to his father's base and establish himself as the new Muslim leader. Husayn set off from Arabia to Kufa with a small entourage of 72 family members and assistants, but his party was intercepted by Umayyad forces at the city of Karbala.

What happened next is another enshrined memory in Shi'i identity. Husayn and his band of 72 decided not to surrender, and even dug a ditch and filled it with fire to cut off their own retreat. But the group was overwhelmed, and as Husayn stood before them with a sword in one hand and the Qu'ran in the other, each man fell under a hail of arrows.[9] The Imam Husayn shrine in Karbala marks this spot, where Husayn is buried. Every year, Shi'i Muslims commemorate these martyrs by observing 10 days of rituals during which they wear black, refrain from celebrations, and perform the Aza, a passion play that reenacts Husayn's murder. "Oh, if only we had been with you," is Shi'is' sad refrain, expressing a collective guilt over not having been present to assist Husayn. Some take to the streets dressed in pure white and beat themselves until their clothes become stained dark crimson with blood.

In contemporary Iraq, the memory of Ali's lineage has continued to affect politics and political symbols. When Saddam seized power, he banned the Aza, forcing Shi'is to perform the passion play secretly in private homes.[10] His secret police took up position inside the courtyards of shrines, confiscating ancient family crypts. At the same time, he plastered posters throughout Shi'i strongholds like the southern Iraqi cities of Karbala and Najaf depicting his own direct descent from Ali as a sign of legitimacy. And in the mid-1980s, during the war with the Shi'i regime in Iran, Saddam unveiled two new missiles: al-Husayn and al-Abbas.

Karbala and Najaf are today nearly entirely Shi'i. Following the first American-Iraqi war in March 1991, the cities were centers of an aborted uprising against Saddam. The ruler assigned the liberation of Karbala to his son-in-law, Husayn Kamil. After killing insurgents holed up inside the Imam Husayn shrine, Kamil is said to have stood outside and declared: "I am Husayn and you are Husayn—see who is winning!"

A Sunni friend from Baghdad recalls the first and only time he visited Karbala: "In junior high school, we took an educational class trip to Karbala to see the shrine of Husayn. I was shocked. All the women were covered, and the vibe was somber. Here was a city one hour from Baghdad, but it was another world."[11]

The House of Abbas

Muhammad's family tree has other branches besides the house of Ali, which also play a leading role in the early centuries of the formation of an Islamic polity. For example, as noted earlier, the Umayyads descend from Umayya, the brother of Muhammad's great-grandfather. As their empire swelled in the late seventh century, the Umayyads came to be regarded by later partisan historians as a self-interested clan ruling over other Arab tribes, non-Arab Muslims, and non-Muslims. Discontent with the regime became widespread, but several attempted uprisings by followers of Ali, including one by Husayn's grandson, were quickly repressed. It would take a deliberate, multigenerational underground movement led by a different branch of Muhammad's family—descended from the Prophet's uncle Abbas (see family tree on page 15)—to unite disparate disaffected groups and overthrow Umayyad rule.

The Abbasids—as the revolutionaries came to be called—planned and extended their revolutionary network in the Persian flank of the Umayyad Empire. Here, Arabs on the outs with the empire allied with Persian aristocrats. Mystery surrounded the Abbasid underground from its earliest days, as activists colluded emerging Shi'i ideologies by describing an enigmatic leader from Muhammad's family waiting to emerge. Grassroots organizing across the empire generated dozens of local Abbasid cells, waiting for the signal to take up arms.[12]

The clandestine movement enjoyed an apocalyptic aura. A document believed to have been written within the decades that followed the Abbasid revolution detailing its secret networks of activists was rediscovered in the twentieth century, in the archives of the University of Baghdad. Titled *The Story of Abbas and His Progeny*, it is a secret history of the Abbasid underground. Among other memorable lines from the political rhetoric of the period as set down in the book in the following: "Surely your *Sunna* (tradition) is the *Sunna* of the Children of Israel," it states, explaining how the Abbasids organized their underground into 12 cells like the 12 tribes of Israel wandering in the desert and metaphorically linking the mysterious Abbasid leader to the messianic line of David.[13]

One of the architects of the underground was Abu Muslim, a slave from Iran who converted to Islam while living in Kufa, Ali's old base and still a hotbed of dissident activity. Abu Muslim was discovered in an Umayyad prison by the leader of an Abbasid cell and liberated to help the burgeoning movement. A humble saddler by trade, Abu Muslim became a shrewd visionary.[14] He established black as the color of the future revolution, as rebels dyed their shirts and clubs black, and waited for the appearance of black banners from the east to herald the start of the uprising.

On June 13, 747, the banners appeared and revolution in the name of the Prophet's unnamed scion quickly spread across Persia and into Iraq. By 750, the Umayyads were defeated, and the victorious Abbasids gathered in Kufa to proclaim their caliph, Abu 'l-Abbas, a descendant not of Ali but his uncle Abbas—a move that would ensure the continuation of Shi'i discontent. The first Abassid caliph soon earned the nickname "al-Saffah," the spiller (of blood), as he hunted down members of the Umayyad family.

Now at the helm of a massive empire, the Abbasids had to turn their coalition of opposition factions into a ruling force. Abu Muslim helped solidify internal security, assisting the new caliph al-Mansur ("the Guided") in quelling a revolt in Damascus. But the initiator of revolution is sometimes among the first to go after the revolution succeeds. Mansur, fearing the Abbasids' chief conspirator might now be their greatest threat, had Abu Muslim assassinated and began an aggressive plan to consolidate his rule in a new capital.

Passing through the plain in central Iraq between the Tigris and Euphrates in search of the ideal spot to ground his imperial center, Mansur was inspired by local Christian monks, who revealed that their holy books predicted a great king would settle in the spot.[15] Mansur ordered a round city to be constructed, and named it Baghdad, from Persian words meaning "Gift of

God." Mansur's vision for a magnificent new capital launched a surge of construction and creativity. Strategically located at the nerve center of the empire's commercial and political traffic, Baghdad was built to celebrate the splendor and detachment of the caliph. Mansur gathered 100,000 workers and artisans from across the empire in July 758. By 765, Mansur took up residence in the city, surrounded by 145-foot thick walls, guard towers, and four grand gates, all centered around the 160-foot-high Golden Gate Palace, capped by a green dome.

The construction of Baghdad from scratch was the largest public works project of its day, and generated ripples across the empire. Suburbs soon sprung up around the Round City. Within decades, Baghdad was a 25-square-mile metropolis, with a population approaching half a million—dwarfing Constantinople and constituting the largest city in the world outside China. A bureaucracy at the caliph's disposal included a judiciary, chancery, tax-collection agency, and army treasury.

As the Abbasid Empire consolidated and expanded, Shi'is came to realize that hopes for restoring the line of Ali as caliph would not be fulfilled under Abbasid rule. Mansur faced challenges from numerous Shi'i insurgents, notably Ali's great-grandsons Ibrahim and Muhammad al-Nafs al-Zakiya ("Muhammad the Pure Soul"). Histories of the Abbasid Empire include stories of intrigue—the caliph chasing rebels from one town to another across the empire. Sitting in Baghdad, Mansur relied on reports from dispersed informants relayed to him through the *barid*, the post and intelligence service. Mansur sent out instructions to capture and kill Shi'i rebels via horseback and carrier pigeons.

But Mansur's empire was filled with secret Shi'i loyalists, who frequently intercepted his messages and alerted Ibrahim and Muhammad in advance. Mansur countered with a grassroots network of messengers and spies, who posed as dervishes and preachers and solicited information from local denizens of the empire's towns and outposts. Eventually, Muhammad emerged from hiding to lead a failed revolt in Medina, dying in battle with Mansur's forces in 762.

Memories of the caliph's pervasive intelligence apparatus assumed mythic proportions. The ninth-century historian Tabari records the legend of Mansur's special mirror that showed where rebels were hiding, something akin to Western myths of a crystal ball. The mirror came from God, according to Tabari, and it had passed from Adam to Abraham to David and eventually to Mansur. It enabled him to differentiate good from evil and friend from enemy.[16]

While repeated Shi'i revolutionary movements in the empire's heartlands did not manage to unseat the Abbasids, far-flung co-revolutionaries met with better success when deployed to the empire's fringes. Abu Abdullah al-Da'i, a thread inspector from one of the markets in Basra, was sent to a mountain eyrie near modern Tunisia in 910 to lead a revolution among the Berber tribes of North Africa. The culmination of 120 years of Shi'i evangelizing among Berber chieftains, Abu Abdullah's mission galvanized a new army that vanquished the Abbasid satellite state in Tunisia and eventually became an empire that swept across North Africa into Egypt. Conquering vast territory, the Berber forces claimed descent from Ali's family and called themselves Fatimids, after Ali's wife Fatima. They built the city of Cairo as the seat for their own caliphate. The tenth century, regarded in hindsight by historians as a "century of Shi'ism," was marked by a cold war between the caliphate in Baghdad and the rival caliphate of Cairo.

This revolt marked one of the last premodern victories of the caliphal form of state-building, in which a charismatic leader preaching a universal religious message unites fractious groups to overthrow the current regime and launch a campaign of territorial expansion. The model had been pioneered successfully in Arabia under Muhammad, generated the Abbasid revolution in 750 that endured until 1258, and spawned the Fatimid revolution in Berber North Africa. (State-building of this sort would not reappear until Muhammad ibn Abd al-Wahhab, mentor of a strident circle of Arabian Sunnis who came to be known as Wahhabis, united many of Arabia's tribes in the nineteenth century, which led to the birth of the modern Kingdom of Saudi Arabia.)

These tales of espionage and political intrigue remain vivid in the minds of Muslims around the world. In Iraq in particular, many of the sectarian differences of today are informed by the political intrigue of yesterday.

A Light in Dark Ages

Sunni clerics in the Arab Middle East today tend to recall the Abbasid period with nostalgia. The caliph Harun al-Rashid ("Aaron the Rightly-Guided"), who ruled Baghdad for two decades during a high point of Abbasid political authority in the late eighth and early ninth centuries, is among the legends of modern Arab Muslim memory. Fascination with Harun extends beyond the Arab world as well. When Charlemagne sent emissaries to Baghdad, Harun sent back an elephant to Paris as a gift to the French king.[17] Tales of Rashid in the *1,001 Nights* charmed Europe and to this day captivate Western audiences, who packed the theaters for Disney's take on Aladdin, his flying carpet, and the *jinn* (genie).

If Aladdin's *jinn* could suddenly appear, snap his fingers, and whisk us back to Abbasid Baghdad, we would find a global capital buzzing with activity, intrigue, and innovation. The city stretched out on both banks of the Tigris River, which was spanned by five pontoon bridges carrying bustling traffic loads (when one bridge collapsed in the ninth century, 1,000 people drowned).[18]

On land, a continuous maze of shops and outdoor stands filled the city, with streets dedicated to specific business sectors. The cloth market included weaving shops selling linens bearing the label "City of Peace," Baghdad's trademark seal, which also appeared on the coins exchanged among money-changers and lenders in the exchange district. Other businesses included soap-sellers, goldsmiths, fruit and flower merchants, and the Canal of Chickens market. Butchers were confined to a slaughterhouse ghetto, complete with its own mosque. Goods available anywhere in the world could be found in Baghdad, which drew artisans from near and far.[19]

Baghdad also attracted the Abbasid Empire's best and brightest. The name Muhammad al-Khawarizmi is still attached to his great discovery, the algorithm. From his Baghdad study, al-Khawarizmi also bequeathed algebra (derived from the famous book *al-Jabr wa al-Muqabalah*) and produced a remarkable map of the known world in 830. He meticulously set about measuring the earth's volume and circumference while constructing clocks, sundials, and astrolabes. Medical techniques were pioneered by the chief of Baghdad's largest hospital, al-Razi, a surgeon who was the first to use opium for anesthesia and write on smallpox and chickenpox in his treatise *al-Judari wa 'l-Hasabah* ("Smallpox and Chickenpox"). The geographer al-Biruni developed ideas about the impact of climate on human development. He would travel to distant ports, from Madagascar to India, and listen to the stories of sailors. A series of tenth-century highway robberies prompted Abbasid bankers to revive an old Assyrian technique of letters of credit and exchange. Rather than carry hard currency, Abbasid merchants used metal tablets to be paid on demand, even as far away as China.

One noted Baghdadi scholar, according to legend, died when a pile of books collapsed on him in his private library.[20] Indeed, massive private libraries and bookstores abounded in Baghdad. Ibn al-Nadim, the son of a prominent book collector, spent years drafting an almanac of the books in his father's store in an attempt to index all books available in Arabic from the birth of Islam to his era. The tome he produced titillates today's scholars with vivid descriptions of ancient classics that no longer survive.[21]

Books filled Baghdad thanks to the patronage of Rashid's son, the caliph al-Ma'mun ("the Trusted One"). With a strong humanist bent, Ma'mun fostered an intricate court culture of syncretism, spurring one of the most ambitious translation movements in human history. Many classical works exist only in Arabic, not the original Greek, thanks to Baghdad's medieval scholars like Thabit bin Qurrah al-Harrani, who translated Ptolemy's *Almagest*, Euclid's *Elements of Geometry*, and Apollonius's book on conic sections.

The enormous wealth of a relatively stable empire in addition to Baghdad's melting pot of Persian, Arabic, and Hellenic intellectual cultures combined to create a flourishing high culture. Intellectuals competed for patronage, often flattering caliphs and merchants by composing panegyrics (praise poetry). Scholars angled for commissions by individual patrons who sought expertise in fields ranging from architecture to mechanics. A project might involve translating and expanding upon Greek knowledge found in a manuscript bought from Byzantine dealers.[22]

Hellenism was only one of the intellectual legacies that contributed to the articulation of Islamic philosophy and systematic theology. Though the seat of a Muslim empire, Baghdad was home to a rainbow of spiritual traditions. Local Christians in particular had an established tradition of studying Aristotelian logic. Their dogma challenged by Christians, Jews, and Manichaeans, Muslim theologians developed discourses of debate infused with new translations of Aristotle and his ideas about polemic and dialectic. Drawing on Persian, Byzantine, and Hellenistic ideas, as well as the canon law of the Orthodox Church, Talmudic, and even old Babylonian law, Islamic scholars and judges developed new legal standards.

Sometimes, despite the enormous ethnic and religious cross-fertilization and atmospheres of tolerance and coexistence unparalleled elsewhere, these standards were also used to separate religious minorities. For example, in the ninth century, the empire instituted laws requiring Jewish people to wear distinguishing marks on their clothing, such as yellow badges and signs around their necks indicating that they were *dhimmi*— religious minorities subject both to the caliph's protection and to laws limiting his political and economic privileges. It bears noting, however, that the more restrictive and humiliating aspects of these laws were only sporadically enforced.[23]

Over the centuries, central government control of local provinces steadily diminished, and new forces from the north emerged now to strengthen and now to threaten Abbasid rule. The reliance on Turkic slave soldiers as an alternative to unruly Arab tribes spawned periods of Turkish military domination of the empire's local and international politics. But imported Turkic fighters were only the first and most benign of newcomers from the northeast. In the mid-thirteenth century, the Mongols invaded with an overwhelming cavalry force that Abbasid foot soldiers could not counter. The Mongol sack of Baghdad in 1258 traumatized generations. The invaders wrapped the caliph in a rug and trampled him with horses, and waged genocide on the city's populace. "I remember when they taught us in school how the Mongols destroyed the capital," recalls one Baghdadi. "We learned that they threw all the books in the Tigris, which turned blue from all the ink. I would drive by the river later and imagine it blue."[24]

Through years of invasions, some Muslim scholars were concerned that all knowledge of Islam could be destroyed forever. The scholar al-Juwayni prepared for this eventuality by drafting a short book designed to serve as a time capsule containing a synopsis of the fundamentals of Muslim law, in case there were no scholars left to teach it.[25] But Islam proved a resilient force. Rather than attempt to destroy it, Mongol rulers embraced the culture of their colonies and converted to Islam. Successive centuries saw continued cultural achievements, albeit of a less profound variety, and waves of conversion and cultural consolidation, amid further foreign invasions and political setbacks.

The early centuries of Islam's history and formative political conflicts occupy a special place in the memories of Iraqis, as well as Arabs and Muslims everywhere. But the physical vestiges of this period are scant in Iraq's capital. Whereas old Cairo, once the seat of the tenth-century Shi'i Fatimid rival caliphate, is still brimming today with architectural remains of the city's days as the capital of an empire, to say nothing of the ancient pyramids that mark the desert landscape, medieval Baghdad is largely lost. Where the Round City once stood, modern Baghdad has long since paved over the ruins and built a train station. The lack of physical remembrances makes the memory transmitted through learning that much more significant, and that much more susceptible to projects of historical reengineering by modern states. While Cairo abides with medieval and ancient landmarks, the most imposing statues and palaces in Baghdad in 2003 were the myriad sculptures, mosques, and palaces deifying Saddam Hussein.

Three

The Soundtrack
to Modern Iraq

Memories of ancient and medieval Iraq described so far have found expression in symbols, images, and words. Another powerful evocation of memory comes through the universal language of music. Like any language, it gives form to the nuances of human experience. Where words convey the subtleties of facts and ideas, music, though by nature less concrete, can stir a range of emotions, sometimes building bridges between peoples and cultures, at other times inciting soldiers to war. The power of music has been known to attract the interest of heads of state as well as to usher in some musicians to the arena of politics. Iraq in the twentieth century provides examples of both, boasting a music scene that is a mirror of the country's recent political evolution.

Iraq's modern music industry has produced artists who evoked unforgettable images through song. Oud virtuoso Nasir Shamma, who lived through the 1991 Gulf War and left Iraq for Egypt in 1993 under the strain of the international sanctions that followed, once recorded a piece of music that forever reminds Iraqis of a tragedy in their recent past. When United States and British war planes attacked Shamma's home city of Baghdad during the 1991 war, one of the sites they bombed was an air raid shelter. Some 400 civilians, mostly children, were killed. Shamma picked up his Oud, and recorded a piece of music to commemorate the tragedy. He began with a sweeping sentimental melody, then grasped the Oud's movable bridge and eased it to the base of the instrument. He rubbed his finger up and down the neck and strummed rapidly to approximate the sound of air raid sirens. He pushed the bridge as far as it would go to the middle of the Oud, to simulate the stinging sounds of crashing explosions, children's screams, and mothers' cries. He then revisited a tuneful yet somber motif from the beginning of the piece to evoke the return of ephemeral calm over the skies of Baghdad.

Who taught Nasir Shamma how to play the Oud, and who built his instrument for him? The music of Shamma's Iraq is a mix of cultural and political memories recent and distant. On the one hand, it stems from the influences of the country's imperial colonizers over the past three centuries. Shamma studied Oud with an elderly musician from Turkey who came to Baghdad as part of the people traffic spawned by the Sunni Ottoman Empire, which ruled the lands of Iraq as three distinct provinces from the sixteenth century onward.[1] The person who built the Oud for Shamma was an old artisan trained by a man from Iran, who made his way to Baghdad thanks to cultural trails blazed by the Shi'i Safavid Empire in Iran.[2] The latter managed to wrest the province of Iraq from Ottoman control for brief interludes. On the eve of modernity, both empires had transmitted more than just political and military institutions to the provinces of Iraq. They bequeathed cultural legacies, consolidated the formation of Sunni and Shi'i political identities, and integrated Iraq into the commercial networks of their imperial heartlands. They also helped invigorate Iraqi music.

On the other hand, Shamma's music has indigenous roots that go back 1,200 years to the time of Baghdad's founding. Shamma's improvised commemoration of the air raid tragedy was based on a series of complex musical scales and motifs known in Arabic as *maqamat* and believed to have been first set down systematically in medieval Baghdad during the Abbasid period. Twelve hundred years ago, Shamma's hometown was regarded as much an exporter as an importer of musical ideas. A ninth-century caliph in Baghdad once tired of his court musician and banished him and his son Zeryab to distant Muslim Spain.

According to some historians, just these two Baghdadis were all it took to launch a new performing style in Spain that spawned the music known today as flamenco.[3]

The movement of peoples and cultures that spawned Shamma's music goes back even farther than the Islamic period. An early intersection between music and politics in Babylon may be found in Psalm 137: "By the rivers of Babylon, we sat and cried as we remembered Zion," expresses the lament of Israelites exiled from their homeland by Nebuchadnezzar. They hang up their harps on willow trees, but their Babylonian rulers ask them to play happy songs: "Sing us a song of Jerusalem." To which the Israelites reply, "How can we sing God's songs in a strange land?"[4] Though it is not clear when the Israelites stopped crying and started strumming, Jews went on to play an important role in the Iraqi music scene until their exile from the country in the 1950s, more than 2,500 years later. According to both Ottoman and British estimates, the Jewish population of Baghdad in the early twentieth century was once as high as 40 percent of the city, the largest single ethnic group.[5] Not only were Jews prominent economically and politically; they were also active culturally.[6] The Iraqi national orchestra of the 1930s and 1940s that Shamma grew up listening to was invariably comprised of many Jewish musicians.[7] Meanwhile, in the mountains of northern Iraq, Kurdish songsters still play the Tar, a lengthy stringed instrument from Iran with a pungent tone resembling a dulcimer, improvising on Kurdish modes believed to be among the oldest scales still in use. Melodies made popular in the twentieth century by Hasan and Muhammad Jazrawi, a family duo in Kurdistan, have long since seeped into the popular culture of Iraq's big cities. And Shamma's piece in commemoration of the air raid tragedy makes use of the *Kurd Maqam*, a mournful scale attributed to the mountain dwellers of the north.

The migration of peoples, cultures, and ideas into Iraq over time has enabled musicians to synthesize sundry sounds into a musical form that fans of Arabic music regard as distinctly Iraqi. But the country's politicians in the twentieth century who attempted to construct a national identity and polity out of the disparate ethnic groups and sects residing within its borders have been less successful. The renewed struggle now at hand to improvise a viable Iraqi state free of brutality and strife has a historic soundtrack, and those who would engage the country politically and culturally would do well to learn how to play along.

A National Orchestra

An observation many Westerners make when they first hear traditional Arabic ensemble music is that there is no harmony or counterpoint; all musicians are playing the same melody in unison. Just because the music is monodic does not, however, make it less complex. Whereas Western classical composers wrote melodies and harmonies mostly in two scales, major and minor, traditional Arabic *maqamat* employ more than 14 different scales and dozens more modes and inversions, with quarter-tone intervals so subtle that the Western piano and fretted guitar cannot even play them. When one tries to impose "well-tempered" Western harmony and counterpoint on Arabic modes, the results tend to be coarse and disappointing.

Political disappointments in confrontations between East and West sometimes run along parallel lines. A few years into the twentieth century, the waning Ottoman provinces of Iraq fell under imperial rule from the European West with the rise of British military and political domination. The British occupation of these provinces disrupted a delicate social stasis established under Ottoman rule, disenfranchising clerics and old landed elites and implanting a new civil service from the British colony of India. The occupation also marked the birth of modern Iraq, one of several mandates carved out from Ottoman provinces and divided between Western imperial powers in the aftermath of World War I. In addition to the provinces of Baghdad and Basra, the British negotiated with the French to add the northern province of Mosul, originally invisaged as a part of French Syria, to what would become known as Iraq. When the League of Nations granted Britain an official mandate for Iraq in 1920, popular revolts erupted in various parts of the country, uniting Sunnis and Shi'is, urban sophisticates and rural tribesmen, Arabs and Kurds, all under the umbrella of opposition to colonial rule.

The British quelled the uprising but soon realized a form of indirect rule was needed. Winston Churchill, the new colonial secretary, convened a conference in Cairo (dubbed "The Forty Thieves") that resolved to form a constitutional monarchy around the figure of Prince Faysal, a Hashemite descendant of the prophet Muhammad and colleague of T. E. Lawrence in the Arabian battle for independence from the Ottomans. Members of the minority urban Sunni community, together with various non-Muslim ethnic and religious groups, would provide Faysal's elite support base. But the Shi'i majority was largely disenfranchised, and the imported prince faced the difficult task of creating harmony in Iraq through a new national identity that was not his own. Britain's superficial attempt at indirect rule did not manage to engineer accord among the fractious ethnic, religious, and class divisions of the country. Nor did British-sponsored efforts to weave together memories of Iraq's complex cultural mosaic into a national history through the educational system prevent Iraq's Kurds from dreaming of a country of their own.[8] Under 12 years of Faysal's rule, the Iraqi parliament went through 15 different coalitions. The growing number of Iraqis who rejected British-imposed efforts at political coalition building instead favored an alluring political alternative that also hailed from the West: nationalism. Many of those who came to favor the ideology's elusive ideal of a single voice to unite Iraqis and all Arabs everywhere also sought to cleanse the country of "outsiders."

But try telling that to Iraq's musicians in the 1930s and 1940s. The music scene in Baghdad at the time was such a thorough blend of cultures and ethnicities from the country's living history that merely the play bill of prominent performers and composers was a nationalist's nightmare. Salima Murad Pasha, one of the country's favorite female vocalists, was an Iraqi Jew, married to Nazem al-Ghazali, the greatest male vocalist at the time and a Sunni Muslim. A young Oud player of great promise, Munir Bashir, had an Assyrian Christian father and a Kurdish mother. His music teachers included a Turk from Istanbul and an Arabian man from Medina. Two of his favorite composers were Salih and Dawoud al-Kuwaiti, Jewish brothers with roots in the country going back two millennia who wrote many of the popular songs Iraqis sing to this day. And the Iraqi National Orchestra, a source of great prestige for Iraq in the Arab Middle East through its weekly broadcasts heard from Morocco to Yemen, had mostly Jewish performers for several years running. A Jewish veteran of the orchestra recalled that one scheduled broadcast in the 1930s had the misfortune of falling on Yom Kippur, the Jewish Day of Atonement. Most of the musicians refused to play, compelling the director of Iraqi national radio to discuss the problem with King Ghazi, who succeeded Faysal. "Fire all the Jews and get some new musicians!" the king said. But it was not possible to find suitable replacements in time for the weekly air check, so the director had no choice but to cancel the show.[9]

It would take more than mere nationalist sloganeering for the proponents of a homogeneous Iraqi polity to excise multiculturalism from the country. It took a good deal of brute force as well. The Iraqi army, trained and equipped by the British, eventually became a support base for opposition to British rule and nationalist activism. In August 1933, Colonel Bakr Sidqi led his forces into northern Iraq to massacre hundreds of Assyrian Christian villagers. Bakr's supporters organized a hero's parade for him in Baghdad, in honor of his success at crushing the Assyrian "threat."[10] A few years later, in 1941, several hundred young Iraqis hailing from the military and security services, German-backed fascist groups, and Baghdad's slums stormed the Jewish quarter and killed nearly 200 Jews. They also killed an even larger number of Muslims, many of whom were fighting to protect their neighbors. Jewish businesses were destroyed and synagogues desecrated.[11]

Anti-Jewish sentiments, blurred together with the resentment of Jewish elites who worked for the British civil service, were further exacerbated by the establishment of the State of Israel in 1948. Stigmatized as "Zionists" and "traitors," about 125,000 Jews fled Iraq for Israel in airlifts and escape routes organized by the Jewish Agency and Mossad between 1950 and 1952, including the musical brothers Salih and Dawoud al-Kuwaiti and most members of the Iraqi National Orchestra. Fewer than 9,000 Jews remained in the country, most of whom departed in the decades that followed.[12] In a throwback to the exiled father-and-son musical duo who left Baghdad in the ninth century and became star performers in medieval Spain, Iraqi Jewish musicians went on to Israel and became the backbone of the Voice of Israel Arabic Orchestra. Broadcast on shortwave, their weekly performances attracted many of the same radio audiences as their Iraqi antecedent.[13] Meanwhile, back in Baghdad, both the monarchy and the country's minorities heaved under the weight of nationalism. After 22 years of repeated efforts by military men to topple the monarchy by coup, General Abd al-Karim Qasim at last seized power in 1958, executed the royal family, and declared Iraq a republic.

From Dissonance to Unison

Qasim won a reputation as a one-man dynamo, spending 14-hour days in his office in the Defense Ministry, micromanaging the country and succeeding where his predecessors had failed. He instituted land reforms and cleared the slums around Baghdad, built large housing complexes for the urban poor, and pushed through social reforms to eliminate child marriage, ban polygamy, and enable women to inherit property. All the while, oil sustained the Iraqi economy, providing nearly half the government's revenue and almost all its foreign currency; the country's traditional base of agriculture ran a distant second.[14] Qasim set in motion a process of nationalization of major industries.

But another coup in February 1963 resulted in Qasim's execution and the rise to power of a new military junta, followed in turn by repeated coups for several years. While Qasim had been ruling the nascent Republic, another nationalist movement was taking shape: the Ba'th Arab National Socialist Party, with an ideology hailing from its sister party in Damascus and tactics resembling the cellular organization of revolutionary Bolshevism in Russia. In July 1968, 10 years and four coups after Iraq had become a republic, the Ba'th took power under the leadership of Ahmad Hasan al-Bakr and his vice-president, Saddam Hussein. Early years of Ba'th control were marked by show trials and executions based on trumped-up charges, such as the public hanging of nine Jews accused of espionage, celebrated in Baghdad's Liberation Square by Iraqi media and the mob. The party also initiated purges of domestic opposition, new laws to curb the power and wealth of non-Arab ethnics, and repeated attacks on Kurdish civilians in northern Iraq undertaken to weaken Kurdish national aspirations and ethnically cleanse the oil-rich region of Kirkuk, a Kurdish stronghold, of non-Arab communities.

While Bakr served as Iraq's titular head, Saddam worked behind the scenes to dominate politics and the public's imagination. He crafted an elusive personality cult, meeting only in private with select party leaders while partnering with journalists to weave a mythologized version of his biography into the national press. He advertised his phone number to the public and encouraged Iraqis to call him with their problems.[15] In 1979, he made his move, forcing an ailing Bakr to step down and name him president. Saddam retained his popularity for several years into his rule, largely through state-owned television, which covered Saddam's random visits to Iraqi households to check on their welfare, sudden violent purges of "traitors" and "conspirators," and afternoons in the countryside helping poor farmers harvest their crops. One Iraqi television viewer recalls, "He had a nice physique at the time, and his scything technique was flawless."[16]

Saddam came to demand more of his public as the country entered the 1980s. His decision to invade Iran and fight a protracted bloody war, while enjoying support from the United States, carried with it a massive mobilization of young men to the front. Exporting youthful energy to the battlefield proved an effective check against dissident political activity at home, but it came at the expense of Iraq's domestic economy, which suffered considerably, and the people's esteem for their leadership, which plummeted. Music played an important role in Saddam's domestic campaign to preserve a veneer of national unity. Where popular songs had once mirrored the varied strains of

Iraqi identity and culture, more of the music that now earned studio recordings was focused on reinforcing the cult of one man's rule. An early pop song of this variety was *al-'Aziz Inta* ("You Are Our Beloved"), a love song to Saddam with the memorable words, "You are our candle . . . You are our homeland's hope." Iraqi diva Ma'ida Nazhad recorded a new song referencing Saddam's young daughter Halah that topped the charts: *Hayyak Abu Hala* ("You're Welcome, Father of Halah"). In the mid-1980s, the song became the subject of a popular joke whispered among Iraqi high school students: a man who can no longer stand Saddam's rule goes to his doctor and asks to be placed in suspended animation until Saddam falls from power. Just before the doctor puts the man to sleep, he hears "You're Welcome, Father of Halah" playing on the radio. Fifty years pass, and the doctor revives his patient. Anxious to know whether Saddam is gone, the man flicks on the radio, only to shriek at the revelation that Saddam's grandson is now in power, as evidenced by the new pop hit: "You're Welcome, *Son* of Halah."[17]

Falling Out of Sync with the Region

Ideas of pan-Arab unity that emerged among speakers of Arabic fostered a sense of connection with the region's glorious past, before centuries of foreign domination, and an Arab identity that transcended the new national borders. The cultural capital of pan-Arabism for many years was Cairo, under the leadership of Gamal Abdel Nasser. Among his many achievements, he sponsored the engineering of Arab cultural unity and solidarity through music. One of the best-loved songs of pan-Arabism from the Nasserist period was the half-hour-long *Basat al-Rih* ("The Flying Carpet"), recorded in an electrifying live performance by the legendary singer and Oud player Farid al-Atrash. The lyrics have Farid and a female vocalist flying on a magic carpet over the heartlands of the Arab world, from the olive trees of Syria to Marrakesh and Tunis. In one climactic moment, Farid sings, "O carpet, let's fly over Baghdad, a land of greatnesses, a land of glories," and the audience cheers. When Iraq's nationalists at last deposed the monarchy in 1958, Egyptian songsters responded with great enthusiasm. Cairo's immortal diva Um Kalthum performed the song "Baghdad" with lyrics extolling the city's historic civilization and long-awaited liberation. Despite the violent excesses of nationalism in Iraq and the notorious brutality of successive rulers, culminating in Saddam, the country remained an integral part of the pan-Arab imagination for years. Saddam's war on Iran was spun by poets and musicians region-wide as a courageous campaign to defend the Arab world's eastern flank from a Persian onslaught. Witness the poetry of the Kuwaiti Su'ad al-Sabah: "Give me the helmet of one Iraqi soldier and take 1,000 poets."

But inside Iraq, the draw of pan-Arabism was less widespread. Neither did it appeal to Kurdish communities, who harbored nationalist ambitions of their own, nor did it win over many of the country's Shi'is, whose complex sectarian identity posed a challenge to Arabism's core definition. In contrast to the far-reaching pan-Arab imagination spawned in Egyptian music under nationalism, many pop songs of Saddam's Iraq had the more direct purpose of inciting Iraqis to sacrifice their lives on the battlefield. Bawdy folk singers from Iraq's populous countryside were recruited to write motivational music in the village style (known as *Aghani 'l-Rif*). For example, the heavyset Sa'di al-Hilli, renowned for graphic love songs, sang a new song with the following lyrics: "O my land, your dirt will be perfume for my body when I die. / At the front line, my machine gun starts to chant." *Rif* war songs might be described as the equivalent of enlisting today's "gangster rappers" to praise America's military engagements in Iraq and Afghanistan. After Iraqi troops won an important battle in Iran, Saddam convened a music festival in Baghdad broadcast on national television. One of the highlights was a chorus of children singing a new song about Iran's supreme leader, Ruhollah Khomeini: "'Aish Jabak Aish Dallak ya 'bn Fayna?" ("Who brought you and who showed you the way, you son of a whore?").[18] Where Iraq's national orchestra once attracted radio audiences from Morocco to Yemen, much of Iraqi popular music now lost its regional appeal. Soon enough, Iraq's national politics followed suit.

When the Iran–Iraq war ended with the status quo ante, Saddam turned his army on the Kurdish north, launching a campaign of genocide that came to be known as the *anfal* ("spoils of war"). Chemical weapons were deployed to kill thousands of Kurdish villagers. Well over 100,000 more Kurds were deported to the south and murdered in camps.[19] Although the *anfal* received scant condemnation in the West or the Arab world, Saddam's invasion of Kuwait in August 1990 made it easy for President Bush to form an international coalition, including numerous Arab countries, to drive Saddam's forces back. The Kuwaiti poet Su'ad al-Sabah, who had written in praise of Iraqi soldiers and once recited poetry to Saddam in private audience, understandably changed her tune. She wrote a new poem called, "The Mongols Will Be Driven Away," likening the Iraqi army to the ravenous invaders of medieval Baghdad.

The Gulf War reduced Iraq's military machine, but the allies nevertheless permitted Saddam's elite Republic Guard forces to crush a popular uprising in March 1991 that briefly deposed the authority of the central government in 15 of Iraq's 18 provinces. Saddam retained power and won a measure of grassroots esteem in the Arab Middle East for standing up to the West. But he became a pariah among the elites of his region and beyond. Beginning in August 1990, the United Nations imposed an economic embargo on Iraq pending its compliance with the disarmament terms of its surrender. During the ensuing decade, Iraq's economy and society deteriorated dramatically. Though the embargo and subsequent amendments allowing for the exchange of oil for food and medicine were designed to provide for the basic needs of the Iraqi people, in effect they brought about poverty and widespread hunger, as Saddam diverted scant resources to the resuscitation of his military and clandestine weapons development. Effectively blocked off from access to the Kurdish north through the U.S. and U.K. enforcement of UN-designated no-fly zones, Saddam devoted political energy and resources to thawing damaged relations with some of his neighbors and erstwhile allies. He managed to reestablish economic and diplomatic relations with several countries in the eastern Mediterranean and the Gulf, and broadened economic cooperation with Russia, China, and France in various sectors.[20] The constellation of factors that led to a new United States-led campaign for "regime change" in Iraq 2003 will best be understood in hindsight over the next few years. For now, it may be said that scenarios bringing about an end to Iraqi-American hostilities stand to end an ongoing war that began in 1991, and which continued for over a decade through what amounted in effect, though not in intent, to siege warfare.

Meanwhile, Iraqi music and musicians are enjoying a new resurgence in the era of globalization. Songs lamenting the human tragedy of Iraq's interior have found sympathetic ears in recent years. Witness the song, *Tadhakkar* ("Remember"), which became a hit in several Gulf states with the memorable words, "Remember the millions of people eating rocks as their bread. / Remember the millions walking the streets wearing only their bare skin." One of the most popular mainstream Arab vocalists in the region today is Kazem al-Saher, an Iraqi heart-throb who lives in exile and sings to sellout crowds all over the Arab Middle East and Europe. He got his start in the Iraqi army's entertainment corps during the Iran–Iraq war but has since won acclaim for songs on universal themes; he carefully has avoided criticizing the Ba'th government for fear of his family back home. The successive waves of exile and dispossession that Iraqi nationalism and Saddam's wars spawned have also created expatriate communities across the globe with their own musical achievements. In Dearborn and Detroit, Michigan, the cities with the largest concentration of Iraqi exiles in North America, Iraqi Christian singer Majid Kakka spices up traditional Iraqi songs with new synthesized sounds and a touch of hard rock. His band, *al-Ajras* ("The Bells"), sings songs of longing for Baghdad that seem to stir both refugees and their children, most of whom know the city only through the memories of their parents. And in Tel Aviv, Iraqi-Israeli Oud player and vocalist Yair Dalal has become the leader of a preservationist stream in Jewish Iraqi music. He plays traditional Iraqi Jewish songs the way they were originally performed in the early twentieth century, when his music teachers still lived in Baghdad, and writes new songs in a similar style. All these voices, scattered over continents, fashion memories into sound in order to express longing for a place from which they have long been cut off. The circumstances under which an alumni reunion concert of Iraq's national orchestra will be possible require creativity and courage on the part of Iraq's new political leadership and sustained support from the international community.

Part II
POWER

Four

The Party's Over

Saddam's Privileged Politicos
and Their Future in Iraq

~~~~

The Middle East might not manifest the American dream, which promises social mobility and celebrates merit, but it is certainly a place where luck or hard work or both have catapulted the lowly to positions of power. In the twentieth century, bedouin of the Arabian Peninsula suddenly emerged on the international stage due to the oil they controlled and their political acumen in leveraging it. Nationalist coups brought to power a villager from the banks of the Egyptian Nile, Gamal Abdel Nasser, and a member of a minority sect from the mountains of Syria, Hafez al-Asad. The Iranian revolution made an elderly man of the cloth, Ayatollah Ruhollah Khomeini, into the country's Supreme Leader. These turns of fate ushered in new privileged classes: the Saudi princes and Wahhabi clerics of Arabia, the army officers of Egypt, the Alawites of Syria, and the Shi'i jurists of Iran. Privileged classes in Middle Eastern states, like those of developing countries elsewhere, tend to distribute power among their families and supporters to the exclusion of others, hindering social mobility and stunting some of the achievements ambition can inspire. The transition of government in the new Iraq presents an opportunity to work toward a more egalitarian distribution of power.

Iraq has its own recent rags to riches story about a particular lot of mostly Sunni tribes from the center of the country who claim kinship to the country's longtime ruler. Members of these tribes attained a share in power through careers in the ruling Ba'th party apparatus and among the five-odd intelligence and security services that competed with one another to discipline the country. For nearly three decades, party members and their bosses as well as spies and their masters have been as powerful in Iraq as clerics in Iran or lawyers in the United States, in a society where neither the cloth nor the law has had any real power at all.

What the Ba'th has stood for over the past three decades has changed with time. The party first articulated a utopian vision of pan-Arab unity infused vaguely with the values of socialism.[1] But over its long years in power in Iraq, the Ba'th twisted and turned its message, with nods to communism early on when a rival communist party was still permitted to function in the country, and overtures to Islamism more recently as tides of political populism across the region shifted toward religion. These changes stemmed less from political debate within the ranks of the Ba'th than from the whims of its permanent chairman. Saddam's frequent speeches and pronouncements set the tone, and the party machine saw to their propagation through the school system and media. As far as the burning issues of the day were concerned, most Ba'this, and indeed most Iraqis, enjoyed freedom from thought.[2]

Those who craved a share in power could begin their ascent in grade school, when teachers and recruiters urged children to join the party's youth groups and compete to show their allegiance to Saddam. They joined the tala'i' ("vanguards") at age 10 and graduated to the futuwwa ("youth organization") around age 15. They wore a green Ba'th uniform to school once a week and helped plan parties to celebrate key holidays: Saddam's birthday, the anniversary of the party coup, and the nation's "victories" over Iran and the United States in successive Gulf wars. They got to play with real guns and visit military camps. In class they received special treats and in many cases preferential treatment, if their teacher happened to be fervent about advancing the party's anointed. But rising to prominence within the Ba'th was difficult in the tender years of childhood, as the most cubs could offer was a demonstration of loyalty to party over family. For example, they could win special points for informing on parents and elder siblings who criticized Saddam in the privacy of their homes. They might lose a father or mother to Iraq's political prisons, but they would earn special recognition for precociously having set their priorities straight.[3]

Then came adulthood. Determined teens won the status of *munasir* ("supporter"), and the one-on-one attention of a mentor. They rarely knew who ranked above their mentor, nor did they necessarily know whom else he or she was mentoring. At this point, they had reached the bottom rung of a cellular power structure shaped now like a pyramid, now like a beeline, depending on the province they hailed from and the division of the party they had joined.[4] They learned to keep secrets and compartmentalize their life. Although the Ba'th party's dark early days as an underground revolutionary movement had ended years ago, its political culture of mystery mastery persisted in broad daylight.

Another lesson young party members learned as they came of age was that membership in the Ba'th was a lifestyle, but not a livelihood. Those who excelled in high school or had the right connections to earn a place in one of the state's public universities could avoid the draft. So could those whose parents were wealthy enough to pay their tuition in a private college. The rest faced three years in the army, a dangerous and low-paying job. Wherever they passed their late teens and early 20s, party membership continued to offer perks. They could study less and score better, fight less and rise higher, as long as they kept feeding their mentors the twin currencies of power: fresh reports on colleagues and friends who disliked Saddam and fresh recruits from among the people who wanted to join the party.[5]

When school or service time was up, some went on to professions or stayed on as professional soldiers and saw their party loyalty pay off somewhat through fast-track promotions. A smaller number who had the right family ties, an impeccable party record, and a penchant for adventure and risk opted to make the party apparatus their profession. They traded in a slightly more stable work environment for an immensely more interesting job.

Every party member, as well as many ordinary citizens in Iraq, periodically served Saddam's five intelligence and security services as informants. But as those who took full-time jobs as Iraqi spooks quickly learned, the rank and file meant as much to the intelligence apparatus as movie ushers do to the entertainment industry: they have a small role to play, but the show goes on without them. The world looked different viewed from a case officer's cubicle at the central headquarters of the *Idarat al-Mukhabarat al-Amma* (Central Intelligence Bureau), a large building complex cordoned off by a tall white wall and flanked by a military airport and Iraq's international exhibitions center on densely crowded Mansur Street in downtown Baghdad. Passersby hurried along past the complex, taking care to avert their eyes. The people inside had a license to hunt down Iraqis inclined to think outside the box.[6]

The intelligence business was a growth industry in Iraq since the Ba'th takeover in 1968. In 2003, available Iraqi intelligence documents surveyed suggest that more than 500,000 people spanning the country's 18 provinces were serving as sometime snitches for the five principal services: special security, general security, general intelligence, military intelligence, and military security. This figure does not include the many more who assisted the Ba'th party's internal security agencies, the civil police forces, and various paramilitary units. But full-time staffers for the five main bureaus were fewer than 45,000.[7] Most were relatives of Saddam, either good old boys from the tribes of his hometown of Takrit 100 miles north of Baghdad, or more distant relatives from one of six small towns nearby. The Dulaym, a confederation of tribal fragments and tribeless peasantry from the northern Euphrates, used to raid caravans of travelers along the road from Baghdad to Aleppo back when Iraq was ruled by Turks. The Jubur and Hawij, both nomadic pastoralists from the north and center, had captured occasional attention for their frequent squabbles with neighboring tribes.[8] In exchange for loyalty to the regime, Saddam's rule afforded these and other hitherto marginal tribesmen 23 years of infamy.

Intelligence higher-ups reported directly to the president. Their mandate to track down "enemies of the state" gave them the pretext to observe nearly anyone in the country. Special Security elites under the supervision of Saddam's son Qusay spied on government ministries and army leaders and supervised operations to kill Shi'i and Kurdish dissidents. They provided physical security to the president, his offices, and his palaces, and helped procure and conceal weapons. General Security, a robust police force, conducted surveillance of the Iraqi public for traces of political deviance, corruption, and crime with a pervasive presence spanning the provinces and a massive database of files on the personal lives of ordinary people. General Intelligence tracked foreign spies, diplomats, journalists, and tourists, and looked for trouble within the Ba'th party and Iraq's professional unions. While Military Intelligence helped Saddam make war on his neighbors, Military Security helped him make war on his own soldiers, if they proved recalcitrant. All these units shared another important task as well: to spy on each other. In so doing they balanced the fear they inspired in their subjects with their own fear of backstabbing counterparts whose reports might incite a higher-up to order their removal, torture, or death.[9]

What made the job interesting was case officers' challenge to build a network of informants in the region or community that fell under their purview. Reined in neither by requirements for a warrant nor by a culture of individual rights, they mixed with people from all walks of life—pimps and their prostitutes, preachers and their flocks, teachers and their students—and leveraged money, access to power, and threats of arrest to confront anyone suspicious. With plausible justification they were free to lock up and torture nearly anyone who lacked the protection of the party. They were also free to rape children and adults of both genders whom chance had delivered to them for questioning. Their powers were well known to the Iraqi public, a fact that afforded them extra perks. They could crash any party. They could demand protection money from a small business, provided their superiors were not wetting their beaks there already. Some of the more powerful Ba'this are known to have seized attractive women at parties, regardless of whether they wanted to go along or happened to be married.

In a country where an exit visa was a privilege not easily procured by most people—travel outside the country was made difficult for the average Iraqi by a $340 government exit tax—many of Iraq's spooks even got to see the world. Most security resources went to thwarting domestic opposition, but there was plenty of work for Iraqi agents in the greater Middle East and beyond. In recent years Iraqi Special Security have scoured the continents of Africa and Asia seeking weapons technology in the black market. So well known are SS procurement efforts in the Arab world that a businessman I know in Beirut was twice approached by black market weapons traffickers offering him uranium samples, just because he was Iraqi. "I'm an American citizen and I can't stand Saddam," he told me. "They assumed I must be another one of those SS guys."[10] Most uranium pitches turn out to be scams anyway, he added. Iraqi government weapons deals have been described by recent defectors as slow going, leaving plenty of time for tourism and rest.

General Intelligence posted as diplomats in Iraqi embassies in the Arab world and Europe meanwhile conducted outreach programs to make common cause with guerrilla organizations hostile to Iraq's traditional enemies, like Syria and Iran—and according to some, its more recent enemies, the United States and Great Britain. They also have been known to carry out assassinations abroad. Three agents of General Intelligence were held responsible by Lebanese security forces for the slaying of an Iraqi Shi'i dissident cleric in Beirut in 1994. Over the years, Military Intelligence agents have killed opposition figures in cities as remote as London, Paris, and Detroit.

The international assignments of Iraqi spooks varied in their level of danger and intensity. Several Arab capitals were wont to intervene as long as the matter at hand was intra-Iraqi politics. A gentleman's agreement among some of the region's heads of state allowed for outstretched hands across each other's borders to crush rebel activity. Over the past 20 years, Ba'thi Iraq exercised these privileges liberally from North Africa to the Gulf states, moving beyond exile politics and seeking to win political sympathy and support from non-Iraqi students, professionals, civil servants, and journalists. Iraqi student guilds in Italy and

Greece were among the main venues for the inculcation and recruitment of Arab students in Europe. The quiet North African republic of Mauritania experienced a bit of a shock in the late 1990s when a group of pro-Ba'th Mauritanian students attempted to stage a coup with funding from Saddam.[11]

Perhaps the country where the party's greatest grassroots recruitment efforts were expended was the desert Kingdom of Jordan, which for many years stood as an ambivalent buffer zone between Saddam's Iraq and Israeli visions of a new Middle East. Iraq's party and security services invested hundreds of millions of dollars in a campaign to win over Jordanians and Jordanian-Palestinians to their leader's point of view and stem Israel's ambition to use Jordan as its economic and intelligence outpost to the Arab world. Jordan's geopolitical importance was matched by its value to Iraq's economy as a major consumer of Iraqi oil under sanctions and a vital way station for smugglers, money launderers, and spies. As a friend at Amman's Iraqi embassy remarked in the autumn of 2002, "Jordan is the lungs of Iraq."[12]

On a quiet street in the eastern part of Amman stands the Assemblage of Jordanian Professional Unions. The imposing edifice houses the Engineers Union, the Lawyers Union, and the Doctors Union, among others. Hanging over the entrance is a placard in large, ornate Arabic letters that sports the unions' motto of solidarity: "No to normalization with the Zionist enemy." Funded in part by Iraq, the building is a testament to Ba'thi efforts to unite Jordanian society around a rallying cry with near-universal Arab appeal.

The leadership of the unions includes many Jordanian nationals who graduated from Iraqi universities and colleges, which offered free education and a stipend to all Arabs who qualified, either through aptitude or through a show of pure zeal for the party. Although Iraq's limited resources under sanctions made it difficult for the country to continue sponsoring foreign Arab students, hundreds of Jordanians were nevertheless enrolled in Iraqi universities in 2003. "Not all of us are particularly pro-Saddam," a Palestinian friend who studied in Baghdad told me. "The universities are easier to get into and the cost of living is cheaper." A Jordanian acquaintance was recruited by an

Iraqi cultural attaché in Bologna. After he finished his studies in Italy, he returned to Jordan and ran the "Society of Iraqi University Graduates" to recruit more students and organize rallies in solidarity with the Iraqi people. As of 2003, he holds a position of some importance in the Jordanian civil service. He has made a habit of passing on information to the intelligence attaché at the Iraqi embassy he felt the Iraqi government would like to know. Scores of Jordanian professionals, politicians, and businessmen maintained these sorts of ties to Iraq's party, some for ideological reasons, some purely for profit, and many for a combination of both.[13]

Another big building in the outskirts of Amman called "Journalists' City" is a compound where many of the country's local reporters have their offices. The late King Hussein started building it in the 1980s and ran low on funds; Saddam stepped in and completed the project. For years Iraq's General Intelligence unit has supplemented the meager salaries of newspaper columnists and talking heads in Jordan who supported Saddam's politics and threatened to harm many of those who did not. Jordanian media people and guild members have come together on television and in the pages of newspapers in recent months to call for the boycott of American products, an end to diplomatic relations with Israel, and solidarity with the Iraqi people in the face of sanctions and war.[14]

The hundreds of Iraqi agents and party members posted in Jordan as diplomats and businessmen have had opportunities over the past few years to enrich themselves by leveraging party ties back home with commercial activities in the shady space between Amman's public and private sectors. They laundered money on behalf of their superiors in the party. They established dummy corporations to import banned "dual use" technologies to Jordan, pocketing commissions for their trouble and skimming off fees to taxi drivers and truckers who smuggled the equipment on to Baghdad.

Ba'thi elites also served their state and padded their paychecks by finding ways to defy the international sanctions regime imposed on Iraq. In December 1996 a UN Security Council Resolution established the oil-for-food program, under which all proceeds obtained from Iraq's closely monitored oil sales were to have been deposited in an escrow account used to purchase humanitarian supplies designated by a special committee. Iraq's oil shipments were limited by a half-annual profits ceiling, which was raised from $2 billion to $5.265 billion in mid-1998 and was eventually removed altogether in 1999. In return for its oil shipments, Iraq was provided with humanitarian supplies—foodstuffs and medicine, agricultural machinery, power equipment, and educational materials. But the Iraqi government with the help of its party members and their business contacts systematically circumvented the UN sanctions. Trade activities outside the UN jurisdiction were principally conducted via three cross-border routes to Jordan, Turkey, and the Gulf. In recent years, Syria has emerged as another overland trade partner. As many as 300,000 barrels of oil per day (bopd) were transported through these channels.[15]

The large volume of oil traded semilegally between Jordan and Iraq under sanctions spawned a mini-industry of smuggled oil exports. It was encouraged on the Iraqi side because it brought additional income to government coffers and was attractive on the Jordanian side because it enabled consumers to cut out the middle man and buy oil almost directly from the source. These activities spawned a thriving gray market between Iraq and Jordan estimated to have employed more than 5,000 smugglers, to say nothing of the merchants and apparatchiks on both sides who made money.

At the Iraqi bus and taxi station in central Amman—where distinctive orange and white cabs from Baghdad wait to carry goods and human traffic across the border—customs officials took a small stipend from the Jordanian government and, in some cases, a larger stipend from the smugglers who paid them to look the other way. Across the street from the parked taxis, a little boy would wave an empty plastic jar up and down. It was a signal to passing motorists that he could lead you to a man who sold Iraqi benzene at well below market prices.

Driving on toward the fringes of Jordan to the Iraqi border, across desert dunes, past Zarqa University, a stronghold of the Muslim Brotherhood, past the occasional free trade zone, fruit stand, and fenced-off military installation, one would reach Azraq, a place of black volcanic stones and desert. Around the bend lies a massive oil refinery, where dozens of trucks with Iraqi oil waited in the hot sun. The truck frames shimmered in the heat rising off the oil-splotched pavement. The truckers also had smaller shipments of diesel fuel, which they brought across in secret compartments and sold well below the going rate to loitering Egyptians and Sudanese, who in turn sold the oil on the black market to consumers. There was no secret where it all came from: gas stations on the Iraqi border, where it was subsidized and cheap. "Very egalitarian," a friend in Jordan's General Intelligence Directorate remarked. "All you'd need is a truck. These gas stations were really export stations, and they would just fill up more than a driver would ordinarily need."[16]

Iraqi cab drivers meanwhile sold other wares in the Iraqi cab station in Amman. On a crisp autumn day in 2002, Kalashnikovs smuggled across the border were available at bargain-basement prices. Who was buying? Bearded men who aimed to smuggle them into the West Bank, or in some cases Saudi Arabia, where Islamists had begun stockpiling for the possibility of an assault. Some people who resided in Jordan and supported extremist Islamist groups were stockpiling semiautomatic rifles in their own basements—not necessarily for any immediate purpose, because after all, Islamists hold seats in the Jordanian parliament—but for the *Sa'ah*, the prophesied hour of reckoning. In addition to weapons, other prized cross-border contraband included artifacts from Iraqi museums, universities, and collectors' homes. A Jordanian agent received a special appreciation from his superiors in 1994 when he intercepted a statue from the Sumerian period that had been sold for 70,000 Jordanian dinar (nearly $100,000) and smuggled across the border, en route to a private collector in Geneva, in a crate of kitchen utensils.[17]

Most Iraqi agents who facilitated smuggling and trade in Jordan and other countries in the Arab world and beyond eventually received a summons to come home and resume their domestic security work, or in some cases to accept various administrative and political appointments in Baghdad and the provinces. More than a few of these are angling to maintain their government jobs after the fall of Saddam's government, and hope to hold onto them for years to come. What may be said about the politics of these more worldly Ba'this? Did extensive contact and trade with people outside the pervasive influence of the party have a moderating effect on their outlook?

In the years of sanctions, Saddam encouraged a degree of political pragmatism among the more trusted members of his clan posted abroad. It is noteworthy that in some of Saddam's speeches, he reveres the eleventh-century Arabic doctor-warrior Usama bin Munqidh, who valiantly fought the crusaders but also forged close friendships with Christians, even traveling to Christendom to treat an ailing friend. Whether Saddam's periodic emphasis on the memory of Osama bin Munqidh betrays an intent to inspire a sort of political flexibility among his party elites is unclear. But a number of credible sources contend that during the Rabin years in Israel, Iraq quietly offered to discuss a peace deal if the Jewish state could persuade America to lift the sanctions. (The United States did not take kindly to the initiative.) Some of the smuggled Iraqi oil in recent years has been known to make its way into Israel via Palestinian intermediaries.[18] A few factories in Jordan's free trade zones have also fostered cooperation of an indirect sort between Iraq and Israel. Israeli textile experts have taken part in joint ventures to manufacture clothes for export to Baghdad, Basra, and Mosul.

On any given day in the late 1990s, Jordanian go-betweens might hold a morning meeting with a Ba'thi from Baghdad and an afternoon appointment with a merchant from New York or Tel Aviv. These contacts sometimes yielded radical plans for thawing relations between Saddam's privileged politicos and the United States. Yusuf Bahlaq, a Jordanian national of Palestinian extraction who has been exporting paper to Iraq since 1981, drew up a radical plan to head off the U.S.-Iraqi impasse in the summer of 2002 and on a visit to Baghdad quietly passed it on to sympathetic Iraqi party men from the armed forces whom he had known for years. Bahlaq's plan proposed bringing American delegations to Iraq, Saddam's recognition of the Iraqi opposition, and inviting U.S. congressmen to lead arms inspections. It might have been a coincidence, but elements of the proposal appear to have been entertained by the Iraqi leadership, which issued an invitation to U.S. congressmen a few weeks later.[19]

Whatever the politics of party and intelligence men, as they returned home from a tour of duty, they always took care to toe the line. If one avoided interagency conflict and paid one's dues through fierce intelligence work, a decade or two in the *Mukhabarat* might yield an invitation to a government position of some importance. A good old boy from the right tribe could reasonably hope to become the appointed mayor of a distant town, political advisor to a minister or governor, or even in time a member of Saddam's cabinet. But there was a catch: promotions to high levels in the party apparatus tended to come as rewards for the kinds of brutal crackdowns on insurgents and other triumphs of state over society that aggrieved ordinary Iraqis considerably. The higher up you were in the administration of a province or town, the less likely your constituents were to like you. There are concerns that a spate of vengeance and bloodletting will take place in Iraq in the wake of Saddam's loss of control, reflecting the long-festering popular rage against the privileged tribesmen of the intelligence services and Ba'th party now poised to come in full view as Iraqis attain a modicum of freedom.[20]

Malice Toward None?

In hopes that it will soon no longer be commonplace to whisper in Iraq when telling a joke about Saddam or his henchmen, allow me to share one with you. A *lablabi* (boiled salted chickpeas) peddler parks his cart in front of one of the presidential palaces, and as he begins to call out, "Chickpeas for sale!" Saddam and his bodyguards walk out the front gate.

"Who is this guy and what does he think he's doing here?" Saddam asks.

"He's selling chickpeas," a guard replies.

"Throw him out of Iraq," says Saddam, "I don't want to see him in the country again."

The next day, 6 million Iraqis show up in front of the palace selling chickpeas.[21]

A minority clique that rules a country with an iron fist must crack down on public ridicule as its first line of defense. The jokes themselves are harmless, but the widespread suffering and rage that make them funny could, if given a chance, stoke the desire to sweep away a ruler and his minions in a roaring revolt. Decades of Ba'thi control have yielded hundreds of thousands of human tragedies in Iraq, to say nothing of neighboring Iran and Kuwait. Hardly a family has avoided the loss of a loved one or theft of assets by the elite of greater Takrit. As power changes hands, the question of Saddam's privileged politicos occupies Iraq's body and soul: the mind wants representative rule, the heart wants justice, and the stomach wants revenge.

All three cravings inevitably bow, however, to the realities of transitional government. Though nary a Middle Eastern state has refrained from exacting retribution on its enemies where possible, most have also displayed pragmatism in salvaging the useful human resources of the regimes they supplanted. The Umayyad tribes of Arabia conquered Syria and Egypt from the Byzantines in the seventh century and inherited a vast bureaucratic responsibility they were ill equipped to meet. So they let the bureaucrats of the old regime keep their jobs, and the administrative language of the first Muslim empire remained Byzantine Greek for nearly a century. Two hundred years later in North Africa, when an Iraqi Shi'i revolutionary led an army of Berber tribes to overthrow an Abbasid satellite state that ruled from the city of Qayrawan, the rebel leader surprised his constituents by asking his erstwhile enemy, the intelligence chief of the deposed prince, to stay on in his post. Some historians of the time believed the spymaster had cut a secret deal to help the rebels months before their victory. Political upheavals in the twentieth century yielded similar surprises, from the bureaucrats and technocrats of Iran's shah, who held together a new government for the Mullahs, to the civil servants of Iraqis' slain king, who put their misgivings aside in 1958 and lent the nascent Republic of Iraq a helping hand. Transitional government happens overnight, but the transformation of government takes time.

These words would infuriate anyone who has known the brutality of the Ba'th or has been to an Iraqi prison. Zainab al-Suwaij, an Iraqi American Muslim activist from Basra who fought in the unsuccessful 1991 popular uprising against Saddam, recalls storming a jail in Karbala: "As I wandered around the jail, I saw some of the instruments that were used to torture people, with instruction manuals posted on the wall. I saw huge, human meat grinders that fed into a septic tank. I saw chemical pools in which people were dissolved. I saw rooms for sexual abuse, and human ovens. The smell in these rooms was putrid, a smell only decades of human torture can create."[22] Even as a war crimes tribunal and system of national reconciliation takes shape in the new Iraq, there are concerns about a repeat performance of the citizen slayings in Iraq's southern provinces and elsewhere that took place in the uprising that followed the 1991 war. Many of the victims could be people known to have worked for the party and *Mukhabarat*.

Many of Saddam's privileged politicos are now increasingly on the run. Their fate in the years ahead will vary from province to province and from person to person. What will come of the operatives of Saddam's security and intelligence apparatus? Will the stigma of party affiliation turn some longtime civil servants with talents to offer the new Iraq into outcasts? Will the bitter memory of war crimes perpetrated by Saddam's supporters lead to new forms of injustice against the country's Sunni Arab minority? What role can newcomers to the country play in facilitating national reconciliation?

The answers to these questions begin with a massive research project. Iraq's security and intelligence apparatus across the country generated tens of millions of memos over the past few years documenting interrogations, torture, and executions, as well as the complex web of serial snitches whose reports helped label colleagues and neighbors "enemies of the state." Just a small fraction of these files numbering 2.4 million pages was confiscated by the United States and its allies in 1991 in northern Iraq and promptly brought to the United States for review. The State Department, in cooperation with the Harvard University Iraq Documentation Project, reviewed them en masse to help prepare evidence for possible war crimes trials against members of Iraq's political leadership for their campaign of genocide against the Kurds.[23]

The value of these dated items from an outlying province pale in comparison to the vast caches of documents likely to become available to Iraq's new government from the intelligence nerve centers of the old regime: Baghdad, Basra, and Mosul. How many documents will have been hurriedly shredded and burned in 2003 remains to be seen. Many if not most documents will probably survive the transition of government, thanks in part to Saddam, who has regarded any measures taken in anticipation of a new government as acts of treason. Nevertheless, moles within the *Mukhabarat* have cooperated secretly with the United States and Jordan to begin smuggling documents out of Iraq for several months running in 2002 and 2003, in exchange for amnesty and perhaps a role in the new Iraq.

A methodical review of Iraq's intelligence archives is the only way to pinpoint violators of international law and exonerate officials who claim to have done no harm. The undertaking will be time-consuming and enormous, with staffing needs ranging from dozens to hundreds of researchers, depending on the definition and scope of the inquiry. Although the occupiers of Germany after World War II took several years to complete their survey of Nazi SS archives,[24] recent innovations in modern technology will help hurry the Iraqi project along. The ability of computers to scan and recognize printed and handwritten Arabic text will enable lightning-quick sorts and key word searches for the names of particular subjects of scrutiny. But more than 50 years after the fall of Berlin, there is still no substitute for human sensitivity and inferential analysis in making sense of spook-speak. The heroes of this dark research project will emerge from their cubicles with a deep understanding of Iraqi and regional power politics past and present.

Meanwhile, ordinary Iraqis have concerns of their own. The deep scar in Iraqi society that stands to be laid bare by Saddam's ouster poses immediate demands for a rooting out of the rule of fear. This means curtains for the staff at spook central. Though elements of General Security and the regular police force may survive the transitional government virtually intact, policy experts and Iraqis far and wide agree that General Intelligence, Special Security, and the party patrols of the regular army had best be dismantled, their personnel pensioned off. But precedent purges in post-Nazi and post-Soviet governments indicate that a pink slip alone will not get every heavy off the stage. Thousands of diehards from the Nazi SS regrouped in a paramilitary organization that became known as the Werewolves. They poisoned defectors and officials of the postwar government, biding their time in hideouts in Germany's forests. Though hunted down year after year by the new administrators of the country, there were still a few Werewolves on the prowl in 1953. Other Nazi intelligence veterans stuck together and attempted to join the new Europe, offering themselves to the service of the new German government. The most famous of these was the Gehlen organization, a Nazi military intelligence clique that joined the American team. The trouble with Gehlen was that pro-Soviet elements who ran the government in communist East Germany had managed to penetrate it thoroughly. Veteran St. Anthony's College scholar Roy Giles, who served in his youth as an administrator in Germany's postwar British sector, offers words of wisdom: "If an organization hands itself to you on a plate, you can bet there will be some bad eggs in it."[25]

Ex-*Mukhabarat* agents and party apparatchiks may keep a low profile in the short term, but a range of opportunities await them inside the new Iraq and beyond. Those inclined to attack the new regime and its defenders may find logistical support and easy funding from foreign sources. Governments and wealthy individuals in the region with an ax to grind in the new Iraq will seek out ex-spooks in order to leverage their networks and expertise in the country to strike at various targets. Political gains for the country's Shi'is will provoke the ire of the stalwarts of sectarian chauvinism. Widespread vengeance wrought upon Sunni tribes will anger the region. A long-term foreign military presence in the country will galvanize Islamists and nationalists far and wide. The training Iraqi intelligence personnel went through did not mold a mind-set amenable to carrying out suicide attacks, but it did create consummate assassins and saboteurs. Justice and national reconciliation in the new Iraq can go a long way in reducing the incentive of former elites to hit back. But popular perceptions in the region depend no less on the slant of Arabic media coverage of the transformation underway. As a new government takes shape under the aegis of an international military presence, hopes for national unity in Iraq will not be fostered by Arab satellite television correspondents who file their stories "live from occupied Baghdad."

Politics aside, the profit motive will lead retired agents in several directions. Many of Iraq's ex-spooks offer area expertise and a contact base that exiled dissidents and regional specialists will be hard pressed to match. Some have already engaged in business activities in the region's gray and black markets for personal gain, on behalf of the old regime, or both. In the rough and tumble of a national work in progress, some will fortify the country's nascent organized crime syndicates with brawn and ruthless, competitive tactics. Others will emerge as translators, advisors, bodyguards, or rainmakers for local and foreign entrepreneurs. As Richard Aldrich writes in *The Hidden Hand*, a seminal study of Cold War espionage, "[The Cold War] was not the first or the last conflict in which secret service personnel quickly found reemployment."[26]

One can only hope that shrewd planning and good fortune will conspire to weave ex-spooks back peacefully into the fabric of Iraq. Achieving the same for the Ba'th party apparatus in the broadest sense poses a challenge many times more massive, because it concerns several hundred thousand people and their extended families. Like any ruling party, the Ba'th attracted some of Iraq's best and brightest who joined for the same reasons that ambitious people everywhere are drawn to the locus of power and wealth. They faced trade-offs that tested their morals and values in ways outsiders can hardly imagine. Who would presume to judge someone's life choices in a state system so cheap and cruel?

Reconciliation and retribution will occur in tandem in the new Iraq. Against the backdrop of war crimes tribunals for the architects of Ba'thi brutality, vigilante justice stands to touch many more lives and reintroduce the cruelty of *fitna*, an Arabic word for civil strife. Longtime detractors of Saddam in Iraq who had disparaged the well-known Sunni tradition of the prophet Muhammad—"One hour of *fitna* is worse than a century of tyranny"—may suddenly come to appreciate its wisdom. But the better instincts of human nature will also put in an appearance. Zainab al-Suwaij recalled treating a wounded Ba'th official while serving as a nurse in Basra during the abortive uprising of 1991. "He was terrified," she said. "He thought I was going to kill him instead of stitch his wounds. I said, 'Don't worry, we are not like you.'"[27]

Stemming extrajudicial violence calls for stern security measures and moral leadership on every level. Subsequent chapters exploring the role of the religious establishment, educational system, and entertainment industry in promoting compassion and forgiveness speak to forces beyond the realm of policy that can nudge Iraqi society in the right direction. As for the systemic questions of power and its distribution, two principles come to mind.

The first is merit. Workplaces in every Iraqi government office deserve the sort of grueling audit that outside consultants are sometimes called upon to carry out on bloated corporations. Sloth is universal, and the trained eye can spot it a mile away. Enough coffee-slurping party hacks will get the boot for slacking off to usher in new blood in short order, while conscientious civil servants who happen to have chosen the party will have the chance to prove themselves on an increasingly level playing field.

The second principle is character. The more unpleasant traits that a one-party system tends to inculcate in its members coincide with some of the well-known qualities organizational psychologists consider toxic to a work environment: lack of initiative, hostility to new ideas, hoarding information, and injecting politics into the workplace. Ex-Ba'this in civil service who defy these stereotypes deserve to stay right where they are; the rest belong at home.

Honing group dynamics in Iraq's public sector also rests on the establishment of camaraderie and trust between co-workers. The presence of *Mukhabarat* and party moles in nearly every government office imposes the responsibility of "lustration" on Iraq's new leadership. The term was widely used in post-Soviet Eastern Europe, notably the Czech Republic and Poland, to denote the process of relieving moles of their day jobs. The sleuth work of tracking down moles falls upon that corps of researchers tasked to scrutinize the archives of Saddam's *Mukhabarat*.

Millions of reports from hundreds of thousands of informants in Iraq's big cities stand to expose countless relationships of trust violated on a grand scale. As part of the process of national reconciliation in former communist East Germany after its reintegration into the German Republic, the government declared that everyone had a right to see their file in the *Stasi* secret police headquarters. At last, people had the opportunity to learn who their anonymous accusers had been and confront them, perhaps forgive them. Whether a similar right granted to all Iraqis would lead to reconciliation or only further retribution is a question only time can answer. True national reconciliation depends on the willingness of Iraqis to reengineer the structure of power in state and society, not by replacing one elite clique with another but by opening the field to everyone.

Questions meanwhile facing the U.S. government in its stated commitment to support Iraq's rehabilitation include the extent to which it may seek to bring about a long-term redistribution of power from the top down by chaperoning the country's political system. America's dilemma stems from the discomfort of confronting inertia: the identity-based criteria reinforced by the British in Iraq in the 1920s, whereby adherents to the Sunni minority religious sect were anointed to govern, have been perpetuated through generations of violent Sunni minority rule in Iraq and the disenfranchisement of its majority Shi'i community. The antique lens of colonial identity politics continues to shape policy-making discourse today, and the sectarian identities of Iraq still loom large in the country's political culture, as the following chapter will show. Viewing Iraq through the additional lens of economics, as a subsequent section will do, reveals the depth of disenfranchisement and the difficulty of truly broadening the arena of power. It is nonetheless a cause worth struggling for, by both the peoples of Iraq and their supporters abroad.

Five

State-Building by the Book

Islamic Leadership in the New Iraq

Every few weeks since 1997, according to a friend in Iran, a mule ambles across the Iran–Iraq border bearing a bearded rider, his water flask, some snacks, and a satchel. A short distance beyond the last Iranian town, the rider reaches the first Iraqi checkpoint, where border guards ask a dozen tough questions peppered with two or three mortal threats. He slips them a generous bribe worth one or two American dollars and continues on his way. A few days later, he arrives at Najaf, the second holiest city to Shi'is. But he is no ordinary pilgrim.[1]

Najaf is not the pulsating center of religious traffic it used to be. Several holy places were destroyed by Saddam in the 1980s. Some of the city's religious authorities were arrested and tortured to death after the Shi'i uprising against Saddam in the aftermath of the 1991 Gulf War. In the center of town in a two-story house adjoining a historic mosque, the highest-ranking Shi'i cleric in Najaf is teaching a young student *tajwid*, a traditional style of chanting Qur'an. Sayyid Ali al-Sistani is the *marja* (religious authority), whose rulings on Islamic law are binding for millions of Shi'is in Iraq, the Gulf states, Lebanon, India, Pakistan, and elsewhere. He gets up to answer the knock on the door.

The man from Iran greets him with kisses on both cheeks. The sayyid's eyes fall on the satchel. He sets it down on the table and removes the documents inside: dozens of e-mails in Arabic printed on A4 paper sheets. They are *istifta'at*, requests from Shi'is all over the world for a religious edict to answer a moral or religious quandary: Can I marry a Jewish girl? Should I settle a business dispute with my Muslim partner in a secular court? Will I suffer in the world to come if I fight in a war against a Muslim country?

The delivery came from the nearest holy city with Internet access: the Iranian religious capital of Qom. Every few weeks, the man with the satchel rides back and delivers answers—a handwritten sheaf of *fatawa*, religious edicts, from the sayyid in Najaf. In an office building across from Qom's main religious seminary, an Iraqi tekkie named Abd al-Karim Kazimi inputs every paragraph into his Web site, *Nahrain.net*, the official clearinghouse of Sistani's latest teachings for pious Shi'is near and far.

"We get 350,000 hits a month," he says, "from all over the Middle East as well as Europe and the United States. They try to block us in Saudi Arabia, but the Shi'is who live there browse our pages by accessing mirror sites in other countries." On a budget of $100,000 a year, mostly from Shi'i almsgivers in the Gulf states, the site employs writers, Web designers, the latest technology, human messengers, and the occasional mule.[2]

The team effort that makes it possible to globalize Sistani's edicts reflects Iraq's endurance as a center of spiritual leadership and innovation. Regardless of events, Iraqis do not stop thinking and talking about God, a topic they have been contemplating for thousands of years. Sumerian temple priests invoked the authority of local gods to rule the first urban communities. The kings and emperors of later Mesopotamia used the gods of the cosmos to overrule the priests and their townships. Time reduced the number of gods to one, with the articulation of monotheism by the biblical patriarch Abraham. Though the monotheistic faiths that came after Judaism were conceived in other settings, their arrival in Iraq transformed them forever. Islam emerged in an Arabian tribal society, but won an empire and urban elites through a revolution that yielded the caliphal capital of Baghdad, where Islam's major legal and mystical schools were formed.[3]

Each religious innovation left its mark on the country, making Iraqi society the most spiritually diverse in the Middle East today. Its multitude of Christian and Muslim sects and its

recently exiled Jewish community have already been described
in previous chapters. But now and then on a visit to contemporary Iraq one even comes across traditions that harken back to
the ancient days before there was one God. For example, not
long ago the people of Basra mourned the passing of a snake
charmer named Abu 'l-Hayya, who made magical ointments and
potions out of venom—a vestige of an ancient Mesopotamian
cult. He kept the snakes in cloth bags at night but let them out
every morning to slither around the house and backyard—"so
they could get some exercise," according to his granddaughter.
"They used to catch birds and rats. They would slither around
our feet, and we'd pick them up and hold them. I remember in
1990 we went on a visit to Egypt and saw the snakes in the zoo.
You could pay the zoo some money to take the snake out and
put it on your head for a picture. It was no big deal for me."[4]

From ancient cults to cutting-edge cross-border Web sites,
Iraqi clerics have manifested resilience under the strain of sanctions and surveillance. But spiritual leadership in the new Iraq
worries people who believe in a separation of religion from politics and fear the maximalist ambitions God has been known to
inspire in the Middle East. The country's multiethnic Shi'i
majority and Sunni minority communities defy easy labels like
"secular" and "fundamentalist," and the clerics who organize
their worship differ in outlook. But one thing most Iraqi clerics
have had in common in recent years was their isolation from
religio-political movements outside Iraq. Although a few important clerics like Sistani found ways to maintain some contact
with counterparts abroad, most clerics inside Iraq were cut off,
due to Saddam's strict control over people flow and information
flow. Now all this will change as Iraq's isolation comes to an
end. Islamic leadership in the new Iraq stands to influence and
be influenced by Islamist movements in the Middle East and
global trends in religion and politics.

A tour of Iraq's Islamic landscape requires some historical context. The premodern world has always lent power and influence
to those who won the job of mediating between society and God.
In late-eighth-century Baghdad the two contenders were the

caliph, who ruled an empire from a throne, and a grassroots class of urban Muslim clerics known as the *ulama* (sing., *alim*). The former sought to consecrate the monopoly his office had traditionally held on the religious articulation of Islam by putting the latter through an inquisition. Those *ulama* who refused to fall in line with his theological views would be banished. But the *ulama* stood their ground and the caliph's successor put an end to the inquisition. Decentralized clerical networks determined Muslim legal and ethical norms from then on, while caliphs saw to the lay rule of the empire.[5]

Ulama codified the traditions of the prophet Muhammad and explained what obligations they posed to ordinary Muslims. They also served the state as bureaucrats and functionaries and the society as teachers, mediators, and leaders of worship. To legislate Islam's message, Sunnis drew from traditions of the prophet Muhammad which Shi'is rejected. Shi'is, for their part, emphasized their own traditions of the prophet as well as those of his son-in-law Ali, the man they revered most after Muhammad. Sunni *ulama* won more widespread support from lay rulers, although Shi'is held sway in times and places where their ideas were in favor. Reaching the fringes of successive Muslim empires, networks of *ulama* were an engine of Islam's premodern venture of globalization, a project that converted millions of people, streamlined cultural norms, and expanded commerce within its vast borders.

Another engine was the Muslim mystics known as Sufis. Some reinterpreted Islam's legal traditions through the prism of spirituality, while others fused the teachings of the Qur'an and its prophet with older ideas about magic and shrines. At times when hardline *ulama* with an ear to the ruler acted to curb radical ideas, Sufi orders were a refuge for philosophical and spiritual innovators. However idiosyncratic the teachings of some Sufis, their distinguished contribution to the propagation of Islam is beyond doubt. They spoke to the old-fashioned sensibilities of villagers and frontiersmen and rallied the caliph's troops at the empire's borders ever outward.

Though *ulama* and Sufis outlived the days of the caliphs, which formally ended with the breakup of the Ottoman Empire

after World War I, new systems of colonial rule and the nationalism that came in its wake largely disenfranchised the cloth from
its privileged place in government and administration. The
twentieth century registered gains for clerics in political systems that leaned on them for legitimacy, notably in Saudi Arabia and Iran, and losses in countries that espoused the values of
secularism, like Turkey, Syria, and Iraq.

Both *ulama* and Sufis endure in contemporary Iraq, tran-
scending ethnicities, Muslim sects, and schools of Muslim law.
The Kurds of the north are mainly Sunni but include Shi'i
minority communities in the southern sections of Kurdistan
and parts of the cities of Kirkuk and Arbil. Sufism reigns
supreme, though Kurdish *ulama* command sizable followings of
their own.[6] The predominantly Arab south is mostly Shi'i, but
includes non-Arab adherents to Shi'ism who trace their roots to
Turkey and Iran, as well as the more modest Sunni Arab communities. *Ulama* of both sects command the largest followings.
All these faiths and ethnic groups are represented in the predominantly Sunni center. The vestiges of the country's older religious communities, including numerous sects of Christianity
and smaller faiths with more ancient roots, survive and continued to yield a few of the country's more important political
players under Saddam. The viability of the minority faiths themselves as a basis for political organization has diminished considerably, however, owing to their adherents' small and dwin-
dling numbers.

A country elsewhere in the Middle East as ethnically and
religiously diverse would surprise no one by manifesting sectarian strife. Witness the frequent attacks by Sunnis and Shi'is on
one another's mosques in Pakistan, to say nothing of attacks by
members of both communities on the country's churches. Those
who have tried to explain the comparative rarity of spontaneous
flare-ups like these in Iraq in recent years usually paid a back-
handed compliment to Saddam, citing his regime's monopoliza-
tion of political and ethnic violence to keep the religiously
diverse communities in check and Sunni elites ascendant. But
Saddam's accompanying historic penchant for playing ethnic
and religious groups against one another makes one wonder

whether more deeply rooted cultures of accommodation might not also deserve some credit for Iraq's relative calm.

Like thoughtful people everywhere, Iraqis identify ethnically and religiously, as well as ideologically and politically. When new ways of organizing state and society hit Iraq in the twentieth century through British rule and subsequent republican army coups, Iraqis drew from the manifold ideas around them and formed political parties. So did urbanites in nearly every Arab country at the time. Minorities and many lay Muslims gravitated to political ideas that shed the baggage of religion and saw all native Arabic speakers as one nation. The spiritual leaders of Islam for their part gave these ideas mixed reviews. While some joined the bandwagon and most stayed aloof, an ingenious few teamed up with lay people to make their own play for political power by melding new ideas of political organization with the old clerical networks that had held sway in society for centuries. Some people have dubbed these movements "Islamic fundamentalist," but that term is unsuitable, because it fails to take into account the modern underpinnings of their political organization. A more appropriate term is "Islamist," which simply denotes a political ideology informed by ideas about Islam.

Most Islamist parties shared a commitment to an appropriation of the Qur'an and prophetic traditions as the legal and political system of the country. But interpretations of Islam's essence differed, as did the parties' political strategies, which ranged from passive resistance to systemic activism to lethal violence. Waves of rural young people who grew up in more traditional settings found Islamism attractive and somehow comforting as they moved into the big cities. In Iraq, elements of every major community experimented with Islamism to varying degrees—Sunnis in the 1950s and 1960s, Shi'is in the 1970s, and Kurds in the 1980s and 1990s—and each experiment yielded a state crackdown with executions and deportations. The three sets of crackdowns left an indelible mark on religious life inside Iraq, and many of the exiled Islamists have not stopped making ambitious plans for the country's future.[7]

The international Muslim Brotherhood movement, which began in Egypt in the late 1920s, filtered into Sunni communities in Baghdad and Mosul by the mid-1940s. Books by the Egyptian Brotherhood ideologues won a wide readership in these cities. The rallying cry of Palestinian liberation that these books espoused resonated in Iraq, particularly after the Zionist movement won a Jewish state in the 1948 war. Muslims at the time in both Iraq and Palestine had shared in the struggle against British mandatory rule, and both countries hosted large communities of Jews—in Palestine mainly through decades of immigration, in Iraq mainly through millennia of continuity. Activism against the British won the Iraqi Brotherhood a foothold in the local coalition that became the new Iraqi Republic, while activism against the Jews established their credentials in the international Brotherhood movement. In the 1960s, successive Iraqi juntas honed a secularist worldview that the Brotherhood roundly rejected. Those who survived in politics did so mainly by turning their agenda outward toward solidarity with Palestine, and in so doing helped ensure Iraq's persistent stand against Israel. But the Ba'th government eventually resolved to rid Iraq of Sunni Islamists. A sustained campaign of crackdowns, tortures, and executions in the late 1960s did not take long to destroy the movement's domestic infrastructure. Some activists left the country, and the members who remained decided to retreat from a conflict they felt they could not win.

The Brotherhood unwittingly weakened Iraq's Sunni *ulama* inside the country by inspiring Saddam's government to reengineer the Sunni religious establishment through government control. Sunni seminaries won government funding but lost their autonomy and faced tough restrictions on topics they were free to teach. The instruction of Qur'an chanting and interpretation of prophetic traditions dealing in personal and family law survived intact. But the prolific literature of Sunni tradition that may broadly be said to address the ethics of religiopolitical leadership faced tight curbs. In early 2003, *ulama* of local mosques still received a note from the government every week with guidelines for the content of their sermons. Their traditional role as mediators within Sunni society eroded, because ordinary people distrusted their close ties to the government. Ironically, the very Muslim sect that claimed Saddam as one of its own suffered from his close embrace. The younger the Sunni Arab cleric in Iraq today, the less well-rounded his exposure to Muslim tradition is likely to be.[8]

Old-timers who cut their teeth on religious texts in the less restricted days before the Ba'th, on the other hand, enjoy enormous respect in Iraq and beyond. And not all of them share the politics of the Brotherhood or the Ba'th. Yasir al-Kubaisi is an elderly Sunni cleric from Baghdad who has become a superstar in the Gulf. For years now he has been able to come and go from Baghdad while residing mainly in the United Arab Emirates (UAE), where he tapes a weekly show on personal and family law for the Dubai Satellite Channel. I met him in the summer of 1999 at a lavish Friday lunch at the home of Seif al-Ghurair, a multimillionaire who owns a bank and some of the UAE's largest trading companies. The 40-odd guests sat sipping juice in rapt attention as Kubaisi expounded on personal ethics, effortlessly interweaving an old-fashioned Iraqi accent Gulf Arabs warm to with quotes from Qur'an and prophetic traditions, while lacing his sermon with original poetry and some jokes.

What are his politics? you might ask. His friends in the Gulf know not to press him on Saddam or even Palestine, because his freedom to come and go in Iraq under Saddam has always hinged on his refusal to weigh in on politics. But mutual friends intimate that Kubaisi and many of his followers are cool to the international Muslim Brotherhood movement and the firebrands it produces. They reject the strategy of suicide bombings adopted by the Palestinian Brotherhood offshoot, Hamas, on the ground that it has not advanced Palestinian national aspirations, in some cases on religious grounds as well. Needless to say, Kubaisi is no friend of the Ba'th party either, and has little love for the Arab republics of Syria or Egypt. The Gulf states of Bahrain, the UAE, and Kuwait are full of politically ambivalent Sunni *ulama* who quietly espouse a liberal Muslim worldview while avoiding confrontations with certain Saudi and Yemeni clerics who toe a harder line. Many are Iraqis; all are deeply respectful of Kubaisi and his ilk. Lacking a country like Saudi Arabia to bankroll their activities, these cliques tend to be hard pressed for cash.[9]

By contrast, the hardcore Iraqi Muslim Brotherhood exiles whose contact with the Iraqi interior has been comparatively thin in recent years enjoy generous funding from Saudi Arabia's Muslim World League, the multibillion-dollar endowment of that country's clerics. In the United States and London, where some of these clerics preside and deliver weekly Friday sermons in Saudi-built mosques, the ideological link between the struggles against Zionism and imperialism in Iraq and Palestine remains inseparable, even though the Jews are gone from one and the British have departed from the other. These *ulama* have in mind to return to Iraq and bring their ideologies with them.

Meanwhile, back in the Iraqi port city of Basra, it is the Muslim festival of *Eid al-Adha.* A girl named Fatima is helping her grandfather, a venerable Shi'i cleric, count wads of cash, holiday alms contributions from friends and neighbors who worship in his mosque. She puts them into envelopes and wraps them together to be sent by messenger to the holy city of Najaf, where that leading Shi'i *marja* Ali al-Sistani who responds to e-mails via mule will graciously accept the contribution. The mandatory Shi'i charity tax of *Khums* yields donations from Shi'is all over Iraq, traditional and secular alike. They remit in private to their local holy man, who passes most of the money on to the *marja* (Shi'i authority). The institution is more than a thousand years old. In the tenth century, when a leading Shi'i *marja* happened to be an imam living underground and struggling to unseat the Sunni caliph, *Khums* served as a grassroots movement to finance the revolution. But most of the money historically went to needy Muslims and to defray the cost of seminary instruction.

In contemporary Iraq, *Khums* is one of the few nonprofit financial networks to survive Saddam, albeit as a shadow of its former self. Through decades of Ba'th rule, the disaffected Shi'i establishment maintained extrasystemic organizational structures that at times enjoyed a measure of autonomy from Saddam's spiritual engineering. "They leave us alone," Fatima said. "Nobody asks me how much money I counted." Sistani submits a budget neither to the government nor to his own flocks. By contrast to Sunni tradition, the school of Shi'i thought to which most Shi'i worshipers in Iraq adhere holds that the *marja* is infallible. He can reason and pronounce ethical judgments freely, and spend the money as he sees fit.[10]

These privileges notwithstanding, Shi'i leadership in Iraq has been no picnic. The community's disenfranchisement dates back to the rule of the British, who largely kept them out of government jobs. The height of pan-Arabism in the 1950s and 1960s saw popular support for Iraq to join some of its neighbors in a new union of Arab states, a proposition Shi'is rejected because the demographic scale of the new confederacy would have tipped in favor of Sunnis. Several Shi'i Islamist parties emerged in the 1950s, in some cases espousing a peaceful campaign of societal transformation, in others calling for a violent overthrow of the establishment. The Shi'i *Da'wa* party of renowned *Alim* Baqir al-Sadr combined both strategies, first espousing a phase of covert organization and political proselytism that spanned nearly two decades, then coming out of the closet in 1979 with a call to take up arms against Saddam.[11]

Sadr and his sister faced execution, scores of Shi'i activists were rounded up and killed, and the party's stalwarts scattered across the globe. Some went east and ceded a measure of political independence to the nascent Shi'i revolutionary state of Iran, where the Supreme Council for the Islamic Revolution in Iraq has maintained a continuous presence. Others went west and established offices in London. Sunni Brotherhood exiles generally hung on to their strident politics wherever they went, while Sunni clerics who would not toe the line have stayed aloof from politics. By contrast, Shi'i Islamist exiles manifest a broader array of views and political alliances. The militants who pitched tent in Iran remained militant, making common cause with Shi'i Hizbullah in its armed struggle against Israel and maintaining a vision of clerical rule in Iraq along the lines of Khomeini's Islamic Republic. Their tentative truce with the United States in early 2003 reflected more realpolitik and less a commitment to shared values. But Shi'i revolutionaries of a different sort in London reached out to the West. Members of the Kho'i Foundation, named after a famous Iraqi opponent to Khomeini's theocratic vision, won a seat in the United Nations and forged ties with American organizations, including the National Endowment for Democracy. Other Shi'i Islamists in London came out unambiguously in favor of democracy for Iraq and joined the Iraqi National Congress, a U.S.-backed umbrella group of opposition parties.[12]

For Iraqi Shi'is inside Iraq, who lacked any systemic option for political dissent, the calculations were different. In 1991, many young Shi'is joined an uprising against Saddam in the wake of that year's Gulf War, on the perceived promise of American support. The United States did not lend a hand to the uprising, and the harsh crackdown that followed left death and destruction in its wake. Tanks that entered Basra, Karbala, and other major Shi'i cities in southern Iraq came adorned with signs reading, "No Shi'is after today." The brutal crackdown was followed by a wave of arrests, tortures, and detentions of Shi'i *ulama*. While Sunni clergy lost credibility with many Iraqis for their relegation to an appendage of the state apparatus, a few Shi'i spiritual leaders who survived have gained prestige among their flocks for their integrity and thinly veiled abhorrence of the state.

The homes of some Shi'i *ulama* in Iraq these days teem with people. The holy man and his family mentioned earlier rarely take a meal alone; guests with special needs are there for breakfast, lunch, and dinner. "People are constantly buzzing in and out," Fatima reports. "Sometimes I want quiet, but I also like the action." Most visitors ask for the *alim*'s blessing or consecration of a life-cycle event. But the judicial services they are called upon to perform with varying degrees of formality betray Iraqi society's search for integrity in a state where the secular legal system is pathetic. When two Shi'is have a business dispute and want an unbiased mediator, the two most sensible options are to consult a venerable *alim*—the older the better—or the *sheikh al-ashira* (tribal elder), either of whom would be far less likely to accept a bribe from the other side than any government functionary. The fact that relatively secular cities like Basra and Baghdad manifest increasing demand for the mediation services of clerics speaks both to the failure of the state and the success of spiritual leadership.[13]

Muslims everywhere bear names that begin, "Abd al-"something: Abd Allah, Abd al-Jabbar, Abd al-Samad, and so on. The prefix means "slave of" or "servant of," and the word that follows is usually one of the 99-odd Arabic names for God. The prefix and suffix together proclaim indenture to God. A distinguished Sufi poet once wondered why so many Muslims aim to be God's slaves, when what God really needs are lovers and friends.

In the rugged mountains of Iraqi Kurdistan, Sufi orders dominate the Islamic cultural landscape and have done so for centuries. The region is less urban than the rest of Iraq, and becomes considerably less urban the farther back one delves into its history. *Ulama*, who distinguished themselves by canonizing Islamic ethics and law, evolved as a class in premodern Muslim cities and towns where demand for new norms and laws was greatest. The rural backwaters of Muslim empires globalized more slowly than the cities, leaving the vestiges of ancient cultures more room to breathe. Kurdish Muslims to this day consider it distasteful to spit into fire; that is a throwback to the sensibilities of Zoroastrian fire priests who used to lead the ancient ancestors of the Kurds in worship.[14] Shrine Sufism, which fused Muslim mysticism with local traditions, was the Kurds' Islamizing engine of choice.

The great irony of Iraq in the past three years is that its cosmopolitan cities have been more isolated than its traditional backwaters—at least as far as information traffic is concerned. While sanctions and Saddam's strict control over information largely sealed off people and ideas from Iraq's south and center, Kurdistan under the aegis of the British- and American-enforced no-fly zone built a cellular phone network and unrestricted Internet cafés all over the north. New technologies enabled Kurds to make new friends and contacts all over the world. But this minirenaissance came on the heels of the greatest Iraqi genocide of the twentieth century, in which the dark underbelly of identity politics played a leading role.

A century before Islamist parties came into vogue in Iraq's big cities, the Kurds of the north rallied behind a Sufi cleric in an armed resistance movement against Iranians to the east and

Ottomans to the west. It was a local order of a transregional mystical movement called the *Naqshbandiyya,* which commands a global following today. The fight was an early play for a measure of sovereignty, which Kurds have sought in struggles passive and active from then until now.[15]

The emergence of Middle Eastern nation-states from urban ethnic groups in the twentieth century left Kurds disaffected. The pan-Arab sentiments of elites in Baghdad and Mosul in the 1950s and 1960s had a tendency to deemphasize Kurdism in the political lexicon. Sunni Muslims as most of them were, some Kurds looked to the Muslim Brotherhood for support at the time. But the movement proved a disappointment due to its unwillingness to help press for a Kurdish national home. When the Ba'th cracked down on the Brotherhood, it adopted a measure of leniency in dealing with the movement's Sunni Arab members, allowing them to disavow the movement and return to a secularist worldview. But Kurdish Islamists were tarred traitors with a broad brush. Government crackdowns on the Kurdish Brotherhood should be viewed in the broader context of Kurdish nationalist challenges to the central government in the 1980s. The central government razed towns and villages, ethnically cleansing them of the Kurds who lived there. It might have seemed strange to the Brotherhood in Kurdistan that their counterparts in Baghdad espoused an egalitarian Islamist ideology, but while faulting Jews for colonizing Palestinian Muslim land failed to wage jihad on the secularist Ba'th party for dispossessing Kurdish Muslims of theirs.[16]

Saddam tried to nurture Sunni Islamist sentiments among the Kurds during the Iran–Iraq war to enlist their help against the Iranian Shi'a. But the movement declared war on Saddam's "infidel regime" instead, triggering Saddam's concerted campaign to exterminate Kurdish men, women, and children beginning in 1986. Saddam's allies in the West and the Arab world looked the other way. With Saddam on the outs after 1991, Kurdish aspirations suddenly won widespread sympathy. Indigenous Islamists from Iraq's north raised monies in the United States and Saudi Arabia for their renewed proclamation of jihad against the Ba'th, although as a movement they played second fiddle to larger secularist groups. Ironically, in recent years, some Iraqi Sunni Kurds with an Islamist tinge to their worldview have allegedly received support from Saddam Hussein to combat American and British enforcement of the UN no-fly zone. Others, mostly subsumed within secularist parties, have won American expertise and training to help fight Saddam, in a program of support bearing some resemblance to America's aid in the 1980s to the holy warriors of Afghanistan to fight the Soviets.

How to Get It Right This Time

By some accounts, the new Iraq is a link in a chain of transformations set in motion by the tragedy of September 11, which was spawned by a movement of Afghan Arab Islamists who once enjoyed American support and training but then turned on their erstwhile backers. That relationship gone sour stems in turn from a long tradition of powers aligning with religio-political movements to fight a common enemy. For policy makers, Islamic leadership in the new Iraq is just another geopolitical problem. For young people and their families who happen to live in the country, it is a force that stands to pervade the public and private spheres of their lives. For the rest of us, it could be the first spiritual venture of the twenty-first century to reward us or merely the next one to punish us.

Old imperial policies die hard. Big decision makers like to whittle their options down to two: Should we back the Shi'is or the Sunnis? Should we prop up the Sufis or bankroll the *ulama?* In the later years of the Ottoman Empire, when decentralization of power and autonomy for the provinces was the modus operandi, Sufis and their syncretism won a measure of state support. But some of these groups became the basis for local proto-nationalist resistance movements. The pendulum began to swing to the other side in the early years of the British adventure in the Arab world, when the desire to wrest Arabia from the Ottomans led to a decision to back a Saudi king and the Wahhabi *ulama* who legitimized him. Never mind the Sufi clerics they attacked or the Shi'i shrines they desecrated.

In the same tradition, the second half of the twentieth century in the Middle East witnessed more joint ventures between pro-Western powers and hard-line clerics, in the face of a common godless enemy. The Egyptian president Sadat granted Islamists power and wealth in the 1970s to counteract Marxist and communist opposition groups, until an Islamist assassinated him. Israel in the 1980s facilitated the growth of the Muslim Brotherhood in Palestine as an alternative to the PLO; the only beneficiaries of this venture were the leaders of the armed movement now known as Hamas.[17] America's support of Afghan Islamists has already been mentioned, together with its tragic punch line. At the dawn of the twenty-first century, some circles in Washington and elsewhere want to allocate monies to help the global pendulum swing back once again toward Sufi movements as an alternative to the *ulama*. Concern about the balance of power between Iraq's Shi'i majorities and Sunni minorities meanwhile remains inseparable from the geopolitics of the United States and its relations with Iran, Saudi Arabia, and the greater Muslim world. All this, and the hopes and fears of Iraqis in the interior, are still absent from the discussion.

The plot thickens. Over the next few years while Iraq remains in flux, the coffers of the Saudi Muslim World League will open to Iraq's Sunni establishment in a venture of reeducation and reorientation. The foundations of Iran's clerical establishment will seek to fortify the great institutions of Shi'i learning with resources and an international political network. Many of the exiled Islamist dissident groups portrayed above will seek to return from Tehran, London, and the United States to reestablish themselves in the country. At best, these forces will help revive traditions of learning that suffered under Saddam and provide members of each Muslim denomination a cushion of political and moral support. At worst, they will foment sectarian violence, attacks on foreigners, and a bellicose foreign policy. Whether it is desirable to expose the country to these forces during a time of transformation is a question worthy of debate. But the debate is moot, because at the dawn of the twenty-first century, sealing off clerics in the new Iraq from their wealthier counterparts abroad is logistically impossible—as impossible as trying to seal off Iraqi consumers from global capitalism.

All this is a lot to take for the venerable cleric's granddaughter in Basra as she wraps wads of Iraqi dinars and sends them on to Najaf this *'Eid*. The home she lives in—where her grandfather arbitrates disputes and resolves blood feuds and provides spiritual guidance to those who need it—is a locus of community leadership with integrity and influence on the society around it. It is also one of the few reliable indigenous institutions of charity in 2003 Iraq. Fatima's grandfather has been too busy doing what clerics do best to plot a coup or coin a blood-curdling phrase. Nor will any amount of money persuade him to shift gears. In the turbulent months of 2003, he will be busier than he has been since the 1991 uprising, when he counseled worshipers not to take up arms against the regime.[18]

In the years to come there will be never a dull moment. Demands on respected clerics for spiritual leadership and counsel will remain unnaturally high in Iraq as long as the institutions of state are perceived as corrupt. Shrewd political leadership of the country would best take the initiative in tasking clerics of every sect to play a role as mediators and bridges to help heal society's rifts. Concern among secularists about clerics' growing esteem in the eyes of their communities should provide incentives to help rebuild the lay alternative: viable Iraqi courts with educated lawyers and untouchable judges, above-board distribution networks for food and social services. The manifold challenges to Iraq's renewal had best be met on the local level through competition in the marketplace of ideas.

Elderly clerics differ from some of their younger counterparts, however. Shi'i *ulama* in their 30s and 40s went through seminary at a time of pervasive state espionage and suppression. Their Sunni contemporaries endured indoctrination in state-run schools light on traditional scholarship and heavy on the politicized pedantry of the party. Both formative experiences stand to make younger *ulama* more susceptible to sales pitches from abroad for a more rebellious new take on religion and politics. They will find opportunities to garner funding from Iranian and

Saudi petro-endowments. Each of these two formidable trusts funds a strident brand of Shi'i and Sunni Islamism, respectively, which has been associated with some of the more militant headline-grabbing movements in the Middle East today, including the Iranian-backed Hizbullah and the Saudi-supported Hamas. One might say that Iranian and Saudi funds are as pervasive in the world's mosques as Coke and Pepsi are in the world's vending machines. The allure of money has a way of making the ideologies these funds support more compelling, regardless of their merit or relevance to a particular society. Recent Iraqi returnees from abroad who have enjoyed these funds for years already aim to facilitate the process. Ideological propagation machines as well greased as these have been known to blow smaller projects out of the water. More modest movements with international networks such as the Shi'i Kho'i Foundation and Sufi *Naqshbandiyya* aim to appeal to hearts and minds as well. Can anyone really compete with Coke and Pepsi, and should wealthy governments and foundations support the effort? Is anybody interested in attempting to break the imperial cycle of propping up religious movements in the Middle East once and for all?

There is a two-part answer.

First, one can level the playing field in Islamic Iraq somewhat by reducing the inflow of strident ideological capital on both the demand side and the supply side. In general, demand for maximalist ideologies stems from one part chauvinism and two parts social disaffection. The more egalitarian Iraqi society and its organs of state become, the lower the demand for sectarian supremacism. It bears noting in this vein that reducing disaffection in Iraq means redistributing some of the economic and political opportunity held overwhelmingly by Arab Sunnis, a process that will anger some members of Iraq's Sunni minority and predispose them to seek support from the region at large. As for the supply side, the governments of Iran and Saudi Arabia are likely to spend less on exporting Islamism in the years ahead for political and economic reasons of their own. That is the subject of another book. Shrewd diplomacy by the new Iraqi government and its allies can meanwhile encourage the two countries to play as constructive a role as possible in Iraq's renewal.

The second part of the answer concerns how and whether to promote other Islamist movements. Iraq's spiritual landscape over the past century has not been lacking in ideologies infused with faith. Nor have the adherents to its manifold religions and sects failed to find ways to reduce, for the most part, sectarian strife. Yet Iraq lacks a modern ecumenical tradition. Fatima of Basra said that her grandfather the Shi'i *alim* rarely interacts with a priest, let alone a Sunni counterpart. "We see them in the street and in our neighborhood," she said, "but we don't know much about them."

On a personal note, my great-great-grandfather, Hakham Avraham Aslan, was chief rabbi of Baghdad in the 1930s, and died there in 1948 at the age of 92. My mother has childhood memories of his kindness and warmth, and my grandmother came to know him well as one of his last star students. Aslan had a reputation for modesty and evenhandedness and was sometimes called upon to resolve political disputes within the Jewish community. He also maintained friendships with members of all faiths, including some of the city's leading Muslim clerics. Yet Aslan lamented the stridency and supremacism that the faith of majority cultures sometimes inspires. His Jewish students came to him seeking advice about growing incidents of discrimination and intolerance emanating from Muslim circles; they felt pressured to convert to Islam or find another place to live. Generations later, as a graduate student living in the Gulf for a year, I enjoyed friendships with young Iraqi Muslim clerics but inevitably faced the same sort of pressure to become Muslim. The pressure stemmed from their sincere concern for my welfare, as they viewed Islam as inherently superior to all other faiths. Lost on these clerics, however, was the basic premise of interfaith dialogue, that all religions have equal merit and no party to the dialogue should attempt to dissuade another of core beliefs.

Embracing ecumenical principles is the only way a heterogeneous society can bridge secularism and sectarian politics, in Iraq or anywhere else. Muslim clerics should have the chance to aspire to political power in the new Iraq, if they trade in the maximalism of the country's old Islamist parties for a platform of values that all denominations share. As for the world's policy makers and grant makers, the spiritual platform to encourage in Iraq and the rest of the Middle East is the one that makes a point of speaking for everyone. Those who consider this goal unrealistic may be right; it is, nevertheless, the challenge ahead. Sufis and *ulama*, Sunnis and Shi'a must learn to essentialize Islam in their hearts and in their mosques while embracing the broadest definition of religion possible in the corridors of lay authority.

Six

About Face

Reengineering the Iraqi Army

Television images of power in Iraq focus on generals with big mustaches and berets, sitting stoically as they watch their leader deliver a defiant speech to the television camera at the other end of the table. They also include soldiers in elaborate military costumes marching rigidly in long parades, and militia women wearing long green tunics, skirts, matching head scarves, and white sashes that read: "At your service, O Saddam!"[1] Perhaps the most visible Iraqi social institution to foreign audiences, the Iraqi army is nonetheless known only by its most superficial features. Behind the impersonal uniforms, anonymous faces, and tank brigades named after Nebuchadnezzar are Iraqis young and old whose lives have been defined by a national draft and years of service. Soldiers hitchhike back to base after a weekend furlough or lounge in bus stations waiting to travel home across the country, while fresh high school graduates report to draft centers. A vast but largely unknown human infrastructure underlies what was once regarded as the world's fourth largest fighting force.

For many Iraqis, military service has meant coming of age. A woman friend from Basra recalls that her father Abu Husayn, a veteran who did his tour of duty in the 1970s, used to spend long summer nights with his children cooling off on the roof of their home in Basra and recounting stories from his army days. Then a young Shi'i man deployed with many friends and neighbors to the other side of the country, Abu Husayn fought in northern

Iraq to suppress repeated uprisings by Kurdish parties. "The military made a man out of me," he said.[2]

Iraq's armed forces have also committed some of the most egregious war crimes of the past two decades, from executing thousands of Kurdish civilians and Iranian soldiers to gang-raping women during the invasion of Kuwait. Some observers regard the Iraqi army as merely a contemporary version of the German Wehrmacht or Japanese imperial forces of World War II, best dissolved and discarded. Yet the army will likely endure and could even help the new Iraq face the momentous challenges of ensuring the country's territorial integrity and instilling national unity and meritocracy in a divided society.

Imagining the transformation of militaries for social ends has a long tradition. Eighteenth-century French philosopher Jean-Jacques Rousseau regarded war as an unnatural corruption of man, yet advocated citizen militias as a vital institution to defend the freedom and independence of Europe's emerging states. Citizen rather than professional soldiers, Rousseau argued, have a vested interest in not going to war.[3] On the other hand, for nineteenth-century British librettist W. S. Gilbert, the transformation of the soldier into an enlightened man of society was an emasculating development to be mocked. The "Modern Major-General" in his satirical operetta *Pirates of Penzeance* was more dilettante than warrior—

> For my military knowledge, though I'm plucky and adventury
> Has only been brought down to the beginning of the century;
> But still in matters vegetable, animal, and mineral,
> I am the very model of a modern Major-General.

—and his rise in the ranks seemed to signal early twinges of self-doubt for the British Empire. Yet as a new day dawns in Iraq, what remains of its battered military will face a project of internal reengineering from an army of suppression and conquest to an army of nation-building and defense. Gilbert's modern major-general may cease to be a laughing matter and become a model worthy of emulation. The leap of faith I am about to describe must begin with a look at the concept of the utility of a standing army in times of peace and war and a review of Iraq's armed forces in recent decades, the social experience of its soldiers, and the security needs of a country in transformation.

Rules of Engagement

An army is a human instrument built for war, and war is hell.

Designed for war's ordered chaos but maintained during peacetime, armies are inherently a bundle of contradictions. While appearing impersonal and imposing, soldier men and women (more often teenage boys and girls) must cleave as a social unit to endure mutual vulnerability in the face of bullets and bombs. Armies at once encourage the basest impulse to kill while honing professional expertise in the most sophisticated technology available.

Popular conceptions of the military are refracted through contradictory prisms. Commercials on American television stress the pride and education derived from service in the army, in which men and women are encouraged to "be all they can be" in a kind of high-tech outdoor adventure. Catch the evening news and admire Colin Powell, exemplar of how the military's meritocracy can provide a unique path to social and political mobility. But change the channel and watch Serbian soldiers tried for war crimes, including sexual slavery and genocide, at the Hague. Pick up *All Quiet on the Western Front* and follow the rude awakening of German boys who become men as they encounter the futile horror of man's inhumanity to man.

The ultimate icon of war's absurdity is, appropriately enough, an Iraqi: Air Force Captain John Yossarian, the protagonist of Joseph Heller's 1961 classic novel *Catch-22* and an ethnic Assyrian. While the ancient Assyrians honed the tactics of totalitarian control and ruthless military conquest, Heller's modern Assyrian struggles to preserve his individuality as he faces a black comedy of violence, bureaucracy, and paradoxical irrationality. A Dilbert in uniform, Yossarian would feel right at home in the modern Iraqi army, where reports indicate that low morale and maddening conditions spawned massive desertions up through 2002.[4]

In fact, systemic problems particular to Iraq's political environment created an especially disruptive military experience. Random call-ups for reservists and even regulars were the norm, designed to keep men subject to the whims of the state. During the Iran–Iraq war, a heavy death toll on the front lines gave rise to wishful rumors that children born during the 1968 Ba'th revolution would be exempt. Purportedly lucky teenagers and their parents threw celebratory parties, but the rumor eventually proved false. The offspring of 1968 went straight to the battle-fields, and many never returned.[5] Once in uniform, soldiers never knew how long their tours of duty would last. Though compulsory service was only two years, in practice soldiers might be retained far longer. Up to one-third of some divisions were composed of reservists, for whom merit offered little hope of advancement. Officers would often withhold information from subordinates, only adding to a sense of helplessness. Soldiers who could afford to bribe their superiors did so, as a generous gift to a commanding officer was one of the few ways to secure better treatment.

Discouraging military valor actually served the political interests of the Ba'th leadership. With its civilian roots, the Ba'th party sought to construct a "coup-proof" army to protect its rule from ambitious generals. Though excellence among privates was expected, initiative and independence among the officer corps were discouraged, and numerous commanders who proved "too successful" during the war with Iran were either demoted or died under mysterious circumstances. Officers who reported on colleagues involved in political dissent received promotions, and the state would occasionally execute division commanders deemed a potential threat.

The military might have made a man out of Abu Husayn in the 1970s, but his son's generation grew up during nearly a decade of war, bearing the scars of fighting under absurd conditions. Abu Husayn's son tried repeatedly to flunk classes, hoping to stay back year after year to defer enlistment. Many of his friends chose to flee, hiding at relatives' homes in basements or secret rooms. One friend who was forced to enlist took matters into his own hands: a few weeks after joining the army, he placed his palm on a small mortar. "It's better to lose a hand than to die," he said, before detonating the shell, destroying his palm but ensuring he would avoid a trip to the Iranian front. With so many young men at the Iranian front in the 1980s, Saddam saw fit to import several hundred thousand Egyptian laborers to take their place working the industries and soil. The presence of these foreign laborers bred popular resentment. "Our men were getting killed so outsiders could come in and earn money," Abu Husayn's daughter said. Many Egyptians were beaten in the streets of Baghdad during this period. "The big cities felt like a military base," she said. "Every other car was a military car, with soldiers coming and going all the time. As kids, my brother and I used to wave at passing military cars with young soldiers in the back. We would flash them with victory signs, but they would shake their fingers at us and make an upside down *V*—the opposite of victory. The soldiers were so bitter; their life was gone."[6]

A Nightmare of Continuity and Change

How the most formidable Arab army became a breeding ground for deserters is a story of historical devolution. More than 80 years have passed since the modern Iraqi army was first established and trained by the British. The story began in the deserts of Arabia, as British officer T. E. Lawrence joined with Arabian prince Faysal to challenge Ottoman forces. The bond they forged is memorialized in the sweeping cinematic epic *Lawrence of Arabia*, and led to Faysal's installation as king of Iraq in 1921. Faysal needed an army, and the British required local guards for their own military installations. In the early 1920s, an Iraqi army was founded to counter a possible Turkish attack from the north, along with a special division of "Levies" battalions to guard British Royal Air Force bases.

The Iraqi army has since the 1920s participated in a host of wars against internal and external enemies in Israel, in the Kurdish mountains, on the Iranian front lines, and on Kuwait's shores. But three basic attributes of the Iraqi military have not

changed much. First, the army has been used since its beginnings for internal security missions, not only against Iraq's
external opponents. For example, the nascent Iraqi forces in
1931 clashed with Mahmud Barzinji, a Kurdish tribal leader.
The Iraqi army has continued to confront Kurdish military challenges for decades. Second, the army has maintained a continu-
ously uneasy relationship with Iraq's political leadership, beginning with the British decision to recruit former soldiers and
officers from the former Ottoman military. In spite of Iraq's
political instability through most of its history, the structure of
the regular army has not changed dramatically. Iraq in 1936 was
the scene of the first attempted military coup in modern Arab
history, and six more followed over the next five years.[7] This
tradition led Saddam's state naturally to regard the army as a
potential opponent. A third continuity has been the army's mission as a uniting force in a country with a troubled sense of
national identity, given its ethnic, religious, and tribal cleav-
ages. As of January 2003, soldiers in the Iraqi army hailed from a
variety of backgrounds: Shi'is, Kurds, Sunnis, Tukomans, and
Assyrians. A closer look at the officer corps, however, revealed
the regime's preference for relying on the Sunni minority, as
Shi'i officers were vastly underrepresented. Indeed, despite
being open to women up through the war with Iran, Iraq's 16
officer training academies remained largely inaccessible to
Shi'is and other ethnic and religious groups the government
deemed untrustworthy.[8] High hopes for the army's potential as
a tool of modernization and socialization date back to 1948,
when the British Advisory mission to Iraq Major General Renton wrote the Iraqi Defense Ministry and suggested that "the
army should be the university of the nation and any man who
has served in it should come out as a better citizen." It was
March 1948. Two months later, the full capacity of the Iraqi
army was occupied in the war on Israel, never to return to General Renton's idea.[9]

In addition to continuities, Saddam's rule has introduced
military innovations. For the past few years Iraq has had not one
but two armies: the regular army and a mix of forces that Saddam deemed to be more loyal, sometimes referred to as the

"Special Army," with the Republican Guard and the Special Republican Guard at its center.[10] The Republican Guard began as a strike force tasked to guarding the president, but during the war with Iran, the Guard was expanded and developed, in effect, to a parallel military. Comprising two cores that commanded seven divisions, the Guard was strategically deployed around the urban centers that the regime considered most crucial for its survival: Takrit and Baghdad, as well as in the Shi'i area in the south that had a history of dissent with the central government. The Guard was better trained, better treated, and better equipped than the regular army. Most of its soldiers and all its officer core were Sunni. In time however, as the Guard grew larger and less trusted, the government established yet another elite force to be entrusted with defending the elites of the state—the Special Republican Guard. This force of about 12,000 to 15,000 soldiers (without reservists that double this number) was based in Baghdad and its republican palace.[11] It had its own armor brigade and air defense system with the sole purpose of defending the regime. All the various forces of the special army amounted to 100,000 to 150,000 soldiers and, together with the regular army, they amounted to about 480,000 soldiers.[12] Calling up all the reservists could enlarge the force to a little over a million, out of a population approaching 24 million.[13]

But as the special army expanded, the regular army became a shadow of its former self. By January 2003, it comprised 16 divisions organized under five corps.[14] Mistrusted by the regime, which supervised the regular army closely through an extensive network of moles within its ranks, it was mostly deployed away from the capital and central cities.[15] In some cases units were not issued live ammunition, as the central government feared a coup.[16] Ten years of sanctions had limited the military's ability to refurbish the material losses it suffered in the Gulf War in 1991. Most of the military's primary weapons systems predated the 1991 war, and had been further destroyed by occasional U.S. and British air strikes, as well as by clashes with Kurds in the north and Shi'is in the south. Combat effectiveness was further limited by the fact that the armed forces were constrained in their training due to poor physical conditions.

Morale was in a perpetual state of deterioration, further diminished by the government's brutal long-term campaign to discourage desertion. In one famous episode, Saddam Hussein appeared on television rewarding a father who had turned in his AWOL son. After the son's execution, the father declared that a boy who walks away from his national commitments is no longer a son. The state also resorted to the persuasive tactic of mutilations. In 1994 Saddam issued an order to cut off the ears of persons who failed to report to their military duty or who left their commissions without authorization.[17] By using this cruel method, the regime evoked memories of ancient times. Section 282 of the world's first code of law, legislated by Hammurabi of Babylon over 2,500 years ago: "If a slave say to his master, 'You are not my master,' if they convict him his master shall cut off his ear." The evocation of ancient laws of slavery unwittingly reinforced many Iraqis' feeling of enslavement to their state. Taking all these elements into account, it is hardly surprising that units of the regular army have so readily surrendered to United States forces. In the Gulf War, most army units surrendered to the United States on first contact. This phenomenon was still evident in the 1995–1996 battle with the Kurds, where in one instance, a large number of soldiers surrendered to their Kurdish foes upon sighting U.S. planes. There is every expectation that similar waves of surrender will greet American troops and their allies in a 2003 confrontation.

A New Mission

Reengineering the Iraqi army begins by redefining the country's "national security." In most industrialized democracies, the concept entails defending the homeland and its citizens from external threats, while law enforcement agencies handle internal security threats. But some South American militaries, for example, have expanded national security to deal with perceived internal enemies, usually political dissidents, and in some developing countries national security has meant promoting modernization, going so far as to make deep inroads into the everyday life of its own citizens. In the Arab world, national security has an even more complex meaning. The external threat to most Arab countries is limited. Rarely have Arab states fought each other; the Syrian invasion of Jordan in 1970 and the Iraqi invasion of Kuwait in 1990 were both aberrations in the past three decades. Aside from engaging non-Arab neighbors like Iran and Israel, Arab militaries have generally served as guardians of their specific national cause. In a country like Iraq, with its fragmented sense of national identity, the army has constituted the most visible and viable state function, demonstrating this by battling domestic ethnic groups from Kurds to Assyrians.

A new definition of national security for Iraq rests on two pillars: redefining the external threat, and redefining the role of the military in relation to the question of territorial integrity vis-à-vis minorities.

Only two of Iraq's neighbors, Iran and Turkey, are large enough to pose a significant external threat. Iran, with a military of over 500,000 soldiers and 350,000 reservists organized in 32 divisions, is Iraq's traditional opponent in the region.[18] Despite the improvement in diplomatic relations in 1990, the two countries still dispute their common border, maritime boundaries, and navigation channels.[19] Iran has hosted the 10,000-strong Shi'i Supreme Council for Islamic Revolution in Iraq, and allowed its armed faction, the Badr Corps, to use its territory to attack Iraq and ally with Kurdish rebels.[20] Iraq in turn has hosted the *Mujahedin-e Khalq* (People's Mujahedin), a 15,000-strong Iranian Marxist resistance movement.[21]

Turkey, Iraq's northern neighbor, has at its disposal an army of over a million soldiers, including reservists.[22] Iraq and Turkey dispute water development plans for the Tigris and Euphrates rivers and have lingering tensions over Turkish incursions into Iraqi territory in pursuit of Kurdish rebels. Yet a new central government in Iraq will likely share a common concern for mitigating Kurdish issues, and can draw on a history of past strategic cooperation with Turkey under Western auspices, notably the 1955 Baghdad Pact initiated by NATO to create an anti-Soviet alliance. Syria, with its 300,000 strong armed forces,[23] has never played a significant part in Iraqi threat perception. Though the countries had tense relations over ideological differences (namely, who truly upheld Ba'th party ideals) and water disputes,[24] they have not collided militarily. Only once, in the mid-1970s, did the two countries conduct threatening military maneuvers along their joint border. Iraq has even served as Syria's ally at times, with two Iraqi armored divisions assisting Syrian forces during the 1973 war with Israel on the Golan Heights.[25] A burgeoning Israeli-Turkish alliance in the late 1990s pushed Syria and Iraq closer together. Syria has no reason to provoke Iraq, particularly as it fears that it might become a new regional target for the United States in its ongoing campaign.

Given the low threat from Syria and Turkey, Iraq's legitimate military needs at present relate to deterring Iran. Recently, a former Iraqi general suggested that about 150,000 soldiers would suffice for the mission.[26] Other estimates take into account Iran's 32 divisions and argue that no fewer than 11 Iraqi divisions are needed, based on the classic 3:1 offense/defense ratio. In any case, Iraq's security needs will ultimately depend on the level of American commitment to Baghdad's security. A full U.S. partnership could mean a defense treaty like those the United States maintains with Japan and South Korea. Or it could mean declaring Iraq to be a Major Non-NATO Ally, like Bahrain and Israel, reflecting Washington's commitment to the country's security and easing arms procurement. Because Iraq's level of military strength depends directly on the extent of America's security commitment, the best option for the United States may be to integrate the new Iraqi army into the security structure of CENTCOM (U.S. Central Command). CENTCOM is responsible, among other missions, for training U.S. forces with local militaries in preparation for mutual war scenarios. Joint Iraqi-American war games offer multiple returns, including professionalizing Iraq's armed forces and sending a clear deterrent message to Iran. With the fragility of some of the pro-Western governments in the Gulf, a professional Iraqi army may prove a vital asset to U.S. security interests in the region.

A second element of threat perception for Iraq's military to address is the maintenance of territorial integrity and deference to the central government. Whether the Kurdish north will welcome full integration into an Iraqi state will depend on the level of autonomy it achieves in the emerging post-Saddam political system. But the semi-independent status of three Kurdish militia forces totaling 60,000 troops raises the question of these groups' resistance to a broader Iraqi national project. In my view, a unified and stable Iraq cannot tolerate the existence of such a large nongovernmental paramilitary. Here, the military, once the frontline enemy of the Kurds, can offer the strongest path to integration. A model successfully employed in South Africa in the mid-1990s integrated the armed wing of the African National Congress into the South African military after 30 years of conflict. The two sides launched a long research phase, in which they outlined their vision of a joint force. The political leadership of both sides then constructed a detailed integration program based on mutual agreement.[27] The gradual structure allowed for a buildup of trust, a realistic adjustment of expectations, and an opportunity for top military commanders to collaborate.

Because the Iraqi army has committed severe human rights abuses against the Kurdish population, killing thousands in the late 1980s, Kurds must win public apologies, payment of reparations, and trials for guilty military officers. Moreover, keeping Kurdish military units in Kurdish areas—but now as part of a new Iraqi army—can mitigate Kurdish concerns about personal security and safety. Clear promotion routes for Kurds in the new Iraqi armed forces and civil service, economic investment in local military-related infrastructure, and use of the military to promote civilian projects like building schools and providing medical aid would serve to strengthen the case. The Kurdish forces, for their part, should commit themselves to Iraq's new political structure. Though far-fetched at first glance, regional and local conditions offer a chance for such a commitment to materialize. While most international and regional powers object to an independent Kurdish state, Kurdish society itself allocates great importance to the preservation and primacy of tribal structures even at the expense of nationalist ambitions.[28] In 1996, the Barazani faction in Iraq's north even aligned itself with Saddam for a while, in order to strengthen its hand within the Kurdish community.

A third, proactive aspect of the new Iraq's national security might harken back to Renton's idea for a military "university of the nation." A watershed in U.S. military history was President Truman's order in the 1950s to desegregate American military units, paving the way for full meritocracy in the armed forces. The genius of Truman's move transcends its first consequence: the improvement of the military. He also managed to reorient the sensibilities of young Americans who went on to impact society as civilians. Truman understood that the tedious process of forging societal integration can be achieved faster through a hierarchical institution that is accustomed to following orders. An analogue to Truman's move in Iraq might begin with an integration of all the country's ethnic groups into the officer corps, from which most have been until now excluded. A hallmark of success would witness, for example, Assyrian and Kurdish officers commanding Shi'i or Sunni troops—a Kurdish Colin Powell. Similarly, international officers and personnel working with soldiers in the new Iraq would best insist on meritocratic procedures, rewarding those officers who perform well and marginalizing the incompetent.

But the university of the nation can teach more than egalitarianism, and might even take a lesson or two from Saddam himself. In early September 2002, he ordered the Military Industrialization Organization to participate in an interagency effort to rehabilitate a water project in Baghdad.[29] In other countries, militaries participate in educational programs to illiterate populations, civil engineering projects, and even agricultural missions. The Chinese model takes this idea a step further, as the People's Liberation Army is an active player in the business arena. With these examples in mind, the new Iraqi military can play a pivotal role in reintegrating Iraq into the international community. Young recruits can be educated while on active duty. Alongside traditional training, the military can address the country's sanctions-era high illiteracy rates. Beyond reading and writing, the military can help promote normative frameworks that will be needed in the new Iraq, including the values of pluralism and entrepreneurship. The military can also, by way of a refined system of military academies, offer a variety of technical

educational programs to train Iraq's next technological generation. Such a change entails not only an altering of the scope of
the Iraqi military, but also considerable resources. In order to
divert resources for a national project of this size, the military
will have to be downsized considerably. Long years of distrust by
the Iraqi people of their armed forces will also serve as a hindrance to implementing such an ambitious plan. The new Iraqi
army will have to convince the population that it is genuinely
demilitarized, and that treatment of soldiers and civilians has
changed. The operative expression is the Arabic, *ma qalla wa
dalla*, which means more or less that less is more. Iraq's new
army can become a powerful tool for regional security and the
envy of the Arab world.

Part III
MONEY

Seven

The Wages of Stability

Stunted Business and Labor
Under Sanctions and Surveillance

Tony Soprano's organized crime family has not extended far beyond the Tri-state area. But just as American audiences have become mesmerized by the travails of this fictional New Jersey Mafioso and his circle, Iraqis in recent years fell for "Abu Alich" and his coterie of Baghdadi heavies. And just as "The Sopranos" became HBO's flagship drama, "Dhi'ab al-Layl"—"The Wolves of the Night"—stands as Iraqi television's epic miniseries of the 1990s.

Over the course of the decade, Iraqi TV sporadically debuted dramatic series, captivating Iraqi viewers each night for a month or two only to flame out in a thrilling final episode. Several dramas focused on gang violence, reflecting the upsurge in organized crime and contraband smuggling that engulfed Iraq in the 1990s under sanctions. Like "The Sopranos," "Dhi'ab al-Layl" featured graphic scenes of violence and partially romanticized the gang itself. Led by a brutal gangster, the "Wolves of the Night" were a motley crew of toughs, each with his own nickname and his own existential struggle. The show's portrayal of the human side of gangsters—ordinary people responding to extraordinary hardship by doing what they must to get by—resonated deeply with Iraqis. "My kid brother would go around saying, 'I'm Abu Alich!'" a friend from Baghdad recalls. "He liked to call himself after 'the bubblegum guy,' the detached gangster who brooded while blowing bubbles."[1] Of course, in the final episode of "Dhi'ab al-Layl," the Iraqi police prevail. During a climactic shootout, Abu Alich and his boys are gunned down in their hideout.

Dead on TV, Abu Alich lived on in reality. His contradictory blend of brutality and humanity, destructiveness and ingenuity, vulnerability and immortality resonated deeply in 1990s Iraq. This was not the Iraq that émigrés from the 1960s, and 1970s remember, a country enriched with oil and legitimate business and employment opportunities for most of its citizens. After a decade of devastating war with Iran and an outrageous miscalculation that led Saddam Hussein to invade Kuwait, the international community had turned against Iraq's leadership and punished the country, first with a crippling invasion, then with a sustained embargo. The project of reconstruction now taking shape in the new Iraq will pick up where Saddam's economy and society left off: a stunted business and consumer culture that was at once beset by rigid restrictions and played by no rules. The following chapter will offer a strategy for Iraq's economic rehabilitation. But first, here is the story of Iraq's economy under sanctions—a tragedy of industry and infrastructure told in numbers, and a dark comedy of workers and entrepreneurs struggling to survive in the strange world of a lawless police state. Here is how so many Iraqis became "Wolves of the Night."

Below Ground Level

Financial and trade sanctions imposed on Iraq by the United Nations in late 1990 brought many of Iraq's economic sectors to a virtual standstill. In the ensuing decade, the country's gross domestic product (GDP) dropped over 50 percent—from around $60 billion just before the 1990–91 crisis to an estimated $25.5 million in 2002.[2] In terms of real GDP growth, the country's economy contracted by 6 percent over the year 2001 and is believed to have shrunk by a further 2 percent in 2002. To Iraq's population of 24 million, expected to reach 31 million by the year 2010,[3] this has meant an even lower per capita income of less than $1,000 in early 2003, placing the country among the poorest in GDP per capity in the world, despite its vast oil reserves.[4] Though exact figures on income distribution are unavailable, it is clear that the vast majority of wealth has been concentrated among a small community of Iraqis primarily residing in the center of the country and close to the ruling clique, while most inhabitants have lately subsisted on annual incomes in the low hundreds of dollars. As of February 2003, more than 75 percent of the country's 2.5 million-strong labor force were working either for the government or for the army. The average civil servant's salary was $5 per month. The private sector is a marginal component of GDP.[5]

The reason one of the highest flying economies in the Middle East plummeted to ground level has to do with a substance that lies below ground level. Large holes in the ground near the northern Iraqi city of Kirkuk have been venting burning natural gas since ancient times. Some historians say this is the place mentioned in the Bible, Daniel 3:27, where the Babylonian king Nebuchadnezzar tosses three of his enemies into a burning fiery furnace.[6] Oil was discovered in Kirkuk in Iraq in 1927 and has been the mainstay of Iraq's economy ever since. There is so much natural pressure in the wells of Kirkuk pushing its oil to the surface that secondary pumps and artificial pressure are unnecessary. For a sense of scale, consider that whereas many American wells yield only 40 barrels per day (bpd) on average, the Kirkuk fields can yield 20,000 to 25,000 bpd. Second in proven oil reserves only to Saudi Arabia, Iraq has some 112.5 billion barrels of crude oil, constituting 10 percent of the world's proven supply, as well as 220 billion barrels of probable and possible deposits. In addition to Iraq's largest fields near Mosul and Kirkuk, smaller fields are found as far south as an area near Basra. Natural gas reserves amount to 3.1 trillion cubic meters, with possible reserves estimated at an additional 4.2 trillion cubic meters.[7]

Oil has been the mainstay of Iraq's economy since the 1930s, when the country's Jewish finance minister Sason Hezqel insisted that the British compensate Iraq for its oil in gold.[8] Long since nationalized and with a total production capacity of 3.5 million bpd, Iraq's state petroleum company earned an annual $15 billion in oil revenues prior to the invasion of Kuwait. At the time, Iraq was also producing up to 20 billion cubic meters of natural gas per year. Oil sector exports equaled 75 percent of Iraq's GDP and provided 95 percent of the country's foreign exchange earnings prior to 1990.[9]

But during the Gulf War, allied bombing raids targeted refineries, depots, and export facilities. "We didn't have a drop of benzene after that for one and half months," recalls a long time employee of Iraq's oil company who now consults privately in Jordan. "With no outside help, we rebuilt the Beiji refinery in just a few weeks time. Can you imagine some of our neighbors in the Gulf doing that with no foreign help? Hundreds of people working with no electricity day and night, using junk and spare parts. Many facilities were 60 percent damaged, meaning we had to dismantle everything and rebuild. That required engineering and technological know-how."[10] For two years after 1991, Iraq continued rebuilding with no outside assistance and by 1993 had brought production levels back to 2 million bpd. But legal oil exports under the sanctions regime have fallen below one million since mid-2002. Several factors have contributed to the drop, including Iraq's periodic unilateral suspension of exports and the absence of an agreement on oil pricing between the Iraqi government and the Security Council's 661 Sanctions Committee.[11]

Despite domestic know-how, Iraq's state-controlled oil industry has deteriorated, lacking access to global capital and new technologies. The infrastructure in Iraq's underdeveloped oilfields has been suffering from a shortage of spare parts and industrial equipment. In early 2003, several more fields were at last undergoing repair. The impact of sanctions on the oil industry cannot, however, be measured in hardware and output alone. "In the 1960s," the Iraqi oil consultant says, "I benefited from a training process that developed over generations, when the Baghdadis who became my professors first began to study engineering abroad. That tradition has been interrupted by sanctions, and the ripple effect will afflict Iraq for generations to come."[12] The foreign expertise Iraq now requires has only begun to become available in recent years, when the UN General Assembly began authorizing foreign oil companies to resume international investment activities in Iraq's oil sector.

Saddam's government managed to reinstate oil supply deals with its former customers Russia, France, and China, in the hope that such sweeteners would entice the three permanent members of the UN Security Council to object to a new military strike against Iraq. Large contracts were signed with petroleum giants from these countries—including the French Total-FinaElf and China's National Petroleum Corporation—to pump Iraqi oil as soon as UN sanctions were lifted. And some 300 Russian firms were known to be operating in Iraq in January 2003, under the UN oil-for-food program, with rights to sell 40 percent of Iraq's oil on world markets once the constraints of sanctions were removed. In terms of development rights, Russian companies at the close of 2002 were estimated to control more than half of Iraq's total reserves. About 10 Russian companies, among them Lukoil and Tatneft, Slavneft, Rosneft, Zarubezhneft, and Gazprom, had development agreements with Iraq, but not all of them were formalized into contracts. One of the largest oil supply deals since 1996 was signed in mid-October 2002, providing Russia's Alfa-Eco with the rights for the future export of 20 million barrels of Iraqi oil. Another Russian oil giant, Lukoil, signed a $20 billion contract in 1997 to drill the West Qurna oilfield, with an estimated 7 billion barrels of recoverable oil. This contract was canceled in January 2003, however, by the Iraqi government to punish Russia for its support in the UN Security Council for the return of weapons inspectors to Iraq. The Zarubezhneft company was granted a potential $90 billion concession to develop the Bin Umar oilfield. Russian firms have also provided Iraq with equipment to extract and process petroleum, while further production-sharing, buy-back, and technical services agreements were in the works. Other contenders for a piece of Iraq's oil wealth included India's Oil & Natural Gas Corporation (ONGC) And even American oil firms, which are supposed to have been excluded from doing business in Saddam's Iraq, managed to get their foot in the door. U.S. petroleum services and equipment firms, such as Halliburton, Baker Hughes, Schlumberger, and General Electric, operated through European—mainly French—subsidiaries and joint venture companies.[13]

But all these contracts and memoranda of understanding were merely agreements on paper that had little actual impact on Iraq's economy. The harsh reality for Iraq's nonoil industries and workers over the past decade of sanctions has been impacted by the sharp decline in the inflow of currency oil had traditionally yielded. For a short period in the late 1990s, Iraq experienced relative economic growth, resulting from a boost in oil production and crude prices. The country's real GDP growth rate reached 12 percent in 1999.[14] However, Iraqi oil exports have dramatically fallen since, and although oil prices keep rising, cash inflow to the country has continued to decline, meaning very little capital available to sustain other sectors.

The Company Store

Besides the impact of lost oil revenue, Iraq's economic woes are compounded by debt. Foreign exchange reserves have been radically depleted by war after war and a decade of sanctions. Iraq's outstanding foreign debt stood at $42.1 billion at the end of 1990,[15] and $180 billion on the eve of 2003.[16] Over one-third of the debt is owed to the Gulf, mainly Kuwait and Saudi Arabia, although Saddam has regarded Gulf finances as grants to support his Iran–Iraq war, which he viewed as defensive war on their behalf. Russia is Iraq's largest single foreign creditor, with $8 billion in debts accumulated prior to 1991. Inflation began its most severe climb in late 1991, when the government printed billions in new currency to fund reconstruction efforts from the 1991 war's devastating bombing campaign. As the dinar fell precipitously, the government refused to adjust. For years, it kept official exchange rates static. It was not until 1995 that the government eased its fiscal policies somewhat, permitting money changers to operate openly. Early that year, $100 was still only worth 33 dinars at the bank, even though it would garner 300,000 dinars on the black market. Eventually, government salaries were raised, but never enough to stay in line with inflation.[17]

Iraq's debt goes beyond that owed to governments. Over the past decade, the United Nations Compensation Commission (UNCC) has processed 2.6 million claims submitted by individuals and companies as well as governments demanding more than $322 billion in reparation for direct injuries inflicted by Iraq's invasion of Kuwait. Nearly $38 billion has been approved by the panel thus far, but as of early 2003, less than $20 billion has been paid. Corporate claimants accounted for 5,685 of the appeals. Companies sought $77.9 billion in compensation for losses ranging from ruined oil equipment to lost jobs and canceled deals. Successful claimants with large awards include companies from Kuwait, Turkey, the United States, Jordan, Russia, Britain, Germany, and Israel. They were awarded $23 billion by the UNCC, although only $3.6 billion had been paid as of January 2003.[18] Since 1999, UNCC records show that some 185 companies have dropped a total of $2.9 billion in claims.[19] These multinationals, including German automaker DaimlerChrysler, British pharmaceuticals company GlaxoSmithKline, Danish pharmaceuticals firm LEO Pharma, Russian energy company Machinoimport, Scottish energy-services provider Wood Group, and Austrian construction company Voest-Alpine MCE, opted to withdraw war-related claims under Iraqi pressure in order to secure contracts to supply Iraq with humanitarian purchases in line with the UN oil-for-food program and in hopes of securing future deals to rebuild the country. In regulating Iraqi oil export earnings under UN sanctions, the Security Council has given priority to war compensation payments over the settlement of external debt. Since December 1996, Iraq has been paying 30 percent of its gross oil sales revenues into the UN Compensation Fund, first to individual claimants, then to corporate ones. Ultimately, it is likely that Iraq would find such heavy obligations too burdensome to bear even under the most ideal of circumstances.[20]

It follows that banking and investment have suffered considerably, effectively blocking the inflow of capital to Iraq. Having nationalized the commercial banking sector in the mid-1960s, Iraq's government created a unified financial institution, the Rafidain Bank, which operated as a monopoly until 1988. In the 1980s, workers would often take out social security and insurance policies at banks, setting aside part of their salaries for future benefit. But Rafidain's considerable assets abroad were frozen following the 1990 Gulf crisis, and the subsequent devaluation of the dinar and rigidity of the official bank exchange rates soon destroyed any incentive to invest. Savings of 2,000 dinars that once would have paid out $6,000 were suddenly worth only $2. Government employees used to pick up their paychecks at the bank. But, as one investor remarks: "Nobody with any sense has money in a bank account—you keep cash in your home or outside the country." Massive inflation did provide savvy dealers with the opportunity to make quick cash in Iraq's liquid market. "If you know how to listen to the news right, you can make good money," the investor explains. "When the arms inspectors went in, currency would go low. When they left, it went up. Everyone listened to the news about the United States. If the United States talked about Iraq, the currency went up. You played off the instability and uncertainty."[21]

In the wake of hyperinflation, the government made efforts in the era of sanctions to mitigate against the deterioration of capital markets. In the 1990s, the country witnessed the establishment of a new state-owned commercial bank, Rashid Bank, followed by the creation of another four state-owned specialized banks—Real Estate Bank of Iraq, Agricultural Cooperative Bank of Iraq, Industrial Bank of Iraq, and the Socialist Bank. Rafidain remained by far the largest commercial bank in terms of assets. The government eventually authorized the establishment of three private banks—the Baghdad Bank, the Commercial Bank, and the Iraqi Islamic Bank for Investment and Development. As of early 2003, the Baghdad Bank was doing comparatively well. It reportedly saw customer deposits grow 50 percent during 2002 and was one of the most traded stocks on the local exchange. With 19 branches, Baghdad Bank's fastest-growing business segment has been domestic money transfers from gainfully employed Iraqis abroad to their families back home.[22] But even these were difficult to manage. International money transfers were banned under UN trade sanctions, and cash transfers within Iraq have been extremely difficult due to excessive paperwork and service charges. Bank clerks took bribes for their services.

Despite modest progress in the banking sector, cold hard cash remained the most common means of trade, whether foreign or domestic. There were no ATM machines or domestic credit cards in Iraq in early 2003, and most banks relied on paper records of clients. Nearly all significant business transactions were calculated and conducted in dollars. For much of the 1990s, Iraqis were not allowed to have dollars by law—"but everyone did anyway," a friend from Baghdad who left in 1998 recalls. "I paid my employees in U.S. dollars. You would even bribe a member of the secret police with dollars, exactly the currency neither you nor he was supposed to have."[23]

Industries Stopped Hiring

The lack of oil revenue and burgeoning debt made many of Iraq's nonoil industries difficult to sustain. The country's historic economic base prior to oil had been agriculture, which remains a major economic sector in Iraq today. Throughout the 1990s into 2003 it employed a rising percentage of the local labor force because so many other industries had stopped hiring. The agricultural sector as of 2003 employs approximately 660,000 Iraqis and accounts for 8 percent of the country's GDP. It has been largely controlled by the state since a land reform plan implemented in the 1960s resulted in increased state land ownership and with it the setting of production quotas and prices. The government's 2003 agricultural policy provided farmers with incentives to cultivate state land, such as a five-year exemption from leasing fees and military service, as well as a disincentive to sloth: unfarmed private land was seized from its owners by the government.[24]

But the sector is suffering. Hit hard by an extended drought, Iraq's vital cereal crops—mainly wheat, barley, and rice—dwindled by nearly 80 percent between 2000 and 2003. The production of dates, one of Iraq's most important nonoil exports, has been virtually cut in half from an annual $75 million prior to 1991. Over the past decade, the country has been transformed from an overall exporter of food to a net importer. On the bright

side, improved rainfall in 2002 seems to have raised Iraq's cereal
output for the year by 15 percent over 2001, to reach 1.4 million
tons. As of early 2003, though 12 percent of Iraq's total land terrain is considered cultivatable, no more than half of this land
area, situated along the Tigris and Euphrates river plains, is actually cultivated; Iraq's arable land is largely dependent on irrigation, and crumbling irrigation systems and ever-rising soil salin-
ity have rendered arable land scarce.[25]

While Iraq's land went dry, the manufacturing industry
ground to a virtual halt. Eighty-five percent of the country's privately held factories have ceased to operate. Allied air raids in
1991 pummeled many factories, causing enduring damage. Of
the country's prewar industrial base, which included petrochemical, arms, textiles, chemical, cement and food-processing factories, only the state-owned chemical manufacturing plants were
fully restored by 2003. Iraq's industrial sector at the end of 2002
accounted for 15 percent of the country's GDP but employed
only 400,000 people. Desperately seeking to address such critical shortages, the government signed $200 million in contracts
with Russia in late 2002 to supply raw materials to Iraq's phar-
maceutical and fertilizer industries. Iraq's petrochemical industry was crippled by air strikes too. Although the key refineries in
the cities of Baiji, Basra, and Dura more recently resumed production, capacity has dropped dramatically.[26]

Prior to 1990, the Iraqi food industry included a range of
products—dairy, sugar, vegetable oil, soft drinks and breweries,
and canning. But as of 2003, this industry is starved out. Date-
based food industries, producing vinegar, ethyl alcohol, date
syrup, and liquid sugar, have been adversely affected by the
declining date crop and the embargo. The canning industry has
been held down by the shortage of cans and packaging materials—plastic, paper, and glass containers. In late 2002, the sector's output was limited to tomato and date preserves. Small private-sector manufacturers adhered to poor quality standards and
increasingly used nonfood-grade chemicals. The nonoil mining
sector, which used to be an important industrial employer
through work extracting phosphates, sulfur, coal, glass, sand,
salt, and gypsum, is down to 100,000 employees. The sector's

output has significantly fallen from pre-1991 levels and barely exports anymore.

The only bright spot in Iraq's manufacturing sector is its state-run pharmaceuticals industry. As of 2003, drug production has gone up 50 percent in some factories that were barely functioning in 1999.

Grids Stopped Connecting

Another impediment to the economic health of the country has been the dilapidated state of its power, transport, and telecommunications infrastructures. Although it is not possible at this writing to assess further destruction resulting from any hostilities in 2003, the situation clearly will not have improved. The need to repair and overhaul grids after damage wrought by the 1991 war posed demand for foreign expertise, but sanctions made the procurement of contracts with many foreign companies illegal or logistically unfeasible. The companies that won contracts to service Iraqi grids were not necessarily the most suitable for the job; they were more often than not the ones that hailed from countries whose leadership maintained the best relations with Saddam and his powerful family and friends.

Approximately 96 percent of Iraq's installed power-generating capacity and national power grid was destroyed during the 1991 Gulf War,[27] which only two of the country's 20 power plants survived. The country's electricity output, mainly produced at the Baiji and Mosul thermal plants and the Saddam hydroelectric dam on the Tigris, as of early 2003 totaled roughly 4.5 gigawatts—an insufficient total considering that demand for electricity in the country is approximately 6.6 gigawatts. The resulting power deficit, compounded by the tattered condition of existing electricity networks, has been responsible for frequent power outages, hampering industrial and domestic functions. To overcome difficulties in electricity supply for essential services, the Iraqi government initially opted to seize industrial emergency generators. With the widening of the list of goods allowed for import under the UN program, foreign firms became involved in the restoration of Iraq's power sector. In mid-2000, an Indian company exported the first gas turbine to Iraq, while a Russian firm began construction works on a power station outside Baghdad. German, Italian, Swedish, Yugoslav, and British companies were all involved in setting up a large-scale power generation plant in northern Iraq later that year. Although full restoration of the national grid still remains far from sight, electricity supply improved overall in 2002, with repair activities partly undertaken by humanitarian relief agencies such as the UN Development Program (UNDP). Works were also being carried out by international companies, through contracts signed with Iraq's General Company for Electrical Projects (GCEP) and subject to UN authorization. Keen to tap business opportunities, quite a few foreign energy companies have opted to open offices in Baghdad since 1999, including the French TotalFinaElf, Italy's Agip, Repsol of Spain, the American Schlumberger, and Russia's Lukoil and Slavneft.[28]

For its part, Iraq's frayed transportation system received a modest boost in recent years with the arrival of over 6,000 trucks, buses, and cars under UN programs. Baghdad bought 500 French Peugeot cars and seven refrigerated trucks from Renault. In the summer of 2002, Iraq took delivery of 28,000 truck and passenger vehicle tires, manufactured by Russia's Nizhnekamskshina, under the framework of oil-for-food deals signed with its major shareholder, Tatneft. Further contracts were pending UN approval in late 2002. Smuggled cars have originated mostly from Asian factories. Others would make their way from the United States or Europe to neighboring Gulf states, where they were resold to Iraqis. Nonetheless, a shortage of spare parts still curtailed development of the country's transportation services.[29]

The railway system's three major lines include one that is linked to that of Turkey; the rest are all domestic. This means that freight delivery by rail through other countries bordering Iraq has not been possible. Plans to restore Iraq's railway infrastructure and connect it to rail networks in Syria and Iran have often been discussed by the countries' respective transportation ministers. While such grand schemes are considered necessary measures to reviving bilateral trade, progress has so far been limited. As for the skies, domestic flights resumed in August 2000 after a decade of closure. In defiance of the UN-imposed no-fly zones, commercial flights to Baghdad soon commenced by Russian, French, Jordanian, Egyptian, UAE, and Yemeni national airlines. Iraq's civilian airline would fly twice a day between Baghdad and Basra, also in violation of the ban. There are international airports near Baghdad at Bamernui and at Basra, and smaller civil airfields at Haditha, Kirkuk, and Mosul. In 2002, the central government drew up plans to construct four new provincial airports over the next decade, in the provinces of Niniveh, Najaf, Kirkuk, and Missan. The Ministry of Transportation drew up a 10-year plan under which domestic passenger numbers were expected to rise from 116,000 a year in 2001 and 2002—mostly expatriate Iraqis—to 450,000 in 2012, the combined result of natural population growth and additional people traffic following a hoped-for lifting of sanctions.[30]

While transport received a small boost in recent years, the country's communications infrastructure remains substandard. In the 1991 war, coalition forces wrecked Iraq's telephone network, largely built by the French company Alcatel in the 1980s. The UN sanctions that followed banned all military and most civilian sales to Iraq and so therefore kept the network weak. Teledensity—the number of telephones per 100 inhabitants—which stood in 1990 at 5.6 percent, had dropped between 1998 and 2001 from 3.3 percent to 3 percent, reflecting the deterioration in services, equipment, and infrastructure.[31] Before the 1991 war, Iraq's international telecommunications system handled some 2 million telephone calls per year. In early 2003, the number of calls was down to around one million and traffic with the West much smaller.[32]

In recent years, the UN 661 Committee, which oversees the implementation of the UN oil-for-food program, began authorizing contractors to rebuild some telecom relay towers and to install microwave equipment to improve intercity connections for humanitarian purposes. In late 2002, the public switched telephone network (PSTN) was in the process of being rebuilt with fiberoptic cable and Internet connectivity through the Turkish backbone. Initial steps toward the rehabilitation of Iraqi telecoms commenced in early 2001 by a Chinese company, Huawei Technologies. A $28 million deal provided for setting up the country's first mobile system by installing 60 base stations in Baghdad with a capacity of 25,000 mobile lines. However, American accusations soon surfaced that Huawei was providing Iraq with dual use equipment that could be utilized for both military and civilian purposes, such as fiberoptic cables and microwave radio systems. By the time American objections had been removed and a UN green light was given to the project, the Chinese firm had pulled out of the deal. Other telecom infrastructure deals were subsequently approved for foreign firms in Iraq. Alcatel began work on a $75 million contract, providing for the construction of an international telephone exchange with a capacity of 1,200 lines and a microwave telephone network linking Baghdad with the central and southern provinces. Alcatel was also due to restore existing telephone links in Baghdad and set up new exchanges with a capacity of 280,000 lines. These initiatives were largely placed on hold.[33]

Recentralized Corruption

Most of the sectors described so far were either controlled or dominated by the state in early 2003. That had not always been the case in Saddam's Iraq, however. Independent of World Bank- or IMF-brokered programs, Saddam attempted to liberalize some markets in the 1980s as part of an effort to deal with the nation's Iran–Iraq war debt. Albeit limited and fragmented, Iraq's privatization drive compared well to similar attempts by other Arab countries at the time. It was implemented quickly and without opposition, and was accompanied by other liberalization policies and structural adjustments.[34] It was also conducted selectively. The government maintained its hold on the largest industries, but let go the smaller, nonstrategic industries. Some state companies were leased on long terms, while others were sold wholly or partially to private investors or went public with stock offerings. In a few cases, the government even turned stock over to company employees. By 1990, Iraq's privatization program encompassed some 80 state-owned enterprises, which were sold to private buyers or converted to mixed-ownership status.[35] The number of private companies operating in Iraq stood at 5,308 firms by the end of 1992, while the government had a minority interest in 42 of these companies.[36] Saddam transferred the poultry industry and fish farms to private ownership. Public transport companies serving the peripheries, the state-run gas stations network and department stores, and some state-run factories were all restructured into private or mixed-ownership enterprises. A decree was even issued for the sale of the majority of Iraqi Airways stakes to the public.[37]

In the past decade, however, Saddam's campaign to recentralize government, taken while the country suffered under the constrictions of the sanctions regime, has resulted in the undertaking of no serious, comprehensive national economic policy. Even if privatization measures were declared, as in the banking or commodity trade sector, they were more strategic than effective economic management policies and in fact functioned as no more than another method of sharing the riches with the governing elite's inner circle.

The Impact on Workers

How the overall failure of the economy played out among ordinary people without government connections is a human tragedy. Throughout the past decade, Iraq's population has been subject to severe economic strains, suffering from a high unemployment rate, hyperinflation, the collapse of many of its businesses, and the downsizing of the civil service. With inflation running at around 25 percent in 2001 and over half the country's labor force unemployed or underemployed, poverty has been widespread in Iraq and the professional middle class has been gutted. Real earnings fell by around 90 percent in the first year of UN sanctions, then fell by a further 40 percent between 1991 and 1996. The monthly wage of an average Iraqi currently stands at around $40. About three-quarters of Iraqis face enormous economic hardship, surviving on just a few dollars a week and relying on government food subsidies. To fill the widening food supply gap, Iraq's government has had to import over 50 percent of its cereal and meat supplies under the framework of the UN oil-for-food program, and introduced a public rationing system for staple goods.[38] Ordinary people competed with one another for just a little food or a few hours' wages. "Baghdad is a relaxed city by nature, but it has become an angry place," one longtime resident said. "So many people are on edge, and can easily break into a fight at any moment. You can see the burden and worries in people's eyes. What will you eat tomorrow? How will you pay your next bill?"[39]

Iraqis who did get paid found themselves counting money the old-fashioned way, because the massive devaluation of the dinar caused a regression to premodern exchange practices: rather than count cash, Iraqis have been conducting financial exchanges by weighing bags of bills. Wage earners sometimes stuffed cash into bulging garbage bags. With no machines to count bills, bank tellers would take a 5,000 dinar tip just to calculate the weight.[40]

The signs of economic hardship were also banal. Many Iraqi homes in late 2002 had no doors on the inside, the wood having been sold off for cash. Some university professors, among the most respected in the Arab world, had to supplement their classroom work by selling cigarettes along Baghdad's dusty streets. In a country where the population is overwhelmingly young—half of Iraqis are under 15 years of age—many women address these post–Gulf War existential pressures by turning to an age-old profession. "There is now more prostitution in Baghdad than any place in the world," a recent émigré who owned a shop in Baghdad told me. "Every day, college and high school girls desperate for money would come to my store to solicit my employees. You can see that they are not prostitutes, just hungry women with no one to support them. We have 600,000 widows, from all the wars and Saddam's crackdowns. Many Iraqi men are crippled or left Iraq with their families behind."[41]

So much human suffering stoked resentment to the central government. Saddam's government reacted to mounting poverty and rage with handouts as carrots to balance the sticks of secret police repression. He used special subsidies to bolster industries and in effect turned the UN-administered oil-for-food program into a personal slush fund to attempt to buy his subjects' loyalty, sharing more than $4 billion in food and goods every year since 1997. Taxi drivers received cars at steep discounts, loyal bureaucrats were rewarded with new laptop computers, and select manufacturers benefited from subsidized rent. But even substantial handouts could not mitigate the post–Gulf War economic pains. "Before the 1990s, there was a culture of laziness," a middle-class Baghdadi observes. "We lived well off subsidies from an oil-rich government. But with inflation and sanctions, we were suddenly faced with pressing daily needs. The state's largesse was no longer adequate."[42]

The Impact on Entrepreneurs

Now imagine attempting to build or maintain a business in an economy as impoverished as that of contemporary Iraq. Add to the description so far of the country's failing economy what became clear in earlier chapters about the pervasiveness of Saddam's brutal security apparatus, and one can easily understand why many of Iraq's entrepreneurs were less than intrepid.

"Just don't call me from your hotel," Hasan says. A Kurdish man originally from Kirkuk, he now runs a small investment company that trades on the Baghdad Stock Exchange, which in the autumn of 2002 listed 115 mostly private and semiprivate companies. Hasan is on his way from Jordan back to Baghdad, where he spends many Saturdays, Mondays, and Wednesdays at the nondescript stock exchange building in the downtown Sa'-dun Park district. He records his transactions manually, like everyone else, and does not experience the same stress that is endemic to the fast-paced exchanges of New York and London. That is because trading regulations set a 5 percent limit on the price movements of shares in a single session. But what does stress out Hasan is his meeting with me in the lobby of Amman's Grand Palace Hotel, where many Iraqis stay for a few days en route to and from Iraq.[43]

We strike up a pleasant conversation, and talk about meeting again on the other side of the border. But it is September 2002, and the United States and Iraq appear on the verge of war. Hassan's paranoia is running high. "Be sure to talk only in Iraqi Arabic," he insists. "And don't say who you are or where you're from." Then he begins to stammer. "On second thought, I think I'd better ask you not to call me."[44]

Hasan's eyes fall on my notebook, and he asks if I can rip out that page where I have written his name and number. When I explain that I also have important notes on the back of the page, he pulls out a black pen, takes my notebook, and starts feverishly scribbling over his phone number. After a whole minute of swift pen strokes, Hasan's number is utterly unreadable. "I'm sorry," he says tersely. "I hope we can meet again in better times."

A businessman's essential asset is his business card, but in Iraq's tense climate in recent years, it could also be a ticket to jail. Indeed, the intensity of Hasan's pen-strokes is only one indication of how Iraq under Saddam and sanctions has produced a most bizarre Iraqi business culture. Effective business practices not only went unrewarded, they were effectively discouraged.

Take advertising and branding, for instance, the essential tools for cultivating and growing a customer base. Both existed only in the most basic form, with a smattering of photoless advertisements in government-controlled newspapers and forgettable TV spots that rarely transcended the grainy quality of cable public-access fare. Most advertisers were local Baghdadi outlets, from clothing boutiques to Nabil's Juice Company to car dealerships (Baghdad has its own auto mile zoned for dealers, the *Ma'arif*). Mindful of the state's watchful eye, ads sometimes began by paying tribute to "the leader, the holy warrior Saddam Hussein" before announcing an upcoming sale. Beginning in the late 1980s, English words were outlawed in advertising. "I produced a really professional advertisement in Amman," recalls a canned goods importer. "When I screened the commercial for the official censor, it was rejected. 'The word ketchup is originally an English name,' he said. I couldn't think of an Arabic name, so the ad ran without any audio—just a model holding my ketchup in silence."[45]

In the late 1990s, TV ad spot rates were cheap, at the equivalent of only $15 per minute. A few advertisers added jingles—changing the lyrics of famous Iraqi songs to praise their product—but slick national branding campaigns were few and far between. Part of the problem was technical, with a dearth of decent graphic design software and decrepit newspapers. "The paper they print on is remanufactured," notes one entrepreneur. "If your hand is wet, it destroys the newspaper."[46] The papers' high propaganda content also meant that they were easily dismissed.

But the biggest obstacle to competitive advertising was the intimidation of merchants. "When you advertise, you show people—especially Saddam's gangs—that you are doing business," confides the owner of an auto parts store who, like many Baghdadi businessmen, was not a member of the Ba'th party. "They will demand their cut from you, and destroy you if you refuse. If you do not have someone to protect you, then you want no one to notice you. If you have the money for a Mercedes, don't buy one. You cannot dare to show yourself."[47]

All those industries described above as "state-controlled" were in effect controlled by members of Saddam's extended family, including his sons and in-laws. No one dared compete in these sectors, and instead relied on flattery and devotion to secure concessions. Those who did manage to create successful ventures on their own had no reason to draw attention to their success. Such intimidation inverts the fundamental values of entrepreneurship, and creates an environment of pervasive uncertainty. "There is no thinking of long-term branding," explains the importer of canned goods. "When you don't know what will happen the next day, you can't organize and plan. One morning you wake up and everything has changed: the dinar collapsed, Saddam invaded Kuwait, your uncle was thrown in jail."[48]

But despite the pervasiveness of Saddam's secret police and network of informants, the regime could never keep tabs on everyone in its sprawling cities. With the onset of sanctions,

which made a good deal of legitimate business unprofitable and
many standard goods unattainable in the lawful market, a
sprawling black market and a minor epidemic of organized
crime evolved—a new social reality reflected in programs like
"Wolves of the Night." The flipside of intimidation became law-
lessness, as a muted anarchy came to underlie the thin veil of a
tightly surveilled society.

Legal and bureaucratic restrictions became increasingly
irrelevant. "You are supposed to incorporate, but if you don't no
one will notice," the canned goods importer said. In 1997, he
began a new product line of *dibis* (liquified dates) and went to
the Ministry of Trade to secure a trademark. "It's a law that you
have to use a unique name for your product line," he explains.
"But I could copy any logo and any label without anyone com-
plaining. You have to trademark the name, but anything else
you can copy. There is no copyright, no bar code, no ingredients,
no inspection certificate." The auto parts dealer's experience
was similar. "I never registered my business," he said. "If you go
the Trade office, everybody will know. So one way to keep a low
profile is not to register your company. One year after opening
my shop, a government inspector came, and I just had to pay
him a bribe."[49]

Recent Baghdadi émigré Omar Dewachi, on the other hand,
spent months and wads of cash in bribes in the late 1990s just to
register his coffeehouse and clear all the bureaucratic restrictions. Even then, problems persisted. "Every two months, we
had intelligence officers, Health Ministry officials, and Tourism
Ministry people all come by threatening us with their own rules
and regulations. They would tell us things like, 'This bar is not
large enough for building codes!' You would have to give them a
bribe. It comes out of the blue, and you can't say anything,
unless someone important is protecting you. But we had no
angel." He went on to describe Iraq's disarray by invoking a kind
of recipe: a handful of socialism, with centralized social services
funded by oil revenue; two cups of capitalism, with a free market and corporations; a dose of fascism, with a police state and a
leader's personality cult; a touch of Nazism, with a party that
transcends the state; all garnished by a round of organized crime,

with smugglers and outlaw power brokers. "One result of this mix is that social categories are not mutually exclusive," he said. "Even party members have to go into business to support themselves."[50]

In fact, the "Mother of Battles" appears to have spawned the "mother of invention"—remarkable ingenuity in the small-time private sector. Forced to contend with limited imports under sanctions, entrepreneurs devised ways to recycle almost anything and turn a profit. Broken hoses were patched and resold. Busted pulleys were fixed up with new balls and new grease. Used disc pads for cars were refurbished with makeshift material. At the auto supply store whose former owner I know, the salesperson would ask, "Do you want the original or the remake?" The remake was always significantly cheaper.[51]

"Iraq imported 100,000 Oldsmobiles from the United States in 1989, our last major shipment of cars," one salesman recalls. "With the sanctions, it's hard to get new cars. So today, in Baghdad, every third car is an Oldsmobile or a Chevy. People have spent a decade refurbishing these old cars. And dealers have adapted to make money off their repair needs. . . . In general, we recycled as many materials as possible back into the market. In the end, we became very resourceful."[52]

Many small-time merchants, especially those not receiving government subsidies, rely on the "taxi service" of smugglers for their goods. "My supplier sends me products via Jordan in trucks," explained a repair shop owner from Baghdad. "The drivers charge you $100—but you are not paying any tax. As for the border guards, just give them one pack of cigarettes and a can of Coke—that's more than enough. They will leave you alone."[53]

The allure of cigarettes in the era of sanctions was no accident. With so much tension built up inside Iraq, demand for cigarettes was unprecedented and smuggling them in became a particularly lucrative informal trade. High-volume traffic began on the eve of the Gulf War and exploded under sanctions. "If you are having financial trouble, become a cigarette middleman," an Iraqi cigarette dealer in Jordan said. "You don't need an office, you just coordinate business. Smugglers come across the border from Jordan and Syria with cartons of cigarettes in their trunks.

One or two packs are enough to bribe the border guards. And you just serve as the local distributor."[54] Emblematic of Iraq's sanctions-era economy has been the proliferation of cigarette roadside stands, known as *chambarchigaya* (smoke stands), which started popping up every 200 meters or so along major roads. Manned by a simple working-class man or university professor grading papers, the *chambarchigaya* consists of a triangular rack with cigarettes, allowing customers to buy one or a few. The ubiquitous stands rarely close before 3 A.M.

Cats of the Embargo

In time, rough-and-tumble competition between small-time smugglers and importers spawned smuggler kings and gangsters who acquired the at once disparaging and envious appellation, *Qitat al-Hisar* ("cats of the embargo"). This nouveau riche turned quick and massive profits by stockpiling goods in countries bordering Iraq and then smuggling them in as prices rose in the turbulence of Iraq's inflation economy. Watching a man in his mid-30s roar by in a new BMW, Iraqis would speculate: "That guy is a cat!" Newspaper cartoonists captured the amoral avarice of the cats by portraying them with bulging bellies and loosened neckties.

While most Iraqis suffered economic hardship, the cats of the embargo stood out as a wealthy elite who had no shame about flaunting just how well they were doing. With deep pockets and high-level connections to some high-ranking Ba'th party official, they were liberated to lead lives of luxury, effectively underwriting the posh fashion boutiques on Baghdad's al-Mansur street, the dealerships specializing in Mercedes imports along the *Ma'arif* auto-mile, and the jewelry stores on Palestine Street in the Harthiya district. But unlike high-ranking Ba'th party hacks who lived mainly off leveraging their government influence, the cats engaged each other in rough-and-tumble competition in what became an underworld's dark meritocracy. They spanned Iraq's ethnic and sectarian rainbow, including many Shi'is and Kurds. Cats hailing from disenfranchised communities maintained a businesslike rapport with the country's political bosses, paying them the bribes they demanded in exchange for autonomy in the black market.

For all entrepreneurs—from cats of the embargo to merchants quietly trying to eke out a living in niche industries—Iraq's business environment is at once an unregulated free-for-all and a most dangerous game. "If you have money, you can do anything you want," said one frustrated merchant who recently left. "Just don't say bad things about Saddam or compete with his family. Keep a low profile. Stay away from his family's businesses. In Baghdad there is no law. You can kill, steal, do whatever you want. You might go to jail, but you just have to bribe the officer. And don't waste time bidding on a government tender against someone who has government connections, even if you give a lower price and better quality."[55]

These merchants and political elites provided the backbone of the regular clientele at the fancy open-air restaurants that dot the Tigris River in the Sulaykh Neighborhood. Here, customers pick their own fish, then watch it cleaned and cooked before their eyes. Alcohol is not sold, but those who bring their own pour it out of flasks under the table. While Iraq is the only Arab country without a mobile phone network (Kurdish entrepreneurs in the northern no-fly zone have since established a rudimentary system in some towns and villages), some people make do with the next best thing: cordless phones rigged with a souped-up signal. Their oversize handsets may not be stylish Nokia flip phones, but they keep them connected up to two miles from home.

One could also find Baghdad's elite in the traditionally Christian quarter of Arasat al-Hindiya. On trendy Arasat Street, young men drive by and show off their cars with bombastic stereo systems thumping, hip boys and girls people-watch, and elegant prostitutes linger on every corner. "People who live here know everyone," remarks one former resident. "For Baghdad's elite, it's a small scene."[56] The scene's ultimate destinations are the country clubs left over from the colonial period: the Hunting Club and the Elwia Club. Founded by British merchants and officials as an elite spot for socializing and recreation, the clubs are shadows of their former sumptuousness, according to old-timers. Nonetheless, they are still the place where many business deals go down. Lounging by the pool or relaxing in the movie theater, Ba'th party bigwigs, embargo cats, and a few professionals from wealthy old families mingle, trying to sustain sophistication in a city howling with the "Wolves of the Night."

Eight

Iraq'n'Roll

Profit and Gain in Iraq's Globalization

Let's rebuild the Iraqi economy. Let's redistribute hoarded wealth inside the country. And let's make a profit along the way. Although Iraq is in a financial mess, the bizarre hand it has been dealt in the past few years and the unique situation in which it stands today vis-à-vis the global economy make it possible for Iraqis and outsiders to work together and pursue all three goals in tandem. The project requires more than an awareness of the quirky legacy of Saddam and sanctions on the country and its scattered peoples; the very quirks have to become part of the project. Articulating a macroeconomic vision to make Iraq commercially viable is relatively easy. The hard part is how to ensure that new money finds its way into new people's pockets.

The predicament of the "Wolves of the Night" has already been detailed. Most of Iraq's industries require injections of capital to rebuild before they can start hiring again. Oil and geopolitical maneuvers must be offset against the country's burgeoning debt before black gold can start yielding for Iraq's people again. And the abject poverty and humanitarian crises that force starving children onto the streets must be mitigated by aid and NGOs before young people can start planning ahead and going to school again. But that is only half the problem. The highest levels of Iraqi business that centrally control the major industries are chronically nepotistic, making the logic of balance sheets secondary in importance in their calculations to cash

earned under the table. And the most egalitarian class of
wealthy merchants, the "cats of the embargo," though more
multiethnic than party hacks, are dangerous to work with; they
cut their teeth competing in a brutal underworld.

There is also a bright side, however, which stems paradoxi-
cally from the excesses of Saddam's rule. To begin with, Iraq still
harbors a labor force with skilled workers relative to those of
other Arab countries and a developed industrial backbone, which
was built to support ongoing war efforts but could quickly and
easily be redirected toward major civilian manufacturing. Second, 4 million Iraqis now reside outside the country, most of
whom fled Iraq's political system and crackdowns on ethnic
groups over the past three decades. The largest concentrations of
exiles correspond to the most disaffected communities inside
the country today, and the many who have achieved success in
their new host countries have a chance to support the ambitions
of their families back home. Though the largest exile communities reside in Jordan and Iran, with smaller numbers in Syria,
Lebanon, Yemen, Libya, and the Gulf states, the wealthiest diaspora Iraqis live in the United States, Canada, Australia, New
Zealand, and Europe. Many are educated and skilled workers:
university professors, doctors, engineers, computer hardware
specialists, architects, and technicians. Research and interviews
suggest that their combined capital could be worth as much as
$30 billion; the more transparent Iraq's financial system
becomes, the more Iraqi foreign capital will make its way home.

Furthermore, one of the legacies of Western countries' crackdowns on alleged terrorist financial networks following the
tragedy of September 11 has been the massive repatriation of
Arab private equity, mostly from the Gulf states, back to local
Middle Eastern banks where Gulf nationals feel it is safer. Some
Arab nationals want to know whether the new Iraq might pose
investment opportunities for them, as Arab bond markets elsewhere in the region are at a junior stage of development and still
not major draws. Worries over the privacy and safety of Arab
holdings in the United States were compounded after the families of September 11 victims filed a $100 trillion suit in August
2002 against members of the Saudi royal family, banks, Islamic

charities, and the government of Sudan. In 2002 roughly $10 billion returned to Arab countries from American banks. This is only a small fraction of Arab funds invested abroad. According to the Merrill Lynch World Wealth Report, 220,000 individuals in the Middle East have $1.2 trillion held overseas. The bulk of these assets are invested in U.S. stocks, bonds, and the real estate market. Concerns about the American economy have provided an additional reason for investors to reassess their exposures. Like many wealthy investors around the world, Gulf Arabs have been diversifying in response to falling interest rates and the tumbling of equity markets. Attracting some of these monies to Iraq requires that new and old players inside the country rally together behind a coherent economic vision.

Cut to the Chase

Plans Western lenders routinely prescribe for developing countries are the familiar mainstay of global capitalism. Iraq's government will require foreign aid and concessions in credit and lending. The cost for these perks will be to open the country to the free flow of capital and trade, liberalize and privatize state assets, and institute the domestic reform policies necessary to foster macroeconomic stability: good governance and the fostering of civil society, open and accountable trade regimes, effective basic services in health and education, protection of the country's resources and the environment, and access to new information technology, with special priority attached to strengthening the institutional capacity of justice and police systems. If government systems fail, lenders will channel their assistance through NGOs and Western multinationals. This high-pressure process will be Iraq's prerequisite for World Trade Organization membership. Its proponents point to gains registered in some East Asian countries that committed to similar reforms: Malaysia's poverty fell from more than half the population to around 7 percent in the 1990s, and Vietnam's per capita GDP doubled. On the other hand, in similar projects in South Asia and sub-Saharan Africa, the number of people living in poverty has grown by tens of millions. Cookie-cutter strategies play out differently in different places. Moreover, privatization and deregulation initiatives in several Arab countries over the past three decades have not stemmed the overall decline in the standard of living or consolidation of wealth into the hands of smaller and smaller groups of people. Iraq could face a similar fate—along with a growing divide between cities, where international presence will be concentrated, and rural areas, where 30 percent of the population resides.

I have little to add to other writings that duly assail the downside of twenty-first-century capitalism. I prefer to emphasize milestones of Iraq's likely road to globalization which are particularly useful for the country. The pressure the world will impose on Iraq to protect the physical security of its citizens and foreign guests is salubrious for a country that has had a special reputation in the Arab Middle East for resolving more than a few business disputes through bloodshed—not only in the violent days of the Ba'th, but also throughout the twentieth century. Bilateral investment agreements with the United States, Europe, and Asia will make Iraq eligible for investment insurance programs, such as those of America's OPIC and the World Bank's MIGA, which guarantee investments against noncommercial risks like civil war and nationalization. Efforts to garner serious foreign investment without offering these guarantees would probably fail. Finally, Iraq would be blessed by an American commitment to designate "qualified industrial zones" (QIZs) focusing on technology, tourism, services, and industry in Iraq. Goods produced by companies in QIZs would be imported to Western markets duty-free if they involve economic cooperation between Iraq and a Western country, bilaterally or multilaterally. This would make investment in these zones particularly attractive for industries whose products are subject to high tariffs when they are imported to Western countries. If Iraq has the good fortune of Jordan, the first country to sign a "free trade agreement" with the United States, it would enjoy the elimination of tariffs on virtually all trade with the world's largest market. There are now 11 QIZs in Jordan that are home to approximately 25 exporting companies. The bulk of exporters from these zones have been textile and garment manufacturers. This modest industry has earned more than $100 million in new investment since 1999, generated over $110 million in exports to the United States, and created nearly 15,000 new jobs.

But the two-way exchange value of QIZs to potential Western and European partners hinges on Iraq's ability to deliver open borders of trade with its neighbors in the greater Middle East, notably the vast export market of Iran. Seeking to break out of its current isolation, Saddam's government signed free trade agreements over the past two years with many other Arab countries—Jordan, Algeria, Egypt, Lebanon, Oman, Qatar, Sudan, Syria, Tunisia, Yemen, and the United Arab Emirates (UAE). In June 2001, the country also signed a four-way free trade agreement with Syria, Egypt, and Libya. Iraq's government should shrewdly maintain these agreements—a complex geopolitical balancing act. The United States and its allies can help strengthen the new government's hand to do so by fostering an advantageous debt relief program and an oil regime of value to the country's industrial base.

Slick Maneuvering

With a high-speed oil industry overhaul supported by the most effective foreign companies, Iraq could boost the country's oil production to 4.5 million bpd within less than three years. By 2010 the country could reach an output of 9 million bpd, transforming it from the world's ninth largest oil producer to the fourth largest. It is estimated that Iraq will have to spend up to $35 to $50 billion over the next decade to raise production capacity to its potential levels.

A question mark looming over international oil markets is whether Iraq would opt out of the Organization of Petroleum Exporting Countries (OPEC). If the new government maintains its membership in the cartel, it is hoped that it could remain exempt from production quotas until it is able to pay off debts and finance reconstruction. Otherwise, it is speculated that a U.S.-backed Baghdad would seek to maximize production to make up for a decade of lost output and could find it in its interests to drop out of OPEC, leading to a dramatic plunge in oil prices. In the long run, however, Iraq is unlikely to remain indifferent to oil prices.

American oil companies are eager to gain access to the world's second largest oil reserves with the help of its new government. At the same time, companies based in Russia, France, and China fear that their recently signed oil contracts will prove worthless after Saddam's fall. Another growth sector in a postwar Iraq would be the import of equipment for the oil and gas industry. Iraq is expected to require some $500 million worth of imported supplies to overhaul the sector and maintain heightened output levels.

Iraq's nationalized oil industry might eventually be headed for privatization in the new Iraq, as part of a more comprehensive structural reform program. The state-run Iraq National Oil Company (INOC), which has monopolized the sector, may be broken down into smaller, competitive enterprises corresponding to its already semiautonomous units. The sector would require separate companies to deal with oil marketing and distribution activities, marine transport (tankers), upstream activities along a regional subdivision, a pipeline maintenance company, downstream natural gas/LPG projects, and gas bottling plants. These new firms would recruit both local and foreign professionals.

There is a clear relationship between calculations regarding Iraqi oil and the dire condition of the country's debt. Iraq's burgeoning combination of outstanding loans and reparations has been building up rapidly. Uncertainty regarding their true value and the fluctuating nature of oil revenues highlight the precarious state of Iraq's economic future. Even under the most favorable terms, Iraq will be incapable of generating oil export revenues sufficient to cover the minimum requirements of debt sustainability. Without substantial relief from external obligations, the deterioration of the Iraqi economy will continue. To avoid a situation whereby the future of Iraq is mortgaged well beyond its means, reparations and debts must be cut to a manageable size. The international community should consider rescheduling Iraq's external debt and forgiving the largest part of reparations payments. In the interest of ensuring a smooth transition from the old regime, it would be necessary to formulate a global settlement plan that would arrange for Iraq to meet its debts without further stalling the country's rehabilitation. The United States is expected to look favorably on a debt relief program. Not quite as affluent as other creditors, Russia is concerned about the debt issue and would require substantial repayment. Arab compensation claimants and debt creditors, most notably the Gulf countries, are likely to forgive or adjust downward their financial demands on Iraq, but may attempt to exact their own political and ideological concessions on the shape of Iraq's new government in exchange.

One possible initiative to settle Iraq's debts would tap the Paris Club, an informal consortium of 19 creditor countries that coordinates strategies for dealing with monies owed to them. Resorting to the Paris Club obliges debtor countries to conclude agreements with the IMF and World Bank. In this way, such a multilateral debt rescheduling arrangement would serve as leverage to press for government accountability and domestic political openness and bring about economic and administrative reform. Negotiations on debt reduction and repayment scheduling would require the new Iraqi government to open its books to domestic as well as international scrutiny. A dramatic reduction in Iraq's compensation obligations could come about as a result of international corporations waiving millions in war reparations owed to them by Iraq. But in return, Iraq would have to reward them by giving them priority in postwar contracts for rebuilding the country and developing its economy.

In short, nearly every government and company that has ever been crossed by Saddam's Iraq now wields enormous economic and political leverage on the country's future. Authoritarian states with clear ideologies and multinational corporations with clear profit motives will predictably press their traditional demands. Less obvious, however, is the agenda America's government and democratic allies will seek to advance in the years ahead, or whether competing ideas within these countries will allow a coherent agenda to emerge at all. For your interest, here is the agenda I propose.

Cut Down Oligarchs and Foster More Elites

An earlier discussion of Saddam's privileged politicos and their
future noted the dilemma the U.S. government faces regarding
the extent of its commitment to a redistribution of power in Iraq
from the top down by chaperoning the country's political system. Unfortunately, the antique lens of colonial identity politics, which is still considered useful in governments' planning of
foreign engagements, tends to induce a lack of depth perception,
which can only be corrected by soldering in the filter of business
and money. It does not matter how few or many Shi'is, for example, hold ministry positions if the majority of Shi'is remain an
impoverished, undereducated underclass. Nor will political
engineering alone serve to decartelize industries held by an
entrenched clique if they and their families still form the most
competent and experienced community of technocrats in Iraq.
In postwar Germany, Nazis were purged from bureaucracy and
business, but many soon returned. By 1948, 85 percent of the
officials removed in Bavaria had been reinstated. It is easy to
imagine that most of the high-ranking technocrats who helped
hold Iraq together over the past decade of sanctions will prove
invaluable to the rapid execution of infrastructure rebuilding
projects, such as restoring the national grid, which could cost
Iraq as much as $4 billion per year over several years. Each infra-
structure overhaul project will come together with lucrative
business opportunities for the elites who broker it, notably big
trade deals with foreign partners to supply the requisite equipment. The liberalization of Iraq's economy could easily serve to
widen the economic gap between Saddam's elites and disaffected
majorities. Far from suffer the slings and arrows of outrageous
fortune, several former princes of the Ba'th may well hold onto
the quiver, while hopeful newcomers to the scene are armed
with the economic equivalent of a peashooter.

That is, unless we fortify their arsenal. Although several
generations are ultimately necessary to usher new communities
fully into the sphere of economic power through education and
the formation of power networks, there are several ways a con-

certed effort on the part of foreign governments, companies, and individuals can meanwhile serve to undercut Iraq's oligarchs. And in the global economy, there are also new tools to foster new elites. The most sweeping device is the enforcement of decartelization laws, which have had the most impact in countries occupied by foreign powers. In postwar Germany, Americans broke up the big conglomerates in Germany's industrial center, the Ruhr region; divided several large firms; and dissolved the company that controlled the film industry. Another measure would tap Iraqi exiles with banking and corporate experience in the United States and London, for example, to run the new operations of multinational companies in Iraq, or structure privatization deals for Western banks. Those returnees who hail from disaffected communities inside the country will naturally turn to their families in Iraq for support and more broadly to facilitate their reacclimation and survival, forming a symbiosis that can congeal into new networks of power and wealth.

A peashooter can be a formidable weapon given the magnifying powers of globalization. One beast of a little tactic for which some incumbent apparatchiks may be ill prepared is the enforcement of intellectual property rights laws. The entertainment and software industries of the United States are approachable on pitches to fund creative methods of securing what some Silicon Valley companies refer to as "found money"—new sales from tertiary markets resulting from the prosecution of pirates. Iraq certainly qualifies as a tertiary market, and in 2003, not a signatory to international copyright laws. America's Commercial Law Development Program, which has already provided assistance in Algeria, Egypt, and Tunisia on intellectual property protection and competition policy, can serve to train young people of modest backgrounds to serve as prosecutors and enforcers. The people best suited for the job are naturally those who have never had ties to Iraq's largest contraband music and software smuggling syndicate, also known as the Ba'th party.

There are many more tactics along these lines, of which two more examples will suffice. First, connections between businesses outside the country and disaffected people inside the country can form the basis for efficient medium-size ventures.

The previous chapter established that the poverty of Iraq under sanctions spawned remarkable entrepreneurial ingenuity among many of its people. The most resourceful among them would be well suited to participate as professionals and as partners in feasibility studies and consulting projects requiring research close to the ground. In addition to multinationals eager to finance the retrieval of information on Iraq's human resources and consumer base, the U.S. Trade and Development Agency (TDA) funds feasibility studies, consultancies, training, and other project planning services. TDA is hardly gun shy about supporting initiatives in the Arab world; in 2001, TDA named Morocco, which has 18 ongoing TDA-funded activities, as its country of the year. The second example stems from the need for viable labor unions in Iraq, the establishment of which could provide a meaningful role for marginalized communist and socialist Iraqi opposition members who wish to return home, as well as usher in the resources of the American labor movement.

A wild card in any campaign to broaden the circle of elites in Iraq is that class of cross-border smuggler kings and gangsters, the "cats of the embargo." As the previous chapter established, cats spanned Iraq's ethnic and cultural divisions, including numerous Shi'is and Kurds. Many of them had not established credentials with the Ba'th party as their staunch supporters, but simply paid them tribute money. The cats over the next few years will have an opportunity to ease out of the black market and prove their mettle in the gray and white markets, perhaps even morph into global tigers. With the analogy in mind of successive generations of immigrants to the United States who made the transition from organized crime to lawful business, one might hope that new power and wealth for cats in the legitimate world could spill over and benefit friends and associates from the marginal groups from which they hail.

Intuitively, the most practical application of cats' hard-nosed expertise working contraband networks at the fringes of Iraq would be their contribution to Iraq's emergence as a regional trade hub for both local and international commerce activities in the sanctions-free future. The government will have to invest in developing advanced sea, land, and air freight facilities that could compete with those offered by the much smaller emirate of Dubai, whose workforce depends on expatriates. But the cats of the embargo could be indispensable to broker the use of these large-scale high-tech port services to importers, exporters, and reexporters. Iraq carries great potential for regional and overseas companies seeking access to the markets of the Middle East, as well as a doorway to regions as diverse as the Indian subcontinent, South Asia, East Africa, and Europe. As a regional center for the distribution of goods, Iraq would have to supply not only terminal services—freight handling operations, bunkering (fuel), hangars and shipyards, warehousing and storage—but also transportation logistics, customs brokering, freight forwarding, trade finance, and cargo insurance services.

Whatever the tactics one chooses, the struggle to break old cartels and support the emergence of new business elites in Iraq is in my view a moral imperative for those who would profit by the country's reintegration in the global economy. The following sample guide to export opportunities to Iraq is based on anticipated equipment needs for the reconstruction of the country's battered industries over the next few years. It is a partial list, and does not include the franchising sector, which I value at an average $500 million per year over the next three years, or the export of luxury items, which depends on the overall economic well being of the country. Ideally the network of importers and traders inside the country who profit by these deals will be as broad as possible.

Grand Opening Spree

The largest nonoil sectors calling for the import of equipment to Iraq are telecommunications, medical services, agriculture, and manufacturing. The overhaul of Iraq's fixed telephony network and unrolling of a new mobile network are both massive projects, calling for foreign expertise, switching equipment and base stations, microwave and fiberoptic technologies, and mobile handsets. The sector's complete revitalization requires investments that could approach $1 billion annually. Meanwhile, the medical equipment sector is worth approximately $450 million per year. This assessment is based on the assumption that substantial international funds will be allocated to health care services in the new Iraq, in an effort to improve the country's poor health care standards. At present, Iraq's medical facilities are no longer able to respond to the population's critical needs. Some hospital buildings are near-collapse, and the number of available beds in Iraqi hospitals totals only 25,000, implying an inadequate overall bed rate of about one per 1,000 people. Iraq's private-sector and international foreign aid organizations are likely to become involved in operating another 10,000 beds. More than 100 new hospitals and medical centers will have to be constructed in Iraq if the population's growing needs are to be met. At the same time, new capital-intensive medical technologies, such as magnetic resonance imaging (MRI), computed tomography (CT), and megavolt radiation therapy, are expected to be purchased by Iraqi hospitals.

In the short term, used and refurbished equipment is likely to make its way into the Iraqi health market, serving as an alternative source for emerging distributors and end-users due to lower prices and shorter delivery time. The use of the build-operate-transfer (BOT) model could also be encouraged as a means of procuring equipment that would enable Iraq to move its health services into the twenty-first century. The BOT model calls for the vendor to install and operate the equipment, receive the revenues from the use of equipment, and finally transfer the equipment at the end of a specified period that covers expenses and profit.

An overhaul of the country's agricultural base is inevitable. Iraq's water distribution network and water treatment systems are inadequate and require urgent repair and development. In order for Iraq to become a major agricultural product trading partner, the country must renew its supply of spare parts, chemicals, pipes, and other vital equipment. In the short term, sanctions-hit Iraq will need to keep up the import of consumer-oriented agricultural commodities, including vegetable oils, wheat, corn, and soybeans. Until a time when Iraq manages to revive its livestock industry, imports of poultry, cattle, dairy, and fish present profitable opportunities for foreign suppliers. In the longer term, the sector's revival would require the support of specialized food technology exhibitions and intensive training programs in modern agriculture and food industry technology.

Iraq's decrepit manufacturing facilities demand building materials. Imports to Iraq will include cement, flooring, prefabricated wall panels, wall paper, doors, windows, paint, insulation, sanitary wares and plumbing fixtures, prefabricated homes, roofing, and siding materials. These materials could also approach $1 billion per year in cost.

Relatedly, the installation and supply of electricity, gas, water, and air conditioning systems is likely to provide rewarding opportunities for both foreign firms looking to do business in the Iraqi market and new Iraqi trading companies. Unique opportunities are also expected to emerge for international construction suppliers, engineering and consulting firms, and industrial and project developers. As for small- and medium-scale private industry, plastic and food processing holds promise, as do assembly lines for cars, home appliances, and electronic equipment. But the local industry's requirements for capital and technology cannot presently be satisfied from domestic sources alone. The renewal of trade and investment finance inflows and the reopening of foreign markets to Iraqi products could best be promoted through strategic partnerships with foreign firms. Such collaboration would also enable Iraqi manufacturers to regain lost export market share faster.

High hopes for new winners in the realms of power and money will doubtless register disappointments as well as some gains. That is why the institutions of truth—Iraqi enterprises of criticism, reflection, education, and justice—will be indispensable.

Part IV
TRUTH

Nine

The Editorial We

Pluralism and Iraqi Journalism

⌒

Iraq's state-controlled daily newspapers for the past 23 years have featured a photograph of Saddam Hussein on page 1 and op-eds by party pundits in praise of his policies. But the lively and complex society around Saddam has received very little coverage. Perhaps the most underreported story in recent years has been the growing income disparity between Saddam's privileged politicos and the rest of the country. Another big scoop, which stems from Iraq's growing poverty, is its burgeoning flesh trade. Here is an example of a story Iraqis would have liked to have known but which never appeared in the local press:

In Amman's ritzy Tla al-Ali suburb, a wealthy realtor named Abu Ahmed, who boasted many clients from the Gulf states, rents out furnished apartments by the week or night and Iraqi girls by the hour. One of his "specimens" is Taghrid, a 19-year-old native of Basra and daughter of a venerable tribe which will remain nameless. The oldest of five sisters, she was sold by her parents and brother to cover the high cost of survival under sanctions. Other girls indentured to Abu Ahmed made the decision themselves. Another girl, Dumu, whose name means "tears," is 15 and from Baghdad, also one of five sisters. Her family fell into dire straits after her father died from an aneurysm, so she decided to sell herself to support her siblings. Dumu had arrived in Amman six weeks before I met her in 2002. Even though she never finished grammar school and can hardly read, she recited from memory an original 15-minute folk poem about a boy she fell in love with back in Baghdad. He had left to visit the UAE for a week, but only returned a year later. The poem is brilliant and heart wrenching. It describes her tears and repeats the refrain, "And you said you'd only be gone a week."[1]

The only time that the trafficking of Iraqi women made front-page headlines in Iraq was when Saddam mentioned it in a speech more than a decade ago, dutifully reprinted in full, as all his speeches have been, by the country's daily newspapers. He did so for a special reason. On the eve of his invasion of Kuwait, he delivered a litany of grievances against the little Gulf country structured vaguely like the American Declaration of Independence and including the memorable line, "The glorious Iraqi woman has come to be sold for one [Kuwaiti] dirham."[2] Ironically, Iraqi sex trafficking did not witness hypergrowth until the hyperinflation that followed the 1991 war under the international sanctions regime. In 1996, Saddam cracked down on the industry and vowed to behead offenders, making Iraqi women that much more precious an export. "If you are obviously from the Gulf, you will be charged around 30 JD [about $42.35] for any girl," explains Nasser, a cabdriver in Amman. "But Iraqi women are more expensive, up to 80 JD per hour."[3]

It would be unfair to single out a particular Arab country for harboring pimps or its press for failing to expose them. Sex trafficking is a multibillion-dollar industry across the Middle East and around the world. Poor countries in North Africa and the Levant offer mainly local girls, while wealthier countries like Israel and the Gulf states import women from Russia and Eastern Europe, the Far East, neighboring countries, or all of the above. The State Department's 2002 annual index of sex traffickers lists Israel and every Gulf state except Oman among the offenders. But if you open a local newspaper in the UAE, Saudi Arabia, or many other Arab countries, you will find a blackout on the subject. For that matter, you will find a blackout on many subjects.

Enter *al-Jazeera*, the Arabic-language international satellite TV news network based in Qatar. In June 2002, a long-anticipated edition of the weekly talk show "Just for Women" (*Li 'n-Nisa'i Faqat*) promised to break this taboo with an investigative report on the region's sex trade and a blunt discussion by female human rights activists from Egypt and Lebanon. It delivered—sort of. The exposé covered the industry in Turkey, a non-Arab country where the press laws are relatively permissive and *al-Jazeera* has a very small audience. The disgraceful situation in Israel earned well-deserved condemnation as well. But no Gulf state was mentioned by name. Farida al-Naqqash, an Egyptian activist who appeared on the program, made prescient points about global capitalism's efficient management of the flesh trade's supply side. On the demand side, however, she seemed to restrain herself. Would anyone care to explore the connection between a conservative society's repression of sexuality and its insatiable demand for prostitutes? Naqqash made an obvious allusion to the Gulf region when she referred to "the granteur states" (*al-Duwal al-Maniha*), and most viewers probably understood what she meant. The network's courage in advancing the discussion this far deserves high praise. Yet three years into the twenty-first century, Saddam Hussein still stands more or less alone in the region for shaming a Gulf country by name in the mainstream Arab media for its sexual iniquities.

Hopes for an improvement in the quality of local media in the Arab world fall upon the new Iraq. A hallmark for a healthy press in the country would be a return to older traditions of social criticism that were once a specialty in Baghdad. An example of an Iraqi who did not mince words was the ninth-century social commentator and essayist Jahiz. He hailed from Basra, where he spent his youth reading books and avoiding gainful employment. He made the big move to Baghdad and acquired a reputation among the city's literati as a gifted writer and intellect. In the bourgeois salons of the Abbasid capital, he listened in on lively conversations about the great political and social controversies of the day, from the conflict between faith and reason and problem of political succession to the young city's sectarian and ethnic tensions. A sort of protojournalist and intellectual entrepreneur, he won commissions from public officials and people of means to write essays, which scholars rank among the most intricate and clever of his day. He maintained a fairly independent voice and expounded on local politics and universal

themes, in one vignette expressing an embryonic theory of evolution a thousand years before Darwin.[4] And yes, he also wrote
about slave girls. His epistle, *The Book of Singing Slave Girls*, is
no Amnesty International report. But like Mark Twain's *Huckle-
berry Finn*, it paints a nuanced and irreverent picture of the psychology of slavery from both the slave's and the master's points
of view. Both Jahiz and Twain were literary pioneers of the young
cultures in which they lived—the early Abbasid Empire and a
consolidating American Union. And now their progeny are on a
course to engage one another in a new cultural frontier.

The Middle East in the twenty-first century is teeming with
the sort of prickly problems and odd situations Mark Twain and
Jahiz would have loved to write about. But something has happened in modern times to subdue more than a few of their
would-be heirs in the region. For starters, many journalists are
slaves to their government. Iraqi media has been through a lot
over the past couple of centuries and suffered considerably over
the past three decades of Ba'th rule, a time of sweeping changes
in Arab media elsewhere. What happens when the reportage of
the interior reconnects with that of its friends and neighbors
will make a good read.

The history of Arab journalism begins with government initiatives. Some Westerners who visited Baghdad in 1816 claim they
saw a local news bulletin there called *Journal of Iraq* printed in
Arabic and Turkish.[5] They say it reported on mostly local affairs
and praised the persona of its publisher, the local Ottoman governor, to a readership of army commanders and elites, the most
literate communities in a semiliterate society. *Journal of Iraq*
would have been the first Arabic newspaper anywhere if the
Westerners' report is true, although scholars in the region have
their doubts and no copy of the bulletin survives. What is certain is that a progressive pasha of Baghdad in 1869 who had been
Ottoman ambassador to Paris brought a printing machine with
him to Iraq and founded a weekly newspaper called *al-Zawra*
("the Curved [city]").[6] It too was a mouthpiece for the empire,
measuring four pages long with ink that stained one's hands.
The occasional edifying article on the advent of electricity or

importance of eating fruits and vegetables played second fiddle to stories extolling the sultan and efficient workings of his government. The editor of the publication had a laid-back life. Once a week he dropped by the police department, government ministries, and local post and telegraph offices, all in walking distance, and wrote up the good news he heard. Occasionally, he even reprinted a story from an upstart Western wire service called Reuters. Similar ventures in Basra and Mosul promoted their provinces too.[7]

While Iraqi journalists enjoyed calm careers in the service of the state, Arab societies of the eastern Mediterranean caught the bug of independent journalism that had been spreading slowly across the ocean from Europe. Lebanese Christians pioneered private presses, weathering the sultan's crackdowns, while ideologues, satirists, and rabble-rousers of most every ethnic and religious group in Cairo established newspapers and journals critical of society and state. Egypt's prestigious daily *al-Ahram* ("The Pyramid"), founded around this time, maintained a measure of independence and helped form a distinctive voice of local indignation at the intrusions of foreign powers in Egypt, from the Ottomans to their successors.[8] A memorable editorial during the British occupation slammed England's inability "to hold to its promise [of quick evacuation] any more than a sieve can hold water." The British shut it down, but thanks to pressure from the French, it reopened a month later and has been publishing since.[9]

Journalistic intrigue of this sort did not reach the banks of the Tigris for a few more years. Besides the Ottoman provincial bulletins, the only periodicals in print before 1908 were benign journals of religion by Dominican missionaries in Mosul and Carmelites in Baghdad.[10] The situation changed when the Ottoman government allowed press freedom in the first years of Young Turk rule. By 1914, there were about 70 independent newspapers in Iraq, many rife with criticism of Ottoman hegemony, a point of view endemic to the empire's Arab provinces at the time.[11] But the permissive policy of the Young Turks proved short-lived. Successive crackdowns first by the Ottomans and later by the British led to the closure of nearly every newspaper in Iraq by World War I. The wobbly empire tried to reestablish Iraqi provincial bulletins, but found audiences for its state propaganda waning. Steam was billowing into Baghdad from the hotbeds of nationalism in the eastern Mediterranean. From now on, Iraqi readers demanded spirited prose. Lebanese and Syrian newspapers acquired followings in Iraq; their round rejection of imperialism and Zionism resonated.

The newspapers that were circulated in Iraq had small but avid readerships and won mixed reviews. Some of the country's Muslim preachers railed against the new technology, citing a tradition of the prophet Muhammad calling upon believers to "avoid gossip, wasting money, and asking too many questions," all of which journalists and their subscribers allegedly did.[12] But preachers' broadsides did little to stem some urbanites' thirst for news. Young readers in Iraq's cities who could not afford to buy a newspaper lined up to share someone else's or rent a copy from a news seller and sell it back later in the day at half price. The latter technique prompted one Baghdadi daily to print the screaming headline, "Damn he who rents a paper from the distributor." However enthusiastic some readers were, it bears noting that most Iraqis at the time could not read at all. Still a predominantly rural country, Iraq had an 11 percent literacy rate for people over the age 5 as late as 1947.[13] The trend did not turn around meaningfully until years later when the Ba'th party introduced stringent measures to fight illiteracy.

The rough-and-tumble factionalism that characterized the days of British domination in Iraq gave parties and cliques every incentive to start newspapers of their own. The British established state organs to explain their occupation of the country, to which mosque preachers and others lashed back in sermons. It was only a matter of time before populist voices turned to journalism. A paper called *Independence* ("al-Istiqlal") appeared in Najaf "to respond to the occupiers' deception, to disquiet them, to reveal their barbaric misdeeds." Twenty four-pagers sprouted up in the 1920s, most as mouthpieces for various parties, others financed by the British, and two in Baghdad claiming an independent voice. Over the next 30 years, the life cycles of journalistic enterprises became familiar to the reading public: papers

too feisty were shut down by the government, only to reopen
under another name. Writers too uppity for the mouthpiece of a
mainstream party found employment with a smaller clique
whose sheets were mangier, while radical writers who mellowed
out switched to more tepid organs.[14] One newspaper named
Time ("al-Zaman"), founded in 1937, won esteem as a voice for
objectivity.[15] For the most part, the sort of freedom writers in
Iraq enjoyed was akin to the freedom of politicians in the United
States today to choose the interest groups that contribute to
their campaigns. You are not a slave if you have the right to
choose your masters, but you are not entirely at liberty either.

The laid-back lifestyle of the Ottoman governor's publicist
in nineteenth-century Iraq had given way only a few decades
later to a newspaper culture as swashbuckling as that of the old
Kansas cow towns or the Tennessee of Mark Twain's youth.
Twain's book *Editorial Wild Oats* describes vituperative
exchanges and gunfights between editors in Tennessee that
might as easily have taken place in Baghdad or Basra, if one just
changed the name of the paper from *The Johnson County War-
whoop* or *The Thunderbolt and Battle Cry of Freedom* to Baghdad's *Echo of Independence* (*Sada al-Istiqlal*) or Mosul's *Call of
God's Truth* ("Da'wat al-Haqq"). Instructions from a Tennessee
editor to his young apprentice: "Jones will be here at three—
cowhide him. Gillespie will call earlier, perhaps—throw him out
the window. Ferguson will be along about four—kill him. . . . In
case of accident, go to Lancet the surgeon downstairs. He adver-
tises—we take it out in trade."[16]

The strident spirit of the small-time press in the American
south lives on (I met a woman from South Carolina in 2002 who
edits her own rag called *The Rebel Yell*), but editorial shenani-
gans like these eventually ground to a halt in Iraq with the consolidation of one-party rule. The 1950s and 1960s saw the proliferation of newspapers, spread of radio, and introduction of
television, lending media unprecedented pervasiveness. The pluralism of yellow journalism had been tolerable to the authorities
during the period of the monarchy in part because it reached
comparatively fewer readers. Jahiz, the ninth-century essayist
of Baghdad, probably felt even freer to express himself partly

because what he wrote had to be reproduced by hand and reached only small numbers of affluent devotees. Public expression through mass media in the days of the Iraqi Republic was another matter. Escalating censorship in the 1960s culminated in a 1969 publications law making media the fourth branch of the government. In line with well-known principles of twentieth-century totalitarianism, Saddam's party in the 1970s asserted that the media's purpose was to win over the hearts of the masses to Ba'thism. There would be no room for lengthy scientific or analytical articles, no domestic political criticism, and no irreverence. In addition to pointed progovernment commentary and reportage, Iraqi newspapers under Saddam have featured poems invariably praising the ruler or mocking his enemies.

The refinement of one-party rule in Iraq has its echoes in the modern republics of Libya and Syria, where media are similarly indentured, and fainter reverberations in the fourth estate of more benign Arab republics that espouse a touch of pluralism. Traditions of an independent press meanwhile survive to some degree in some of the region's kingdoms and emirates, where censorship and society's mores work in place of outright government ownership to streamline political spin. In general, external adversaries beginning with Israel win the most coverage; local politics, the coverage of which is more problematic for rulers, receives the least.

Now here comes the surprise: the Iraqi state's war on pluralism did not destroy the power of journalists in the country; it simply rechanneled their talent. It is true that those writers who survived Saddam's crackdowns and wished to retain the right to express criticism had to leave the country and become involved in the expatriate opposition press or non-Iraqi media ventures. But journalists willing to sign on to the state media's unambiguous message were free to throw all their creativity and energy into the means of conveying it.[17] They became practitioners of the craft of journalism without actually generating journalistic content. For these voices, the power of words and images became a tool for social mobility. Some of the most powerful people in Saddam's government hailed from media backgrounds. Tariq Aziz, foreign minister during the 1991 war, had been editor of *The Revolution* ("al-Thawra") in the early years of the Ba'th. Muhammad Sa'id al-Sahhaf, a foreign minister and later information minister, had been director of Iraqi television and radio. Naji Sabri, the last foreign minister of the Ba'th state, cut his teeth as a writer and editor. Hasan Abd al-Hamid, a person with whom I spent a few hours when he was serving as director of cultural programming for Iraq's satellite channel in late 2002, struck me as a tireless devotee to the craft of television. The media profession in a one-party state can be rewarding and fun for those who learn to love their masters.

But Iraq's reading public was not impressed. The experience of growing up in a one-party state breeds skepticism of all voices that claim to speak for "the people," as in Iraqi radio's signature *Voice of the Iraqi People*, or "the truth," as in the words *Voice of the Truth* that used to appear under the frequently televised image of Saddam seated on a throne ad-libbing. There's a joke going around in northern Iraq: a Kurd walks into a repair shop with a broken TV set. The repairman takes a photo of Saddam off the wall and glues it onto the screen. "There," he says, "now it works."[18] Iraqis who lived through the American air raids on Baghdad in 1991 recall scuttling down to the safety of their basements and turning on their radios for coverage of the situation, only to hear hours of music instead, while broadcasters waited for orders from the top on whether to report that the city was under attack. Audiences knew well what the national press was good for, besides washing windows: to understand Saddam's perspective on current events. They also tuned in their shortwave radios to alternative viewpoints from America's "Radio Liberty," which they presumed to be the authoritative source on George W. Bush's perspective, and the BBC Arabic service, perhaps the authoritative source on Tony Blair's perspective. Decades after the fall of small-time local rags that spoke for the leaders of local factions, Iraqi audiences sensibly came to project the skepticism those rags inspired onto the international newsstand.

The globalization of spin in the greater Middle East has meanwhile spiraled out of control. The advent of the Internet in Arab countries where information flow has traditionally been curtailed makes the prospect of streamlining sensibilities more difficult to manage, at least as far as the 3.7 million and count-ing Web browsers now online in Arab countries are concerned. The telecoms advisory firm I work for predicts that the Arab world will host about 30 million Web browsers by 2007, out of a forecast total population of 336 million. This means that Iraq's twentieth-century literacy rates in its early years of editorial pluralism roughly equal the region's twenty-first-century com-puter literacy rates in the coming days of Internet hyperplural-ism. And the schizophrenic policies of the region's rulers with respect to Internet control bear striking resemblance to the fits and starts with which the British Mandate used to attempt to rein in Iraqi editorial wild oats. The ragtag group of tekkies who founded Amman-based *Albawaba.com*, the leading online Ara-bic-language news and information portal in the region today, would also belong in an essay by Mark Twain. Once they ran a piece slamming corruption in the Saudi educational system which led the Saudi kingdom's national Web server to block local browsers' access to their site. But *Albawaba* is one of the most popular Web sites in Saudi Arabia, and its young fans quickly sprang into action. They bombarded the government with e-mails of protest and showered the Web site with moral support. They established "mirror sites" in the UAE, enabling them to access the site indirectly, right under the noses of the Kingdom's national filter. *Albawaba* elected to keep the contro-versy out of the headlines and enter into quiet negotiations with the Saudi government. The Kingdom asked that exposés of inter-nal conditions in Saudi Arabia end; *Albawaba*'s leadership refused. They reached the compromise of a commitment by *Albawaba* to separate the public discussion forums from the portal's news Web site, so that at least the occasional propagan-distic postings by various Saudi opposition groups would not be misconstrued as news. The government lifted the ban shortly thereafter.[19]

As unruly as it is, the Internet remains merely a nuisance and not an existential challenge to the stability of Arab govern-ments, as in the case of old Iraq's small-time rags, due in part to the medium's small audiences. This fact did not stop Saddam from limiting public access to a few Internet cafés in Baghdad,

Basra, and Mosul, the use of which was priced beyond the means of most Iraqis. But there is another reason why the Internet on its own is no sledgehammer to the status quo: however revolutionary the phenomenon of hyperpluralism may be, the noise it makes will not stop humankind from blocking out noise and homing in on signals and symbols. Here is where the craft of the Arab world's indentured journalists remains superior to the public diplomacy efforts of hired hands from Madison Avenue. They understand the symbols that move local audiences and have years of experience transforming them into signals on behalf of their masters. When they throw off the yoke of their government and gain a measure of autonomy, their voice makes an impact. The Qatar-based satellite television network *al-Jazeera*, which reaches many more viewers in the Gulf states alone than the Internet's audience in the entire region, is staffed by people who hail from the BBC Arabic service, the advocacy organs of various states, and the populist streams of Islamism and Arab nationalism. For example, Islamabad correspondent Ahmad Muwaffaq Zaydan used to be a staff-writer for *al-Jihad*, the mouthpiece of Usama bin Laden's mentor in Afghanistan, Abdullah Azzam. The fusion of voices like these and the power of television have enabled *al-Jazeera* to reinforce a regional consciousness focused on the centrality of the Palestinian issue and concerns about American hegemony in Arab countries onto an international platform. As noted earlier, the network also takes on other subjects with a frankness state programming lacks, although it dances around some hot button issues that would turn off certain viewers or lead to its permanent censure in wealthier Arab consumer markets. The network's predicament mirrors the predicament of Arab societies.

Would the team at *al-Jazeera* have hired the ninth-century Iraqi essayist Jahiz if he sent them his resume? He too sought to balance the indulgence of his own creativity with the sensibilities of wealthy elites who paid his bills. But the irreverent worldview he espoused and his propensity for bluntness would put him squarely in the "not-ready-for-prime-time" category in contemporary Arab media. Furthermore, he seemed to have ideas about the value of a broader culture that would not lend themselves to the articulation of an Arabist or Islamist populist message. He wrote a satirical essay on "The Skills of the Guild-Masters"—love poems and battle accounts told in the lingo of various professions of the time—to poke fun at the excesses of jargon that stem from social conditioning. A modern update on the essay might have had Usama bin Laden delivering an ode to a woman he loves in the never-never language of al-Qaeda's hyperbole and threats. There is a market for a modern Jahiz in the Arab world today, as there always has been and always will be. But there is also a dogma of sternness and severity that would stonewall him into silence.

The situation is about to change, however, in the new Iraq, and there are hopes that the change may be contagious else-where in the Middle East. Over the next few years, as Iraq encounters an inflow of ideological capital, returning expats, and newcomers from various states in the region and beyond, the country will sustain a twenty-first-century reprise of *Editorial Wild Oats*. Media organs espousing the viewpoints of competing agendas will supplant the monotonous ventriloquism of Saddam. Returning refugees and others who write for a living will at last have the chance to reach Iraqi readers through the prism of the local organ they like best. Longtime residents of the country who used to rule out careers in journalism because of their distaste for the profession's ground rules under Saddam will have an assortment of new bosses to choose from. And many journalists who worked for the Ba'th will have a chance to reinvent themselves in a new marketplace of images and words.

Moreover, whereas Japan after the Second World War was sealed off for years from international media, Iraq will become just as porous as any other Arab country. The ownership of satellite dishes was rare and illegal on penalty of five years' imprisonment under the Ba'th; their introduction to Iraq en masse will win Western and Arab satellite channels new audiences. Internet browsing was severely restricted in recent years; its widespread availability will end Iraqis' famine for information on a range of subjects, the ranks of which will shrink, and taboos. Both these manifestations of new media stand in turn to serve as a check on the integrity of conventional local media. But the robust competition for hearts and minds played out inside Iraq, as in contemporary Lebanon, will fuel the demand for independent local publications of record.

Arab countries with permissive laws on local media might at last manage to rid themselves of editors' and journalists' need to garner ideological funding when they establish an industrial base capable of sustaining profitable independent news organs through advertising. *Al-Jazeera's* major underwriters—the state-owned Qatar Petroleum Company, Qatar Telecommunications Company and Qatar National Bank—are no substitute for a panoply of private sponsors. For reasons explained in an earlier chapter, Iraq is the Arab country with the brightest prospects to achieve such a transition over the next decade, although the entrepreneurs who attempt it may face great humiliation and risk early on. The people who will be doing the humiliating are the sort of locals whom Mark Twain refers to as "the village smarties" in his *Oats* story about a strange young printer named Nicodemus Dodge. The village smarties play various tricks on him, but to no avail. As a last resort, they attempt to scare him to death by procuring "the skeleton of the late and only local celebrity, Jimmy Finn, the village drunkard," and placing it in Dodge's bed before bedtime.[20] Unfazed, the young printer takes the skeleton out to market and sells it to a traveling quack. He uses the money to buy some things he needs, including an old harmonica, which he uses to play himself to sleep.

Ten

Babylon Take Two

New Iraqi Cinema and Entertainment

⁓

Back in the 1960s when Saddam was just another ambitious young torturer, Woody Allen was just another promising comedian. Violent he wasn't, but his standup routines in American night clubs put audiences in stitches. Once he told the crowd about an argument he had had with the IRS over whether he could write off his psychoanalyst's bills as a business deduction. "The government said it was entertainment," he said. "We compromised, finally, and made it a religious contribution."[1]

Translated into Arabic, his joke might have resonated in Baghdad 1,200 years earlier. The backbone of the Iraqi entertainment industry at the time was a band of storytellers (*qussas*) who held court in some of the city's mosques and public squares. They captivated thousands of people every Friday at the end of a hard week's work. They delivered sermons about the prophet Muhammad and his predecessors or expounded on a Qur'anic verse. Many of them also recounted the travails of caliphs and the underground movements that brought them to power. But they were more than just preachers; they were also standup comics in headgear with no qualms about jazzing up the oral tradition. Their mischievous take on religion and politics in Islam's formative years troubled clerics and political leaders alike.[2] Storytellers might have had as much impact on the denizens of eighth-century Baghdad, Basra, and Mosul as television and movies do on worldwide audiences today.

Then as now, the tension between political authority and the power of storytelling made entertainment in the Middle East a dicey business. There is evidence that dissidents and rulers alike offered bribes to storytellers to slant their take on current events. Their penchant for accepting money from both eventually won them the boot. Ali, the prophet's son-in-law, kicked the storytellers out of Basra en masse and sought to replace them with more pedantic preachers. Similar crackdowns occurred over the century that followed until the mosques of Iraq had been purged. But some scholars believe the storytellers had the last laugh. The theory has been put forth that much of what we know about the Abbasid revolution and other key events in early Islamic history stems from medieval transcriptions of storytellers' Friday sketches.[3]

Now fast-forward your VCR 12 centuries and imagine the enduring unease between the Arab world's power brokers and storytellers in the age of TV and cinema. An old movie house on Baghdad's al-Rashid Street in autumn 2002 is showing black-and-white Egyptian melodramas, Indian blockbusters, and the occasional American thriller, but hardly anyone is there for the show.[4] The golden paint that flakes off the building's elaborate white façade betrays an industry stripped of its luster. A few blocks away stands the Iraqi Artists' Union, one of the few public places that still serves a stiff drink after Saddam banned pubs in 1993. Hasan Abd al-Hamid, the director of cultural programming for Iraqi television, is toasting a playwright who just won the prestigious annual Saddam prize for theater. And in little cinemas across the city where movies used to play before sanctions, actors and comedians are putting on burlesque shows laced with subtle political satire for audiences large and small.

The story behind Iraq's stars of stage and screen is only part of a Middle Eastern epic now paused at a cliffhanger. As Iraq reintegrates into the world community, some people wonder whether the story will have a Hollywood ending.

The curtain rises in North Africa. Arabic movie industries grew out of cultural collaborations with European filmmakers that began during the First World War. Modest silent movies were produced from French Algeria and Morocco to Syria and Lebanon.[5] But one country eclipsed them all: Egypt, which was rivaled in the Arab world only by Iraq as a capital of music and storytelling for centuries. By 1917 the country had built 80 movie houses, which drew in big crowds for Egyptian and foreign productions.[6] Though the earliest local films were silent dramas based on popular novels, the lightness of spirit for which Egyptians are known made for compelling comedies and musicals as soon as sound hit the big screen. Some of the first Egyptian movie stars were vocalists already known across the region through radio broadcasts: Farid al-Atrash, the son of a Druze prince; Leila Murad, a Jewish woman; and Um Kalthum, the heavyset Muslim woman whose booming voice stirred listeners across the region. The film industry also had the benefit of a government that lent its artists a modicum of freedom and its film executives a steady stream of capital. The proliferation of Egyptian movies region-wide spread an affinity for Egypt's distinctive dialect of Arabic and lent the country added prestige as it entered its era of nationalism. The musicals and comedies of the 1930s and 1940s gave way to more heavy-handed melodramas in the 1950s and 1960s, which portrayed conflicted heroines and heroes in a world of good and evil.

Meanwhile, the advent of cinema elsewhere in the Middle East was earning mixed reviews. Mullahs in Iran reacted viscerally to the innovation as early as 1904.[7] They campaigned against it as an import from a godless West and a rival to the mosque, eventually inciting followers in the city of Abadan to burn down a movie house in 1978, killing 400 people. Reactions to colonialism across the region triggered the suspicion in Arab countries controlled by European powers that films funded or produced by foreigners had embedded into their storylines a message of cultural hegemony. As Algeria, Tunisia, and Syria threw off the yoke of imperialism, their new political leaders came to see film as a tool to mold a new national identity, and proceeded to commission screenplays along these lines. Running in tandem were the first Zionist productions in Palestine and early Israel, which drove home themes of Jewish nationalism to Hebrew-speaking audiences.

Iraq was a late bloomer. Small Turkish theater troops used to visit Baghdad before the First World War, and Egyptian silent movies came to Iraqi screens by 1927.[8] But it was not until after the Second World War that an Egyptian-Iraqi joint venture made the first Iraqi movies. Wholly local studios came into play by the mid-1950s, and 20 feature films had been made by 1964. Most were Egyptian-style musicals and melodramas, but some drew inspiration from Iraqi folklore, including an epic drama on the life of the Babylonian king Nebuchadnezzar.

Movie stars in the Arab world became cultural icons. Some embraced the political ideals of their country's leadership; others sympathized with dissidents. Not for the first time in the region, politics and storytelling clashed as cinema came of age. Nearly every government in the Middle East over the past 30 years has expelled artists who eschewed the party line, whatever it happened to be. One country's loss was another's gain. Like German refugees Peter Lorre and Marlene Dietrich who came to Hollywood from Berlin in the 1930s, left-wing Egyptian actor-director Karam Mutawwa fled Sadat's Cairo and moved to Baghdad in the early 1970s.[9] But the notion of Iraq as a haven for creative freedom became comical only a few years later. Iraqi actress Fakriyya Abd al-Karim starred on stage and screen in Baghdad and campaigned for communism well into the party's struggle against the Ba'th. She fled Iraq in 1979 for communist-leaning South Yemen and later moved on to Syria before winning asylum in Sweden, where she died in 1998, still dreaming of Iraq in black and white after decades in exile.[10]

Why bother making a movie anyway? Filmmakers everywhere seek to challenge their audiences as well as entertain them. That often means tugging on the reins of the state's agenda or society's mores. In the Arab world, both state and society are inordinately well equipped to tug back. Censors region-wide have a mandate from families and clerics to squelch explorations of sex and religion and from ruling elites to cut out political content. "Taking into account the various crippling limitations facing Arab filmmakers," writes critic Nana Asfour, "it is surprising that films get made at all."[11] From around 70 films a year produced by studios in Egypt in the 1960s, the annual number since the year 2000 has dwindled to around eight.[12] Arabic movies have lost some of the esteem of their audiences, from the lowbrow who would just as soon see an American blockbuster to aficionados like Palestinian director Elias Suleiman, who recently declared that new Arabic movies do not appeal to him.[13]

Since the 1980s, most Arab governments rarely bankroll local films, leaving directors at the mercy of foreign investors and granteurs. Decades after the fall of its empire, France is once again the main backer of North African and Lebanese cinema. Though some critics accuse artists who accept these funds of playing into the hands of cultural imperialists, filmmaker Ziad Doueri begs to differ. He asserts in an interview that *West Beirut*, his gripping portrayal of teenagers during the Lebanese civil war, enjoyed French funding with no strings attached.[14] Great movies still get made from time to time in Arab North Africa and the eastern Mediterranean. But where mildly repressive political systems have earned the Western label "moderate," the movies they spawn often attain the description "mediocre."

More of the region's great cinematic achievements in recent memory hail from the countries of its political periphery, where state attempts to repress artistic expression are either among the most extreme, like Iran, or the most lax, like Israel. Iran's entertainment industry has received numerous Cannes Film Festival awards over the past few years. Abbas Kiarostami's films contain stunning indictments of Iranian society and state and testify to a local artist's struggle to defy the Ministry of Islamic Guidance. But they also transcend the local setting and strike universal themes—casting doubt on the existence of an afterlife, finding beauty in the imagination of children. Other films no less piercing are the work of some of the clerical government's erstwhile defenders, like Mohsen Makhmalbaf, who abandoned a career in "public diplomacy" at the government-controlled Islamic Artistic Theater Center in favor of secular cinema. Interviewed after the release of his 1987 film *The Peddler*, one of the earliest post-Revolution movies to openly criticize the regime, he declared, "I've discovered cinema, and it has changed the way I look at the world."[15] Israel, for its part, yielded films critical of state policies and societal inequities as early as the mid-1960s. Both countries became exporters of visions to the world. As scholar Kamran Talattof explains, "[Iranian cinema] has been able to satisfy a need beyond the thirst for understanding other cultures, beyond entertaining the idea of the Other . . . it has been able to say something beautiful about life, and this has made Iranian cinema desirable not only to Iranians, but also to the West."[16]

Filmmakers in Iraq under Saddam produced several works of great creativity and charm. *The Princess and the River*, released in 1982, is a full-length animated feature set in the world of Akkadian mythology. Three sisters compete to become queen by crossing the harsh landscapes of ancient Iraq—river, mountains, and desert—and evading mythical monsters along the way. The girls' distinct personalities tellingly reflect a traditional Iraqi conception of the range of feminine character: haughtiness, vanity, and wisdom. For the most part, the docket of 1980s movies interspersed propagandistic Iran–Iraq war films commissioned by the Ministry of Culture with Egyptian-style melodramas. *Fa'iq Gets Married* (*Fa'iq Yatazawwaj*) is an example of the latter. It stars two middle-class bureaucrats who fall in love but cannot afford to marry given the high cost of living. One of the first scenes stands out for its profanity—a man gets a woman drunk and she strips down to her lingerie—and ran in Iraqi cinemas but fell to the cutting room floor before the movie's television debut.[17]

One of the country's best-loved comedy serials in the early Ba'th years was a weekly sit-com performed live and broadcast on Iraqi public television called "Under the Barber's Knife" (*Tahta Mus al-Hallaq*). Some viewers felt that the title subtly connoted piercing scrutiny or careful consideration—an idiomatic Iraqi way of saying "All Things Considered"—beyond its obvious connection to the stars of the show, an elderly barber and his sarcastic young assistant. The series took on contemporary issues with gentle digs at the government and its effort to construct an Iraqi national character. The Ba'th party's Comprehensive National Campaign for the Compulsory Eradication of Illiteracy was spoofed in one memorable episode wherein the elderly barber has to endure an Arabic reading lesson from a schoolboy in the neighborhood whom he knew before the child could even talk.[18]

The actors and playwrights behind these productions enjoyed a privileged position in Iraqi society, thanks in part to Saddam's high regard for the arts. Early in his presidency, Saddam manifested numerous talents and skills, but acknowledged in a memorable speech that he could not draw or paint for his life and held in awe the people who could. More than once in his career, he collaborated with Iraqi writers to produce modern-day myths intended to engineer public consent for some of his policies. One of the first films produced in Iraq after the 1991 war presented Iraq's 1930s King Ghazi as a hero for having attempted to foment rebellion against British rule in Kuwait, viewing the Gulf emirate, as Saddam did, as a rightful province of Iraq. Another politically loaded story, *Zabiba and the King*, was an allegorical novel allegedly penned by Saddam that was performed on stage in the late 1990s. It also advanced the Iraqi government spin on Saddam's invasion of Kuwait and the subsequent war. Saddam commissioned foreign filmmaker Terrence Young, who directed three James Bond films including *Dr. No*, to make a 2003 documentary on Saddam's life.[19]

Saddam knew from experience that artists could subvert public sensibilities unless they were either co-opted or intimidated. Over 23 years, he sought to do both. In 1993 even as he shut down most of the professional unions in Baghdad and banned drinking in public, he permitted the artists' union to stay open and function as a speakeasy. Artists generally had more freedom to poke fun at low-ranking public officials than most anyone else. But the measure of autonomy they enjoyed came with strings attached. Most films that won funding were those that served to promote the government's new social agenda, like the transformation from an agricultural system of landed elites to Soviet-style collective farms.[20] Films that praised the honest virtues of the farmer and the rural working man, as opposed to the bourgeois middle class, also won funds, such as the 1977 feature *The Experiment*, which showed a farmer valiantly trying to cultivate his lands despite harsh weather conditions. As often as possible, artists had to find ways to promote the strident party line on issues like America, the Jews, and inter-Arab politics—over all of which Iraqi artists are in fact divided. Underneath the thin veneer of Ba'thi patriotism, a counterculture of defiance pervaded the artistic community and subtly surfaced here and there, especially when resources became scant in the era of sanctions.

In addition to the overall lack of funds available in Iraq for creative ventures during the sanctions years, filmmakers suffered a further hindrance: the so-called dual use items banned for import to Iraq by the UN embargo included some of the chemicals necessary for the development of film.[21] What resources the government could spare for its artists went mainly to documentaries that depicted the bravery of society and state in the face of an international siege—a project Iraqi artists warmed to. A 30-something friend who used to work as a cameraman for Iraqi public television but now has a gig at the Abu Dhabi Satellite Channel, recalls shooting footage for a documentary about the rebuilding of bridges and factories after the destruction wrought by the United States in the 1991 war. He had the privilege of producing an interview with Saddam as part of the project. "He was really casual with us," my friend said. "He talked to us between shoots like just another young guy. But when he asked us nonchalantly with a smile on his face whether we had all the equipment we needed for our TV work, we knew the correct answer was, Yes, Mr. President, even though the truth was we were working with crap."[22]

In the absence of movies to show, many of the small privately owned cinemas became venues for small-time live burlesque shows. Hundreds of young actors from the Academy of Fine Arts and a few of their mentors developed short slapstick comedies akin to early-twentieth-century American vaudeville. Skits poked fun at rural Iraqis and their distinctive dialects, particularly those who hailed from villages in the south and had made the big move to Baghdad. Social issues like the disintegration of the family under the economic pressure of sanctions, corruption among bureaucrats, and the rise of organized crime gangs were among the most common themes. This young industry, known commonly in Iraq as "commercial theater" (*al-Masrah al-Tijari*), was implicitly critical of aspects of the Iraqi state. Some of the darker sketches depicted agents of Saddam's intelligence and security services and the fear they inspired.[23]

Less widespread and more sophisticated than neighborhood burlesque was the older industry of "serious theater" (*al-Masrah al-Jad*), staged mainly at the al-Rashid Theater in Baghdad near the headquarters of Iraqi public television. A two-hour soliloquy called *al-'Alawi* (*The Minibus Station*) depicts a mother during the Iran–Iraq war who has a stand at a bus stop selling *bagilla*, boiled salted fava beans. As soldiers arrive back from the war front, she asks after her son, who has been gone for months without a trace. The play depicts her gradual deterioration to a state of delusion, defying the state's propagandistic images of women stoic and unflinching in patriotic fortitude. A sanctions-era play about beggars exposes the organization of disabled children and war veterans into beggars' syndicates, with bosses who drop them off downtown at 5 A.M. to beg all day and then pick them up 20 hours later to collect a percentage of their earnings.

Not for the first time in Iraq's history, storytellers under Saddam drew inspiration from the suffering of a battered society and extracted tragedy and humor that resonated with local audiences. A millennium earlier, tenth-century scholar al-Mas'udi recalled scenes of storytellers and bindle stiffs begging together at the doors of mosques, and the contemporaneous compiler of prophetic traditions in Baghdad Ibn Hanbal wrote, "The most mendacious of men are the storytellers and the beggars."[24] Even as the memory of the Ba'th begins to fade, the Iraqi muse endures.

Meanwhile, elsewhere in the Middle East, the muse appears to have taken a vacation. It is Ramadan 2002 and I am on a business trip in Cairo, staying at the Flamenco Hotel on the Nile, lying in bed. I turn on the TV and see bearded Jewish rabbis sitting in a living room speaking Arabic. But the topic of conversation is strange. They are lamenting that a copy of *The Protocols of the Elders of Zion*, a secret book detailing a Jewish plot to enslave the world, has fallen into the hands of gentiles. The program is episode 21 or so of the 41-part *Horseman without a Horse*, a locally produced epic based on the premise that the *Protocols* are real, not an anti-Jewish forgery by the Russian secret police.

Is this racist assault on the Other the most edifying message Egyptian actor Muhammad Subhi can come up with, in a region brimming with compelling stories and talent? I am reminded of something Tunisian filmmaker Nouri Bouzid said about the challenge ahead for Arab cinema: "We must face our memory, judge it, unveil it. Change comes from knowledge. We don't dare see ourselves in the mirror, we look for someone else, we're not proud of what we are. . . . Our history is bound by memory and prohibition. We must unveil what we keep hidden in order perhaps to know who we are."[25]

No less predictable than the plot of *Horseman* is the chain of events I imagine will now transpire in real life. The show will make headlines in the United States, where relatively few have ever seen an Egyptian movie. Most Americans do not know that the star lineup in Cairo in the 1940s was as ethnically diverse as any other film industry, and even included a Jewish songstress. Their first lesson on Arabic entertainment will be that the Egyptian government subsidizes playwrights fixated on the belief that Jews wish to use the blood of Arab children for their Passover Matzoh. And the just national cause of the Palestinians will further suffer from the Jew-baiting of some of its supporters.

As I continue watching *Horseman*, I notice something else: the show is mediocre. Despite its generous funding, the actors are hams, the plot is confusing, the writing is bad, and the lighting is off. I later learn that most Egyptians who saw it felt the same way; after an initial spike in ratings due to international coverage of the controversy, a lot of viewers tuned out. Though *Protocols* enthusiasts have produced great cinema in the past, beginning with Nazi Germany's *Triumph of the Will*, Muhammad Subhi is no Leni Riefenstahl. He's merely the Ed Wood of anti-Semitism.

Another movie that came out a few months earlier in neighboring Israel, *A Trumpet in the Wadi*, portrays an Arab woman in Haifa and a reluctant Jewish immigrant from Russia who fall in love and decide to defy the conflict around them and get married.

The film is based on a story by Sami Mikhael, an Iraqi novelist and unrepentant Communist transferred to Israel with about 125,000 other Iraqi Jews in the early 1950s. The actress who starred in the film came to the United States this Ramadan to speak through a translator in Arabic-accented Hebrew to attendants at a film festival. "Coexistence is something you can learn," she said, "like learning to walk. Artists have a responsibility to lead the way, to act things out ahead of their societies."[26] But you will not find *Trumpet* playing in a movie house in Egypt or any other Arab country. One of the few people in Cairo who has heard of it is playwright Ali Salim, an embattled humanist who sits and writes nearly every day in the café at the Flamenco Hotel. When we get together, I sometimes wonder what has to happen before the grant for a 41-part epic goes to him. I stare across the Nile and imagine the aroma of the Euphrates.

The circumstances under which massive bursts of creativity arise are often bizarre and sometimes born out of suffering. Many film critics have dubbed the past few years a golden age of Iranian cinema, in the same league as German expressionism, French New Wave, and Italian Neo-Realism.[27] It is possible that the Mullahs' war on creative expression served to multiply the number of stories to be told and intensify Iranian filmmakers' lust to tell them. If so, then the emotional minefield of Arab Middle Eastern societies promises to contribute more than just a few more bombs to the world's stage in the years ahead. According to Sabaab al-Musawi, a cinema expert at Baghdad's Academy of Fine Arts, "we have many ideas about films we could make about the past 10 years to translate what has happened to a cinema audience. We are not short of ideas, we just need the opportunity."[28]

The radio program "A World Transforming" (*Alam Muta-hawwil*), broadcast to Iraqis from Prague on America's Radio Liberty Arabic edition for the past few years has given Iraq's isolated societies a chance to hear about ongoing changes in global technology and culture. Since the animated Akkadian mythological feature *The Princess and the River* premiered in Baghdad in 1982, a thriving industry of feature-length Japanese animation has come to enthrall audiences east and west, sometimes fusing ancient and medieval Japanese mythology with the technology of today. *Metropolis*, a recent anime adaptation of a 1949 Japanese comic strip Fritz Lang inspired, even borrows from Babylonian myths, referencing Marduk, the ziggurats, and Babel. Sumerian motifs mix seamlessly with science fiction in cutting-edge radio dramas from the ZBS audio theater company and novels by Neal Stephenson. Is it unreasonable to hope for new Iraqi contributions to these hybrid artistic worlds?

Or perhaps conjuring ancient dreams will hold less immediate appeal to Iraqi artists eager at last to vent unambiguously about the modern hell of sanctions and surveillance. The truth behind the stories they tell will challenge Western and Middle Eastern audiences alike, at once laying bare the dark underbelly of oil realpolitik and the painful excesses of Arab nationalism. Sami Mikhael's lead actress told moviegoers that artists can act out scenes of progress before their societies would deign to live them. The challenge of overcoming animosity between Jews and Arabs will mainly play out in Israel and Palestine, but hcr message resonates in the broadest sense everywhere. Iraqi cinema can take the lead in fostering in its society what Germans call an *Ausarbeitung*, a working out of the self, by breaking taboos of silence on women's issues, ethnic tensions, the tragedies of Ba'thi Iraq, and the odyssey of a country in flux.

Struggling to break taboos through film is the best course world cinema anywhere can possibly chart. The venture is both salubrious for domestic audiences and pragmatic for the business of marketing to foreign audiences. A lesson to draw from modern Iranian cinema is that by delving deep into the very personal and the very local, one can extract something universal. And it happens that sound advice for Iraqi entertainment entrepreneurs is also a cheap and effective alternative to censorship. For those who would seek to strong-arm the youngest cultural ministry in the Arab world into engineering consent for new policies through art, I offer this one-liner: the best defense against the mediocrity of *Horseman Without a Horse* is an engaged international audience that rewards high-quality entertainment at the box office.

Speaking of which, the lucrative movie consumer markets of Saudi Arabia and the Gulf are in for a special treat. For centuries, Iraqi storytelling traditions have mixed with those of India and Iran as the great forces of urban civilization that influenced the nomadic cultures of Arabia's wide open spaces. Although each of these three old urban centers has a modern national identity, only foreign-language movies from India and Iran have lately made their way to Gulf Arab audiences, alongside more distant American blockbusters and Egyptian films. Local moviegoers' affinity for the sensibilities conveyed in Iraqi Arabic is far greater. In Kuwait, Bahrain, and the central Saudi region of Hijaz, people still greet one another as they do in Baghdad by saying, "Shlonak." Idiomatically the expression means, "How are you?" but literally it means, "What is your color?"—a vestige of medieval Iraqi doctors who learned from ancient Greeks that a person's health depended on the balance of different colored humors in the body. Traditional Gulf veneration for urban Iraq bears some resemblance to "hillbilly" awe of America's big cities and Persian-speaking Afghani mountain dwellers' enthusiasm for the high culture of Iran. When the visions of Iraqi filmmakers at last start flickering again, they will find ready audiences in the movie houses of those Gulf states that sanction profane entertainment and around the personal DVD players of those that do not. If you care about moving the Saudi heart, worry about stimulating the Iraqi mind.

Which brings back into focus the question of Arabic cinema's viability. Cairo's embattled liberal playwright Ali Salim will finally win his grant for a 41-part epic not the day after the hell of sanctions freezes over, but the moment Iraq reemerges as a regional capital of entertainment. The slow beginnings of Iraqi cinema's rebirth call for a leap of faith and a harnessing of human and financial capital. The asylum so far granted to dissident artists from one Arab country by another has not netted the sort of consolidation of international talent in one city that happened in Hollywood before the Second World War, because most Middle Eastern states expel more artists than they ever take in. Nor has any Arab country since the advent of film managed to project the mix of cultural fascination and leniency toward artistic expression that attracted "lost generations" of writers to Paris in the 1920s and Prague in the 1990s. Cairo has the former but lacks the latter; Dubai, which recently founded a "Media City," has the latter but lacks the former. For the new Iraq, personal security and creative freedom are cheap door prizes to dispense in exchange for the return of diaspora Iraqis and others with a knowledge and contact base to share from film capitals near and far. For those who have stuck it out inside Iraq, it is not a question of teaching them how to make movies; it is a question of reequipping them with the tools, resources, and networks their visions require. And it is only a question of time.

As you might have gathered by now, I am not so worried about how to stem American cultural imperialism in Iraq. Instead, I am trying to figure out how to foment Iraqi cultural imperialism in the Middle East and beyond. Anybody want some popcorn?

Eleven

Teachers and Judges of Truth

In this century of information technology, knowledge is growing faster than ever before, but wisdom is unchanging. Wisdom is something people in modern times regard as the outcome of life experience, and life still moves along as slowly and as quickly as it ever did. One benefit of wisdom is its value in sorting through knowledge and ideas to discern what is right and judge what is true. As always, wisdom is in short supply. Iraqis who experienced Saddam's rule have as much life experience as anyone else, but their educational system in recent years has been substandard in terms of its conveyance of knowledge and propagandistic in its attempt to control the formation of ideas. As for the country's formal judges of truth, they have held court in a failing legal system. Given the formation of a more benign state in Iraq, the years ahead will show whether the wisdom its people have accumulated through life will translate into effective reforms in education and law. One place from which they can draw inspiration is the country's distant past, a time when teaching and judging were organically linked.

In the eleventh century, there was a remarkable man named Tanukhi, who was born in Basra but lived and worked in various parts of what is now Iraq and western Iran. He hailed from a family of transmitters of *Hadith*, the traditions of the prophet Muhammad's word and deed that together with the Qur'an form the basis for Islamic law. But Tanukhi was inclined early on to study the profane literature of the Arabic and Islamic city culture that was emerging around him, also a respected pursuit at the time. He learned from some of the most important scholars of his day and acquired a well-rounded medieval education, which used to be called *adab*, a term that meant the sum of stories, ideas, and knowledge necessary to make a person courteous and "urbane." This kind of education was meant to foster balance and a sense of fairness. Still a teenager, he won the sensitive job of inspecting weights and measures at one of the empire's mints. He moved on to bureaucratic work near Baghdad, and within a few years had earned the post of judge.[1] Medieval Baghdad was not a place that atomized knowledge and pigeonholed people into specialized fields; it was a place where a belief that you were wise could win you an appointment in the courts.

Tanukhi left more than a trail of rulings behind him. The stories he heard from witnesses and defendants fueled his fertile imagination, and the experience of reasoning his way through cases refined the color scheme of moral gradations he saw between right and wrong. Like all judges everywhere, he met people who had suffered and hoped for a little relief. He found himself meting out wisdom and advice as well as judicial pronouncements, and eventually saw fit to share his insights with a broader audience through writing. He chose as his vehicle an edifying style of entertainment that goes by many different names and never falls out of style. Back then it was called "Relief after Distress" (*al-Faraj Ba'd al-Shidda*), although in today's pop psychology terms, we might call it "Post-Traumatic Joy." In volume after volume of collected works, Tanukhi wove together memories and stories to demonstrate that bad times do not last forever and people can always reasonably hope for relief—a courtier saved from execution by his boss in a moment of compassion, a husband reunited with his estranged wife by a stroke of luck. The hope that Iraqis today will encounter relief after many years of distress makes Tanukhi's idiom all the more prescient.

How would Tanukhi have judged the educational and legal systems of Iraq under Saddam? Of his own day, he registered the following complaint: "The desire for learning is wanting, and there is a lack of noble aspirations. The populace are distracted from such things by care for their living, while the magnates are satisfied with the gratification of brutal passions."[2] The poverty of Iraq in 2003 and the moral depravity of its departed rulers make these comments relevant again. As for knowledge taught in Iraqi schools, Tanukhi might have found fault with much of it, beginning with the Iraqi pledge of allegiance. For several generations now, children in the country's schools have worn mandatory blue-gray uniforms and gathered once a week around a flagpole. They have watched one of their classmates raise the Iraqi flag while a teacher clutching a megaphone led the following call and response:

"Our President?"

"Saddam Hussein!"

"Our slogan?"

"One Arab nation with an eternal message!"

"Our goals?"

"Unity! Freedom! Socialism!"

After which one lucky youngster with a semiautomatic rifle got to fire a round of blanks over the heads of his classmates.

Imagine the legacy of a morning salute like this on Iraqi children. The tender years of childhood never leave us; they form the prism through which we view the world. Whereas between family and teachers, Tanukhi's upbringing exposed him both to the tenets of Muslim tradition and to the complexities of urban society, enabling him to parlay the two brilliantly into a legal and literary career, Iraqi families centuries later continue to emphasize education, but recent generations of young people in the country have a set of classroom memories that parents and outside observers find distressing. They have come of age in a society conditioned to locate truth and pursue justice in the persona of one elusive man—a man who has neither taken kindly to critical thinking nor valued the concept of litigation. A recent issue of the Ba'th state's legal gazette contains a quote from Saddam on the cover page: "Justice is above the law."[3] In light of the legacy of Saddam's sensibilities, the educational and legal systems Iraqis attempt to build over the next few years require an overhaul for the children of today and relief for the children of yesterday.

All this is not to say that the Ba'th party has completely flunked its challenge to educate Iraqis, or that blame rests solely with Saddam's government for the deterioration of the school system under sanctions. On the contrary, the state maintained and enhanced Iraq's reputation as a standard-bearer of teaching in the region for years. Arab countries from Mauritania to Djibouti used Iraqi textbooks to teach Arabic grammar and other subjects into the 1980s. The Ba'th party's "Comprehensive National Campaign for the Compulsory Eradication of Illiteracy" brought reading and writing to the poor and disenfranchised of both genders in cities and rural areas alike. The campaign spanned years and harnessed the after-hours energies of those who could read to serve as tutors to those who could not, on penalty of imprisonment. It won praise from UNESCO and countries as far west as France. The government reports that it managed to raise the national literacy rate from 42 percent in 1975 to 87 percent in 1985.

You might say that Saddam aspired to be "the education president." His party called for revolutions in teaching as a cornerstone of its national agenda when it came to power in 1968. By the time the Ba'th had taken control of every school in the country five years later, its pedagogy committee had crafted a strategy to harmonize the educational system with its ideological principles. The strategy included calls to coordinate skills training and economic planning—"a special stress on science and technology in education . . . to provide personnel required in the various fields of development," according to a press release from the Ba'th congress of 1974.[4] It also included a mission for humanities departments from grade school on up: to mold the mind-set of Iraqi boys and girls in the image of their leader.

An Iraqi father of two in Cleveland, who left Iraq in 1998, remembers what class used to be like when he was a sixth grader in a private elementary school in Baghdad in 1972. "We used to take trips to the library twice a week and go to the theater as a class once a week," he said. "We read the poems of

Mutanabbi in Arabic and Shakespeare in English and turned in writing assignments comparing the worlds of literature to the world around us."[5] He made me wonder whether my friends or I in New England would have even cut it in his sixth grade class, as we did not begin reading Shakespeare until high school. "Parents played an active role in our education too," he went on. "They used to read to me ever since I can remember, and when I started elementary school they came to all the parent-teacher conferences." Science classes were tough and not his favorite subject, he said, but the full-color textbooks of plant and animal taxonomy were a pleasure to look at.[6]

School life changed over the years that followed. As the Ba'th consolidated its hold on teachers, students had to absorb for homework a new corpus of wisdom: Saddam's evening radio and television appearances. For example, when in the early 1990s the president said in a speech on foreign policy, "I swear I am going to burn down half of Israel," elementary school children were required to explain their love for Saddam's words and report on their parents' reaction to them for 15 minutes the following morning; as has already been established, many Iraqi teachers filed reports for the state's intelligence apparatus. Another jewel of the curriculum was "National Culture" (*Thaqafah Qawmiyyah*), a mandatory civics class in secondary schools. It presented the zenith of Iraqi history as the rise of the Ba'th and heroism of its leader. Teachers supportive of the party trained their ears on children's offhand remarks about politics at home. Guidelines from Saddam to teachers in a book on education from 1977: "Teach the student to object to his parents if he hears them discussing state secrets. . . . You must place in every corner a son of the revolution, with a trustworthy eye and a firm mind."[7] Rather than partner with parents on the upbringing of the new generation, the party sought to stem the bond between parents and children and plant paranoia in classroom and household alike. As the classroom became a kind of inculcation headquarters, the overall quality of instruction declined. The Cleveland Iraqi I mentioned notes that his son's sixth grade class in Baghdad in the early 1990s had not reached the level of English proficiency necessary to understand a declaration of war by President Bush, let alone a sonnet by Shakespeare.

The country's 10 co-educational public universities and 20 technical institutes meanwhile hobbled along. The University of Baghdad enjoyed a reputation as the Harvard of the Arab world from its beginnings in 1956 and into the 1980s, with schools of medicine, engineering, agriculture, and law yielding graduates who became leaders in their fields across the region. For decades and to this day, higher education in Iraq's state universities is free for all Arabs who win admission, regardless of the Arab country they hail from. As noted in an earlier chapter, Saddam expanded this generous program to include stipends and free housing for students. As cash grew tighter through successive wars, however, the doling out of largesse acquired a logic that was not egalitarian. Merit came to be measured by loyalty to the state and membership and activism on behalf of the party. Many Iraqis sympathized with Saddam's new law in the early 1980s to reward the children of military servicemen with 10 extra points on their college admissions exam. But the "Friends of Saddam" program created 10 years later to bestow gifts and better grades on the most loyal party members aggrieved those students who happened to prefer hitting the books to engaging in political activism. Several fine private colleges have had permission to operate in the country since 1987 and provide degree programs to those who did not win admission to a public university, but the tuition lies beyond the means of most Iraqis.

The creeping decline of education under the Ba'th took a plunge at every level in the era of international sanctions. Official statistics tell the story the Iraqi government wants to tell: from 11 percent literacy in the 1940s to 87 percent in 1985, the figure had slumped again to 45 percent by 1995 and continues to fall in 2003. Salaries for teachers and professors fell dramatically relative to the skyrocketing cost of living, making it impossible to earn an honest living through teaching alone. This resulted in rapid brain drain. Of those teachers who remained in the country, many came to accept increasingly heavy heaps of paper cash from students in exchange for better grades, lending new meaning to the term "grade inflation." Respected teachers and professors could be seen driving taxis and selling cigarettes on the streets to supplement their income. Family demand for child labor meanwhile reduced free time for homework or extracurricular activities, and resources for the acquisition of basic learning materials, from textbooks to pencils and pens, grew ever scarcer.

Why bother struggling for an education in an economy of unemployment approaching 90 percent? In a departure from the country's long-standing tradition of urban learning, the disincentive to work for a degree has fueled cynical attitudes toward education among many Iraqis. Since the deadly years of the Iran–Iraq war, the most compelling reason to win admission to college has become the chance to avoid military conscription. And the attribute of erudition lost its appeal among some families. "Priorities have changed," says a veteran of Iraq's oil ministry who now resides in Jordan. "A lot of Iraqis who used to value a young man's education and demeanor now are more concerned to see their daughter married off to someone wealthy."[8]

The man's daughter, as of late 2002 still at work on a doctorate in molecular chemistry at the University of Baghdad, has family and friends among Iraq's 4 million-strong diaspora community to thank for the acquisition of scientific textbooks and other sources integral to her research. Iraqis who travel back and forth are accustomed to bringing home books for the young generation. Sanctions may have fueled a massive outflow of teachers and other professionals over the past decade, but enough ambitious students remain in the country to keep thousands of comers and goers engaged and concerned about their future.

Flipping Precedents

Most prayers for relief from the distress wrought by Saddam and sanctions have gone unanswered for years running in modern Iraq. But now and then, a person has encountered relief after distress and retold the story of his good fortune to countless others. The following story, which I heard from a Baghdadi friend in Jordan who used to do translation work for the Iraqi government, sounds like a contemporary analogue to the medieval stories told by the judge Tanukhi. It is also a telling example of the workings of the Iraqi legal system in 2002:

Students at the University of Baghdad who can afford it sometimes have a burger for lunch at a spot not far from campus. The man who flips the burgers is a friend of my friend. In addition to the restaurant, he also owns some land, but for several years was unable to reap any financial reward because he and his brother were fighting over the title deed in court. One day in the 1990s, some new customers pulled up in front of the burger joint in a motorcade. Seated in the backseat and flanked by bodyguards was Saddam Hussein. He wanted lunch. The owner of the restaurant flipped burger after burger for his guests. Saddam had a bodyguard taste one first, then tried it himself. He was very pleased.

"Now pay the man," Saddam said. A bodyguard asked the owner for the bill.

"I will not accept your money," said the burger man.

"What do you mean?" Saddam replied. "Tell us how much we owe you and we'll pay."

"O, Mr. President," the burger man said, "how can I take money from you when I owe you for the very air I breathe around me?"

This response made Saddam smile. "I like this man," he said out loud. "What can I do for you, my friend?"

This gave the burger man pause. "The pleasure of serving you is the most I could ask," he said.

"Now, now," said Saddam, "really, what can I do for you? Just tell me."

"Well," said the burger man, "now that you mention it, I have a certain dispute over land with my brother, and it's tied up in the courts . . ."

Saddam did not care to hear the rest of the story. He simply gave his cohorts the order to tell the judge to resolve the case in favor of the burger man, and the motorcade sped away.[9]

Of course, relief for the burger man spelled distress for his brother, and the question of which brother was in the right is irrelevant to the story. The burgers were delicious, the owner of the restaurant was charming, and "justice," as we have already established from the Ba'thi legal gazette, "is above the law." Stories like these starring other rulers have found their way into eleventh-century essays by Tanukhi and memories of justice ancient and modern elsewhere. Yet there is something particularly tragic about the degeneration of justice in contemporary Iraq, the place where the rule of law was born and which managed to set legal standards in its region as recently as a few decades ago.

On the eve of Iraq's 1958 military coup, the country rested on concentric legal codes. Civil and criminal courts drew precedents from the Ottoman canon of the late nineteenth century and newer traditions introduced by the British Mandatory government. Aspects of personal law also fell under the domain of Sunni and Shi'i religious courts and spiritual councils for Christians and Jews.[10] Outside the bureaucratic structure of the state, tribal judges offered mediation services according to patriarchal legal traditions known as *urf*, for those who agreed to waive the right of appeal to higher government authority. Amid all these competing legal codes, intellectual life for Iraqi law professors and students sparkled with hybrid vigor. The University of Baghdad faculty of law attracted students from across the region and rivaled its trend-setting counterpart faculty in Cairo.[11] An Iraqi Civil Code was formed out of the country's Islamic, tribal, and imperial traditions in 1951. Its author was a noted Egyptian jurist who spent a lifetime melding layers of law into new national codes and had already done so for Egypt, Syria, and Libya.[12] He remarked that the Iraqi project was his masterpiece. Both the 1951 Civil Code and the three Iraqi legal cultures it appropriated retain some relevance 52 years later.

But now they are all bent out of shape. The Ba'th party took the authority to appoint judges and select cases away from the Civil Code's high court in 1977 and gave it to the 22-member Revolutionary Command Council and its appointed minister of justice. Saddam in turn formally appropriated that authority for himself in 1990 when he proclaimed a new constitution. His practice of ruling by decree and writing new laws to punish dissidents provoked resistance early on from some of the high court's judges. Those who objected inevitably found themselves out of work.[13]

A three-tier court system along the lines of the 1951 Civil Code remained in place for decades and into 2003. But so did a parallel network of "revolutionary courts" born of Ba'thism, which had the right of first dibs to any case and a more reflexive disposition to rule according to the whims of the political leadership.[14] The latter corps of gavel-happy judges punished the accused and rewarded the well-connected with the sort of swiftness Saddam liked best. As for their colleagues in the regular courts, they were no less susceptible to political pressure and equally subject to Saddam's whims.[15] But they had even less relevance to ordinary people. Neither did they face frequent demands from party higher-ups for doctored rulings, nor did they enjoy much respect from Iraqi citizens with arbitration needs who fell below the party's radar screen. Like teachers under sanctions, most judges earned more money accepting bribes than meting out impartial justice. "Lawyer" and "fixer" came to be used interchangeably, and modest people who needed genuine arbitration more often turned to esteemed clerics and leaders of tribes.[16] Fifty years after an intellectual architect of Arab nationalism built a modern Iraqi civil code, the legal systems that retained the most integrity were the ones that stemmed from the distant past.

The burger man will continue flipping burgers for hungry students, but their appetite for truth remains unsated. The three faculties of law in Baghdad, Mosul, and Mustansiriyya have suffered a loss of prestige because success in the profession they certify hinges on political acumen and connections alone.[17] Relief for the country's distressed legal system means more than one brother winning a ruler's favor to the detriment of the other. It means engaging every member of the Iraqi family in a commitment to inverting the current precedent and proclaiming that the law is above the justice of the ruler.

Wising Up

All this will take time.

Memory, the universe born of experience and learning that shapes the way we live, is the great engine of continuity through time that haunts us even as it helps us along. When my mother used to speak to her mother in their distinctive dialect of old

Iraqi Arabic, she occasionally punctuated her speech with expressions incomprehensible to Arabs outside Iraq, because they stemmed from older Aramaic and Hebrew words passed down quietly over thousands of years. One can delve into the archeology of memory and divine its many layers, but one cannot remake them once they are embedded in the soil. Only the tender surface remains a work in progress. The telling of stories and the laying down of ground rules are essential components in the program of parenting. But the most powerful tools parents can give their children are a sense of personal worth and the freedom to think critically and question authority. Those who form memories of struggling and criticizing as young people can always find their way. And those who remember blind obedience are lost. That is the enduring tragedy of Saddam's self-appointment as judge and father to the Iraqi nation. It is also an ongoing tragedy elsewhere in the region and beyond.

Generations of Iraqis who passed through the Ba'th educational system in their formative years have special needs in an economy of reconstruction. Those who have stopped learning require vocational instruction in skills useful to the coordinated redevelopment of the country's physical infrastructure—in effect, a partial application of the party's own centralized training strategy, which had called for the marriage of education and economic planning. Those who are still learning deserve to experience a swift readjustment of the culture of the classroom, from dogmatic frontal teaching to a learning partnership. And those who have yet to begin can do no better than grow up around mentors who consecrate the Iraqi family as the country's greatest enduring educational institution, rather than deploy children to spy on their parents. Firebrand teachers hardwired in the ways of the Ba'th should be pensioned off. Exiled Iraqi teachers now searching for relevance in countries other than their own should be given incentives to return. And an unlikely duo of potential helpers who grew up in an altogether different learning environment—Iraqi grandparents and foreign volunteer teacher-trainers—should find their way into a new coordinated learning project, whether in homes or in schools or both.

One of the benefits of the freedom to think critically is the innovation it inspires across disciplines. Nasser Isa al-Sarrami, a Saudi friend who writes on telecommunications and information technology for the daily newspaper *al-Riyadh*, has this in common with the eleventh-century Iraqi judge Tanukhi: he hails from a family of Muslim clerics and has broken with tradition to challenge mores through writing. We share a belief that traditional and avant-garde learning—in Arabic, *Ulum al-Naql* (transmitted knowledge) and *Ulum al-Aql* (reasoned knowledge)—are inextricably linked. The liberation of the humanities in Iraqi schools will complement the teaching of science and hasten the day when the country will reclaim its place as a locus of technological innovation. Needless to say, the lifting of sanctions and reintegration of Iraq into the world community will make the acquisition of technology and tools vital to the teaching of science feasible once more.

But memory makes this transition complicated. Competing identities and ideas dominate Iraq's cultural and intellectual landscape, and the sensibilities of the global village present conceptions and expectations of their own. When one man ceases to unite the country's pedagogy under one ideology, what unifying themes will take its place? Is it right to decentralize the formation of curricula and relax the bias toward building a national memory? Is it wrong to sanction the establishment of *madrasas*, religious schools, which at best strengthen the ethical foundations of spiritual life and at worst promote parochialism and militancy? Iraqis and others will fight over these questions. They will not be easily resolved, nor will the regional and international politics that fuel them cease to impose pressure. My personal bias in humanities teaching would be toward the promotion of role models to further a culture of humanism. The great twentieth-century Iraqi sociologist Ali al-Wardi merits a place in Iraqi textbooks. So does his intellectual ancestor, the eleventh-century geographer al-Biruni, arguably the first humanist intellectual in history. So do Martin Luther King Jr. and Mahatma Gandhi. Constructions of memory can justly face ongoing revision in the years to come, provided the inculcation of critical thinking becomes a fixture in the new Iraq. The teachers of truth should always be well-meaning adults, and the judges of truth should always be their fickle children.

Justice feeds on memory too. However harsh the threat of punishment for breaking the law, a society's strongest deterrent against chaos is an ingrained sense of personal morality. Yet bitter experiences and dire poverty in recent years have led many Iraqis to regard their government as corrupt and the system as worthy of being cheated. Iraq is not Japan in 1945, where citizens wearily maintained their loyalty to state. Nor is Iraq Germany on the eve of its surrender, where courts sullied by totalitarianism and racism nonetheless functioned above board. Like various transitioning countries of Latin America in the 1980s and Eastern Europe in the 1990s, 2003 Iraq has a gutted legal system and a gutted moral code. Restocking both is a multigenerational project. Over the next few years, the lay legal system will strive to establish its independence while clerics and patriarchs stand in for the rule of fear with flawed yet effective institutions of traditional justice.

The world has been through this before. An industry of international legal reform institutions that grew out of the World Bank, European Union, and American Bar Association, among others, have stepped into war-torn areas in the past and supported local projects with mixed results. Injecting the rule of law is still an art and not a science, because complications are distinctly local and vary according to time and place. But a few lessons may be gleaned from recent memory:

First, stick with the program. Though the twenty-first-century legacy of modern Iraqi law is encrusted with Ba'thi amendments and secret clauses, it stems from a twentieth-century civil code that is basically sound. When Kurds recently gained a measure of autonomy in northern Iraq through the American and British enforcement of no-fly zones, they enacted a formal return to the Iraqi legal system as it stood at the time of the 1958 constitution. The rest of the country would do well to follow suit, and also, reintroduce the "Personal Status Law" that was codified in 1963. These laws are already familiar to older Iraqi lawyers and judges who may be induced to return to the legal profession given the leeway to judge according to their conscience. They also inform the content of Iraqi legal textbooks still in circulation. In Romania after the fall of Ceaucescu, laws by reformers went through such frequent rewrites and redactions that lawyers lost track and businesses new to the country lacked the clarity of procedure they needed. In Albania over the past few years, scant indigenous legal talent was too heavily taxed by demands by the international donor community for new bankruptcy laws to focus on the more pressing local needs of fighting corruption and strengthening the judiciary.[18] For Iraq, memories of viable local law form the most practicable basis for further progress.

Second, import the universal tools of legal reform that have proven themselves elsewhere. The World Bank has carried out surveys of court use in Mexico and Argentina, yielding surprising results that contradicted preconceptions about the sluggishness of the judiciary, enabling the Bank to focus its reform efforts on more pressing problems.[19] The American Bar Association has succeeded in invigorating legal education through dynamic training and mock trial programs for law students in developing countries. Although preachier lectures on law by short-term visitors unfamiliar with Iraq's predicament may turn off certain audiences, intellectual engagement infused with humility will be winsome. The abolition of secret courts, enactment of separation of powers laws, and formation of an anticorruption wing for the judiciary are critical tasks for which newcomers not entrenched in the system are ideally suited. NGOs specializing in human rights law can support local initiatives to check the excesses of the emerging security apparatus. And multinational corporations which already boast a track record of government partnerships to fight piracy in the Arab world can engage the new government and its private sector to fund and foster respect for international copyright laws.

Third, be mindful of the flaws of institutional modeling. Rachel Belton, a Rhodes Scholar, has tracked legal reform projects by international organizations in various developing countries. "Non-profits and even large international organizations are sometimes insufficiently in tune with the opportunities and pitfalls imposed by local politics," she observes, "and tend to place equal weight on achieving small reforms, such as the passage of an anti-corruption law, and major reforms, such as the creation of a funded watchdog body to guard against corruption in the courts."[20] The European Union used some of its political capital in Romania in the 1990s to push through a worthy law decriminalizing homosexuality, but meanwhile lost multiple opportunities to push through legislation to make the judiciary more independent while a reform-minded justice minister was at the helm.[21]

The institutions of truth in Iraq will take time to gel. Neither are they as fluid as the transfer of power nor are they as solid as the redistribution of money. Iraqis will encounter truth when they win back the freedom to build their own memories. The encounter will bring relief to generations that have known mainly distress, in a story Tanukhi might have liked to tell.

There is a sad irony to Tanukhi's own life story. After years of writing stories to assure people that bad times do not last forever and they can always reasonably hope for relief, he fell out of favor with the court of Baghdad's ruler, who placed him under house arrest. He fled Baghdad after his release but eventually returned, only to live out his days in isolation and poverty.[22] Whether Iraq's future will more closely resemble Tanukhi's stories or the fate of the man himself remains unclear.

Epilogue

A Time to Relax

This was not a book about a new Middle East.

The past decade has not been the first to witness the crumbling of utopian visions. I propose that we relegate utopia to sweet dreams at night and proceed with the messy work of fomenting accord in Iraq and beyond. This book represents an effort to win over readers to the cause of Iraq's renewal. My remaining words are a sermon to the converted: now that you're willing to engage, relax. Sort of. As an ancient rabbi said, "You don't have to finish the job, but you are not free to quit either."[1]

In the great American Star Wars myth, Han Solo says to Luke Skywalker, "Kid, I been from one end of the galaxy to the other and I seen a lot of crazy things, but I never seen anything that'll make me believe there's some all powerful force controlling *my* destiny." Unlike Han, I believe in The Force; I am skeptical about the power of modernity and technology to restore balance to a tumultuous world. In a few short pages, you have been from one end of Iraqi history to another, but have you seen any technology more amazing than the cycle of generations and transfer of culture and ideas from mothers and fathers to sons and daughters?

Transition comes overnight, but transformation takes time. It demands that we make peace with the possibility that the changes we hope for may not materialize in our lifetimes.

The struggle for patience defines the difference in temperament between secularism and religious extremism. The former is a denial of the world to come; the latter is a distaste for the world we live in. The rush to hasten the fulfillment of prophecy, whether of the religious or the secular variety, stems in part from a sense of urgency which stems in turn from a lack of faith. True faith breeds patience, and patience offers perks in this world and the next. Words fitly spoken by the Shi'i Imam Ja'far al-Sadiq: "Patience is to faith what the head is to the body: the body perishes without the head, and so too when patience goes, faith also disappears."[2]

The slow pace of change need not be a reason for pessimism. For me, it is a reason for optimism and more optimism, provided a heavy dose of patience. It means that the hell Iraqis have endured in recent years may mean very little in the grand scheme of things. It also means that the political and economic ambitions of Iraqis, their neighbors, and the world at large may in the long run hold less value than the building blocks of human progress: listening to the voices of your grandparents, engaging the spirit in contemplation, and building a family to the best of your ability.

These are more or less the words of the preacher, the son of David. He also cautions against going overboard in any direction, even the pursuit of knowledge: "In much wisdom is much grief, and he who increases knowledge increases sorrow."[3] Words apparently heeded by Douglas Macarthur, who is said to have remarked upon returning from Japan, "The more we would have known, the less we would have gotten done."

Neither would I presume to tell you everything you need to know about Iraq nor would I advise you to regard its future as a slave of its past. The future is always a bunch of teenagers struggling with their parents and the world around them.

Notes

❧

Prologue

1. Frank Lloyd Wright, speech at San Raphael High School, San Raphael, CA, July 1957.

2. Naji Sabri, ed., *al-Kitab al-Sanawi li 'l-Jumhuriyya al-Iraqiyya 1988* (Baghdad: Dar al-Ma'mun, 1989).

3. Edward Said, "Israel, Iraq, and the United States," *al-Ahram Weekly*, Internet edition <http://www.ahram.org.eg/weekly/2002/607/focus.htm>. Accessed January 2003.

4. Frank Lloyd Wright, *Frank Lloyd Wright: Collected Writings Including an Autobiography 1930–1932*, ed. Bruce Brooks Pfeiffer (New York: Rizzoli, 1993).

5. Tabari, *Ta'rikh al-Rusul wa 'l-Muluk*, vol. 29, trans. J. D. McAuliffe (Albany, NY: SUNY Press, 1995), pp. 100, 398.

6. D. Sourdel, "Barid," in *The Encyclopedia of Islam*, vol. 1, electronic edition (Leiden: Brill, 2002), p. 1045a.

7. Interview with "Dhiya," Rafha, Saudi Arabia, June 2002.

Chapter 1: The Legacy of Ancient Iraq

1. Interview with "Abu Abdullah" in Tehran, July 1998. "Abu Abdullah" is the name by which the diplomat asked to be referred. It also denotes the fact that he has a son named Abdullah.

2. See Naji Sabri, ed., *al-Kitab al-Sanawi li 'l-Jumhuriyya al-Iraqiyya 1988* (Baghdad: Dar al-Ma'mun, 1989), p. 25. The great Iraqi sociologist Ali al-Wardi, an emeritus professor at the University of Baghdad, has written a voluminous work that constructs the character of Iraqi society through lucid, living memory. It deserves a full translation. See Ali al-Wardi, *Lamahat Ijtima'iyya fi Ta'rikh al-'Iraq al-Hadith* (London: Dar Kufan, 1992).

3. H.W.F. Saggs, *The Greatness that was Babylon* (London: Sedgwick & Jackson, 1988), pp. 11–19, provides a concise overview

and analysis of theories regarding the origins of the Sumerians and their language.

4. Ibid., pp. 10–11.

5. Samuel N. Kramer, *History Begins at Sumer* (Philadelphia: University of Pennsylvania Press, 1981).

6. Saggs, *The Greatness that was Babylon*, p. 19. During this period, it is estimated that Erech grew to a population of around 50,000.

7. Kramer, *History Begins at Sumer*, pp. 32–34.

8. Saggs, *The Greatness that was Babylon*, pp. 47–48. Although according to Kramer's translation, Sargon was a "cupbearer" for Ur-Zababa, king of Kish (see Samuel N. Kramer, *The Sumerians* [Chicago: University of Chicago Press, 1963], p. 60), Saggs argues convincingly that Sargon was probably involved in irrigation.

9. Ibid., p. 46.

10. Ibid., p. 50.

11. For examples, see Revelations 17:2; 18:3; 19:2.

12. Saggs, *The Greatness that was Babylon*, pp. 74–75.

13. Ibid., p. 75.

14. Ibid., p. 76.

15. Interview with Professor James Russell, Department of Near Eastern Languages and Civilizations, Harvard University, Cambridge, MA, August 2002.

16. H.W.F. Saggs, *The Might that was Assyria* (London: Sedgwick & Jackson, 1984), pp. 233–239.

17. R. S. Stafford, *The Tragedy of the Assyrians* (London: Allen & Unwin, 1935), p. 201.

18. The site www.Iraqi-mission.org was accessed by my researchers in January 2003. It is conceivable that the site may be revised sometime this year.

19. S. K. Eddy, *The King is Dead* (Lincoln: University of Nebraska Press, 1961), p. 24.

20. Ibid., pp. 109–110.

21. Georges Roux, *Ancient Iraq* (New York: Penguin, 1980), pp. 383–384.

22. Eddy, *The King is Dead*, p. 136.

23. For a broader appreciation of the aphorisms, personalities, theology, and themes of Talmudic and early rabbinic literature, I recommend William G. Braude's lucid translation of *Sefer Ha-Aggadah*. See H. N. Bialik and Y. H. Ravnitsky, eds., *The Book of Legends: Sefer Ha-Aggadah* (New York: Schocken, 1992).

Chapter 2: The Struggle for Islamic Iraq

1. J. Sourdel Thomine, "Irak," in *Encyclopedia of Islam*, vol. 3, electronic edition (Leiden: Brill, 2002), p. 1250a.
2. See Abu 'l-Faraj al-Isbahani, *Kitab Maqatil al-Talibiyyin* (Cairo: Dar Ihya al-Kutub al-Arabiyyah, 1949), pp. 484–489.
3. The cemetery of Najaf stretches for miles. Millions of Muslims over the centuries have been brought here for burial from all parts of the Muslim world. The population of Najaf is around 500,000.
4. Interview with Ahmed H. al-Rahim, lecturer, Department of Near Eastern Languages and Civilizations, Harvard University, February 2003.
5. Gavin Young, *Iraq: Land of Two Rivers* (London: Collins, 1980), p. 129. The battle of Qadisiyya has played an important role in the political rhetoric of contemporary Iraq. Saddam frequently evoked memories of the battle during the Iran–Iraq war, which came to be known in the state media as "Saddam's Qadisiyya" (*Qadisiyyat Saddam*). Furthermore, the daily newspaper in recent years most closely associated with the Iraqi army is called *al-Qadisiyya*.
6. Some traditional accounts of Ali's murder are recorded in *Kitab Maqatil al-Talibiyyin*, pp. 64–65.
7. Ira Lapidus, *A History of Islamic Societies* (Cambridge: Cambridge University Press, 1995), p. 160.
8. Zainab al-Suwaij, "Iraqi People Yearn to Taste Freedom Again," *USA Today*, January 13, 2003.
9. Young, *Iraq: Land of Two Rivers*, pp. 118–119.
10. Interview with Zainab al-Suwaij, executive director of the American Islamic Congress, Cambridge, MA, February 2003.
11. Interview with Omar Dewachi, graduate student of medical anthropology, Harvard University, who left Iraq in 1998, Cambridge, MA, November 2002.
12. For more information regarding the origins and development of the movement, see Moshe Sharon, *The Social and Military Aspects of the 'Abbasid Revolution* (Jerusalem: Max Schloessinger Memorial Fund, 1990).
13. Moshe Sharon, *Black Banners from the East* (Jerusalem: Magnes, 1983), pp. 191–192.
14. Ibid., p. 201.
15. André Clot, *Harun al-Rashid and the World of the Thousand and One Nights* (London: Saqi, 1989), p. 19. This is one of many

legends associated with the decision of Mansur to build Baghdad in its location. For more information, see Jacob Lassner, *The Shaping of 'Abbasid Rule* (Princeton: Princeton University Press, 1980), pp. 163–175.

16. Tabari, *Ta'rikh al-Rusul wa 'l-Muluk*, English translation, vol. 28 (Albany, NY: SUNY Press, 1995), pp. 112–114.

17. Clot, *Harun al-Rashid and the World of the Thousand and One Nights*, p. 104.

18. Gaston Wiet, *Baghdad: Metropolis of the Abbasid Caliphate* (Norman: University of Oklahoma Press, 1971), p. 18.

19. Ibid., p. 22.

20. The scholar's name was Amr b. Bakr al-Basri al-Jahiz. He was born in Basra in 776 C.E. and moved to Baghdad, where he worked at the court of the Caliph al-Ma'mun. His work included zoology, Arabic grammar, poetry, rhetoric, and lexicography.

21. See Bayard Dodge, ed. and trans., *The Fihrist of al-Nadim: A Tenth Century Survey of Muslim Culture* (New York: Columbia University Press, 1970).

22. For more information, see Dimitri Gutas, *Greek Thought, Arabic Culture: The Graeco-Arabic Translation Movement in Baghdad and Early 'Abbasid Society (2nd–4th/8th–10th Centuries)* (New York: Routledge, 1998).

23. For more information regarding the use of the badge as well as the theory and practice of *dhimmi* laws, see Bernard Lewis, *The Jews of Islam* (Princeton: Princeton University Press, 1984), pp. 24–32.

24. Interview with Ahmed H. al-Rahim, Cambridge, MA, February 2003.

25. Professor Hossein Modarressi, Department of Near Eastern Languages and Civilizations, Princeton University, seminar course, Autumn 1997.

Chapter 3: The Soundtrack to Modern Iraq

1. Shamma's teacher was the Turkish Oud player Jamil Bek Atamburi. He also studied under the Arabian cellist Muhiyy al-Din Haydar al-Sharif.

2. Muhammad Fazil Awad built the Oud. He was trained by Mullah Ali, a renowned Iranian artisan and musician.

3. The Abbasid court musician was Abu Is'haq al-Mawsili.

4. Memories of Babylon have made their way into other modern political ideologies outside Iraq as well. Psalm 137, inspired by the Babylonian exile, was the theme for Verdi's early opera

Nabucco (1842)—a piece composed and performed against the backdrop of European nationalist revolutions. One of the opera's songs, "Va, pensiero . . .", "And the slaves . . .", became the anthem of the Zionist movement prior to "Hatikvah."

5. Elie Kedourie, *The Chatham House Version and Other Middle Eastern Studies* (Hannover: University Press of New England, 1970), p. 437.

6. Ibid., p. 300. The historical factors that led to the prominence of indigenous Jews in the birth and development of modern Iraq are richly explored in a volume of collected essays, B. Braude and B. Lewis, eds., *Christians and Jews in the Ottoman Empire: The Functioning of a Plural Society* (New York: Holmes & Meier, 1982). In particular, I would highlight the contribution of Professor Charles Issawi.

7. Interview with Yair Dalal, Jerusalem, Israel, April 2001. See liner notes to Dalal's album *Samar*, Magda Music, 1998.

8. One of the architects of the intellectual construction of Iraq was Getrude Bell, whose life in letters has at last been translated into Arabic by the seminal Iraqi scholar Namir al-Muzaffar.

9. Interview with Yair Dalal, April 2001.

10. Khaldun S. Husri, "The Assyrian Affair," *International Journal of Middle East Studies* 5 (1974): 352.

11. Nissim Rejwan, *The Jews of Iraq: 3000 Years of History and Culture* (London: Weidenfeld and Nicolson, 1985), p. 222. For more information, see Kedourie, *The Chatham House Version and Other Middle Eastern Studies*, pp. 307–310, and Rejwan, *The Jews of Iraq*, pp. 217–224.

12. Ibid., p. 248. Mordechai Ben-Porat, *To Baghdad and Back* (New York: Gefen, 1998), p. 283.

13. Interview with Yair Dalal, April 2001. See the liner notes from the albums *Samar* and *Salim al-Nur*, Zuta Music, 2000. This information was also related to me in an earlier interview with Yusef Ya'qub Shem Tob at his home in Israel, July 1998.

14. Phebe Marr, *The Modern History of Iraq* (Boulder: Westview, 1985), p. 173.

15. Ibid., p. 229.

16. Interview with a Baghdadi intellectual, Amman, Jordan, September 2002.

17. Interview with Zainab al-Suwaij, executive director of the American Islamic Congress, Cambridge, MA, February 2003.

18. Interview with Zainab al-Suwaij, February 2003.

19. Kanan Makiya, *Cruelty and Silence* (New York: W.W. Norton, 1993), pp. 152, 168.

20. Charles Tripp, *A History of Iraq* (Cambridge: Cambridge University Press, 2002), p. 279.

Chapter 4: The Party's Over

1. Kanan Makiya, *Republic of Fear: The Politics of Modern Iraq* (Los Angeles: University of California Press, 1998), pp. 189–197.

2. Ibid., pp. 229–257.

3. Ibid., pp. 76–77. Christine Helms, *Iraq: Eastern Flank of the Arab World* (Washington, DC: The Brookings Institution, 1984), pp. 97–98.

4. Helms, *Iraq: Eastern Flank of the Arab World*, pp. 86–87.

5. Interview with Tammara Daghestani, mother and resettler of Iraqi refugees, Amman, Jordan, September 2002.

6. Ibid.

7. Ibrahim al-Marashi, "Iraq's Security and Intelligence Network: A Guide and Analysis," *MERIA* 6, no. 3 (September 2002).

8. Sh. Longrigg, "Djubur," in *Encyclopedia of Islam*, vol. 2, electronic edition (Leiden: Brill, 2002), p. 570b.

9. Ibrahim al-Marashi, "Iraq's Security and Intelligence Network."

10. Interview with Iraqi businessman, Beirut, Lebanon, October 2002.

11. Interview with "Samir," a retired officer of Jordan's General Intelligence Directorate, September 2002.

12. Interview with consular officer, Iraqi embassy, Amman, Jordan, September 2002.

13. Interview with "Samir," retired Jordanian GID, September 2002.

14. Ibid.

15. Sadashi Fukuda, ed., *Politics, Economy, and Sanctions in the Persian Gulf States* (Chiba, Japan: Institute of Developing Economies, 2001), p. 28.

16. Interview with "Samir," retired Jordanian GID, September 2002.

17. Ibid.

18. Interview with Patrick Clawson, deputy director, Washington Institute for Near East Policy, August 2002.

19. Interview with Yusuf Bahlaq, Palestinian businessman in Jordan, September 2002.

20. Interview with Tammara Daghestani, Jordan, September 2002.

21. Interview with Zainab al-Suwaij, executive director of the American Islamic Congress, Cambridge, MA, February 2003.

22. Ibid.

23. All of these documents can be viewed on Harvard University's Iraq Documentation Project website, <http://www.fas.harvard.edu/~irdp/>. Accessed February 2003. Around 350,000 of the 2.4 million pages have already been annotated.

24. Telephone interview with Professor Roy Giles, St. Anthony's College, Oxford University, October 2002.

25. Ibid.

26. Richard Aldrich, *The Hidden Hand: Britain, America and Cold War Secret Intelligence* (London: John Murray, 2001), p. 180.

27. Interview with Zainab al-Suwaij, February 2003.

Chapter 5: State-Building by the Book

1. Interview with Abd al-Karim Kazimi, Qom, Iran, March 2001.

2. Ibid.

3. Ira Lapidus, *A History of Islamic Societies* (Cambridge: Cambridge University Press, 1995), pp. 3–10.

4. Interview with a Basran woman and her grandfather during their visit to Damascus, September 2002.

5. Lapidus, *A History of Islamic Societies*, pp. 123–125.

6. For more information, see Sami Shourush, "The Religious Composition of the Kurdish Society: Sufi Orders, Sects, and Religions," in *Ayatollahs, Sufis, and Ideologues: State, Religion, and Social Movements in Iraq*, ed. Faleh Abdul-Jabar (London: Saqi, 2002), pp. 114–139.

7. *Ayatollahs, Sufis, and Ideologues*, pp. 149–176.

8. Interview with Zainab al-Suwaij, executive director of the American Islamic Congress, Cambridge, MA, February 2003.

9. At a conference of the International Congress for Islamic Law held on January 12, 2003, in the UAE, the permissibility of suicide bombings was hotly debated. Egyptian Muslim Brotherhood cleric Yusuf al-Qaradawi supported the tactic and reportedly won over most participants, but one scholar, Hasan Safar, maintained that the weight of Muslim law negates suicide bombings. He added that suicide bombings targeting civilians in Israel have been both un-Islamic and politically inept, allowing people to delegitimize the Palestinian nationalist movement as terrorist in nature. I have had the opportunity to build a network of scholars who share the views of Hasan Safar, some of whom provided me with their own unpublished manuscripts of liberal Islamist scholarship. They deserve a courageous publisher.

10. Interview with a Basran woman and her grandfather during their visit to Damascus, September 2002.
11. *Ayatollahs, Sufis, and Ideologues*, pp. 155–156.
12. Ibid., pp. 211–219.
13. Interview with a Basran woman and her grandfather during their visit to Damascus, September 2002.
14. *Ayatollahs, Sufis, and Ideologues*, p. 114.
15. Ibid., pp. 140–145.
16. For a treatment of religion and politics in Iraqi Kurdish society, see Sami Shourosh's articles, "The Religious Composition of the Kurdish Society: Sufi Orders, Sects, and Religions" and "Islamist and Fundamentalist Movements Among the Kurds," in *Ayatollahs, Sufis, and Ideologues*, pp. 114–139, 177–182.
17. For a grounding in the history of Islamist movements in Palestine, see Ziad Abu Amr, *Islamic Fundamentalist Movements in the West Bank and Gaza: The Muslim Brotherhood and Islamic Jihad* (Bloomington: Indiana University Press, 1994).
18. Interview with a Basran woman and her grandfather during their visit to Damascus, September 2002.
19. *FBIS*, October 7, 2002.

Chapter 6: About Face

1. Neil MacFarquhar, "A Spiffy Army of Volunteers Parades in Praise of Hussein," *New York Times*, January 8, 2003.
2. Interview with Zainab al-Suwaij, executive director of the American Islamic Congress, Cambridge, MA, February 2003.
3. Stanley Hoffman, "Rousseau on War and Peace," *American Political Science Review* 57, no. 2 (June 1963): 317–333.
4. *al-Sharq al-Awsat*, March 26, 1997.
5. Interview with Zainab al-Suwaij, February 2003.
6. Ibid.
7. Kanan Makiya, *Republic of Fear: The Politics of Modern Iraq* (Los Angeles: University of California Press, 1998), pp. 21–29.
8. *FBIS*, May 10, 1996.
9. Khaled Salih, *State-Making, Nation-Building: Iraq 1941–1958* (Goteberg: Goteberg Studies in Political Science, 1996), p. 61.
10. Anthony Cordesman, *Iraq's Military Capabilities in 2002* (Washington, DC: CSIS, 2002), p. 3.
11. Ibid., p. 4.
12. Conference: "Demobilizing, Reforming, and Rebuilding the Iraqi Armed Forces & Dismantling and Transforming Iraq's Military Industries," American Enterprise Institute, November 15, 2002.

13. Shai Feldman and Yiftah Shapir, *The Middle East Military Balance* (Cambridge, MA: MIT Press, 2001), p. 153.
14. Cordesman, *Iraq's Military Capabilities in 2002*, p. 3.
15. Ibid.
16. Ibid., p. 6.
17. *al-Hayat* (London), August 4, 2002.
18. Feldman and Shapir, *The Middle East Military Balance*, pp. 314–316.
19. Barry Posen, *The Sources of Military Doctrine* (Ithaca: Cornell University Press, 1984), p. 13.
20. Feldman and Shapir, *The Middle East Military Balance*, p. 147.
21. Ibid., p. 161.
22. Ibid., p. 315.
23. Country Indicators for Foreign Policy Project, Carleton University, Canada.
24. Peter Yolles and P. H. Gleick, "Water, War, and Peace in the Middle East," *Environment* 36, no. 3 (1994): p. 6.
25. Kenneth Pollack, *Arabs at War* (Lincoln: University of Nebraska Press, 2001), pp. 167–180.
26. Conference: "Demobilizing, Reforming, and Rebuilding the Iraqi Armed Forces & Dismantling and Transforming Iraq's Military Industries," AEI, November 15, 2002.
27. Anja Manuel and P. W. Singer, "A New Model Afghan Army," *Foreign Affairs* (July–August 2002).
28. Hakan Yavuz and Michael Gunter, "The Kurdish Nation," *Current History* (2001).
29. *FBIS*, October 7, 2002.

Chapter 7: The Wages of Stability

1. Interview with Omar Dewachi, graduate student of medical anthropology, Harvard University, who left Iraq in 1998, Cambridge, MA, November 2002.
2. Iraq CountryData 2002, The Economist Intelligence Unit (EIU).
3. World Bank, World Development Indicators, 1997.
4. "Market Information and Analysis Section," Department of Foreign Affairs and Trade (DFAT), Australia.
5. Telephone interview with Baghdadi industrialist, December 2002.
6. Daniel 3:1–30.
7. *Middle East Economic Survey (MEES)* 45, no. 2 (January 14, 2002).
8. Mir Basri, *A'lam al-Yahud fi 'l-Iraq al-Hadith (Prominent Jews in Modern Iraq)* (Jerusalem: Rabitat al-Jami'iyyin al-Yahud al-Nazi'in min al-Iraq, 1983), pp. 33–34.

9. *Middle East Economic Survey (MEEs)*.

10. Between June 2002 and January 2003, my researchers and I maintained contact with a number of Iraqi industrialists who come and go between Amman and Baghdad. Much of this chapter is based on information graciously provided by them, on condition that they not be identified. Henceforth, information sourced to these individuals will be cited as *al-Jama'ah*.

11. *al-Jama'ah*.

12. Ibid.

13. Ibid.

14. "International Energy Annual 2000," Energy Information Administration (EIA), U.S. Government.

15. "Iraqi Memorandum to the United Nations Security Council," *Middle East Economic Survey (MEES)*, May 13, 1991.

16. *al-Jama'ah*.

17. Interview with Omar Dewachi, November 2002.

18. United Nations Compensation Commission records.

19. *Wall Street Journal*, June 19, 2002.

20. *al-Jama'ah*.

21. Interview with recent Iraqi émigré from Baghdad, Cambridge, September 2002.

22. *al-Jama'ah*.

23. Interview with recent Iraqi émigré from Baghdad, Cambridge, November 2002.

24. *al-Jama'ah*.

25. Ibid.

26. Ibid.

27. *Middle East Economic Digest (MEED)*, January 26, 2001.

28. *al-Jama'ah*..

29. Ibid.

30. Ibid.

31. Joseph Braude, *Capacity and Content: Internet Opportunities in the Arab Middle East* (Cambridge, MA: Pyramid Research), 2001. Since this report's publication, I have revised our Internet forecasts in light of changing economic realities in the region.

32. *al-Jama'ah*.

33. Ibid.

34. Fred Lawson (ch. 7) and Kiren Aziz Chaudry (ch. 8) in Iliya Harik and Dennis J. Sullivan, eds., *Privatization and Liberalization in the Middle East* (Bloomington & Indianapolis: Indiana University Press, 1992).

35. OPEC, *OPEC Bulletin* 23, no. 4 (April 1992): 40. Brought by Ahmed M. Jiyad, "The Social Balance Sheet of Privatization in the Arab Countries," presented before the Nordic Middle East Conference on Ethnic Encounter and Cultural Change, Joensuu, Finland, June 19–22, 1995.

36. OPEC, *OPEC Bulletin* 24, no. 9 (October 1993): 49. Brought by Ahmed M. Jiyad, "The Social Balance Sheet of Privatization in the Arab Countries," presented before the Nordic Middle East Conference on Ethnic Encounter and Cultural Change, Joensuu, Finland, June 19–22, 1995.

37. Barbara Nimri Aziz, "Nation for Sale: In Iraq, War and Embargo Have Cleared the Path for Privatization," April 1997. <http://www.Al-Bushra.org/temp/aziz.htm>. Accessed February 2003. Iraq Country Study and Country Guide, The Library of Congress Country Studies, United States.

38. *al-Jama'ah.*

39. Interview with recent Iraqi émigré from Baghdad, Cambridge, November 2002.

40. Interview with recent Iraqi émigré from Baghdad, Cambridge, September 2002.

41. Ibid.

42. Ibid.

43. Interview with Hasan, Amman, Jordan, September 2002.

44. Ibid. An infamous instance of Saddam's persecution of business-people in the era of sanctions is his 1992 execution of 42 merchants, allegedly for profiteering from hyperinflation at the expense of ordinary people. See Ofra Bengio, "Iraq," in *Middle East Contemporary Survey* ed. Ami Ayalon (Boulder: Westview, 1995). Bengio argues convincingly that the executions marked an attempt by Saddam to identify a scapegoat for hyperinflation. Friends in *al-Jama'ah* add that many of the 42 merchants had attempted to form trade syndicates of their own without paying protection money to Saddam's family.

45. Interview with recent Iraqi émigré from Baghdad, Cambridge, September 2002.

46. Ibid.

47. Ibid.

48. Ibid.

49. Ibid.

50. Interview with recent Iraqi émigré from Baghdad, Cambridge, November 2002.

51. Interview with recent Iraqi émigré from Baghdad, Cambridge, September 2002.

52. Interview with recent Iraqi émigré from Baghdad, Cambridge, November 2002.

53. Interview with recent Iraqi émigré from Baghdad, Cambridge, September 2002.

54. Ibid.

55. Ibid.

56. Interview with recent Iraqi émigré from Baghdad, Cambridge, November 2002.

Chapter 9: The Editorial We

1. Interview with "Dumu'," Iraqi prostitute, Amman, Jordan, September 2002.

2. For a comprehensive treatment of political discourse and popular press in Iraq under Saddam, see Ofra Bengio, *Saddam's Word: Political Discourse in Iraq* (New York: Oxford University Press, 1998).

3. Interview with "Yasir," Jordanian cab driver, Amman, Jordan, September 2002.

4. Ch. Pellat, "Al-Jahiz," in *Abbasid Belles-Lettres,* ed. Julia Ashtiany (New York: Cambridge University Press, 1990), p. 87.

5. Ami Ayalon, *The Press in the Arab Middle East* (New York: Oxford University Press, 1995), p. 13.

6. Ibid., p. 25.

7. Ibid.

8. Ibid., p. 43.

9. Ibid.

10. Ibid., p. 25.

11. Ibid., p. 65.

12. The Hadith is the well-known "Ijtanibu Kathiran min al-Zan . . ."

13. Ayalon, *The Press in the Arab Middle East*, p. 95.

14. Ibid., p. 92.

15. Ibid., p. 95.

16. Mark Twain, *Editorial Wild Oats* (New York: Harper & Brothers, 1905), pp. 23–24.

17. The phenomenon of agency as a principle of intellectual engineering is comprehensively explored in James E. Block's new book, *A Nation of Agents: The American Path to a Modern Self and Society* (Cambridge, MA: Harvard University Press, 2002).

18. Interview with a recent Kurdish émigré from Sulaymaniya, Washington, DC, October 2002.

19. Interview with Hani al-Jabsheh, CEO of Albawaba.com, Amman, Jordan, February 2002.

20. Twain, *Editorial Wild Oats*, p. 39.

Chapter 10: Babylon Take Two

1. Woody Allen, *Woody Allen: Standup Comic*, Rhino Records, 1999.

2. C. Pellat, "Kass," in *Encyclopedia of Islam*, vol. 4, electronic edition (Leiden: Brill, 2002), p. 733b.

3. This statement represents a simple summation of a complex and nuanced hypothesis put forth by Jacob Lassner in his book, *Islamic Revolution and Historical Memory: An Inquiry into the Art of 'Abbasid Apologetics* (New Haven: American Oriental Society, 1986). See pp. 10–13, "From Propaganda to History: A Hypothesis."

4. Rory McCarthy, "Baghdad's Dusty Silver Screens," *The Guardian*, November 15, 2002.

5. George Sadoul, *The Cinema in the Arab Countries* (Beirut: Inter-Arab Centre of Cinema & Television, 1966), pp. 69–125. Notes from BBC Channel 4 TV printed on the Internet: <http://www.al-bab.com/media/cinema/film1.html. Accessed January 2003.

6. Notes from BBC Channel 4 TV.

7. Mamad Haghigat, *A History of Iranian Cinema* (Paris: Georges Pompidou Center, 1999). Printed on the Internet: <http://www.unesco.org/courier/2000_10/uk/doss21.htm>

8. Sadoul, *The Cinema in the Arab Countries*, p. 117.

9. Interview with a Palestinian friend who is an accomplished musician, a movie aficionado, a restauranteur, and a psychiatrist in Amman, Jordan, September 2002. He asked not to be named.

10. Abdul-Hadi Jiad, "Breaking Taboos in Iraq" (obituary of Fakhriyah Abdul-Karim), *The Guardian*, September 18, 1998.

11. Nana Asfour, "The Politics of Arab Cinema: Middle Eastern Filmmakers Face Up to Their Reality," *Cineaste*, December 22, 2000, vol. 26, 1.

12. Interview with Professor Viola Shafik printed on the internet: <http://www.cafearabica.com/culture/cultureold/articles/culshafiq2x3.html>. Accessed February 2003.

13. Asfour, "The Politics of Arab Cinema."

14. Ibid.

15. Mamad Haghigat, *A History of Iranian Cinema* (Paris: Georges Pompidou Center, 1999). Printed on the Internet: <http://www.unesco.org/courier/2000_10/uk/doss21.htm>

16. M. Wadsworth, "Cultural Countermeasures: Make Way for Images of Beauty and Liberation, Straight from the Middle East," *The Tucson Weekly*, April 27, 2000.

17. Interview with Hasan Abd al-Hamid, director of cultural programming, Iraqi satellite channel, Amman, Jordan, September 2002.

18. Interview with Omar Dewachi, graduate student of medical anthropology, Harvard University, Cambridge, MA, November 2002.

19. Mark Bowden, "Tales of the Tyrant," *The Atlantic Monthly*, May 2002.

20. Rory McCarthy, "Baghdad's Dusty Silver Screens," *The Guardian*, November 15, 2002.

21. H. Ditmars, "Frontline—Baghdad—Now Playing at the Iraqi National—Carmen," *The Independent-London*, May 31, 2000, p. 18.

22. Conversation in October 1999 with "Ali," a cameraman who used to work for Iraqi public television. When we met, he was employed at a nonprofit institution in Dubai. He now works for Abu Dhabi Satellite Television.

23. Interview with Omar Dewachi, November 2002.

24. Pellat, "Kass," p. 733b.

25. Notes from BBC Channel 4 TV.

26. The actress is Khawlah Hag-Debsy, a teacher at Nive Shalom, a kibbutz in Israel devoted to fostering peace and understanding. She spoke at a film screening in Brookline, MA in November 2002.

27. Mike Hertenstein, "Revolutionary Cinema: Iranian Filmmakers Continue to Test Boundaries and Upset Expectations." Printed on the Internet: <http://www.flickerings.com/2002/films/iranianfilms.htm>. Accessed February 2003.

28. McCarthy, "Baghdad's Dusty Silver Screens."

Chapter 11: Teachers and Judges of Truth

1. H. Faehendrich, "Al-Tanukhi," J. Sourdel Thomine, "Irak," both in *Encyclopedia of Islam*, vol. 10, electronic edition (Leiden: Brill, 2002), p. 192b.

2. D. S. Margoliouth, trans. Tanukhi, *The Table-Talk of a Mesopotamian Judge* (London: The Royal Asiatic Society, 1922), p. 6.

3. While sitting in the waiting room of the Iraqi embassy in Amman, Jordan, in September 2002, I flipped through a recent

edition of an Iraqi legal journal that bore this quote on the title page. The journal was among paraphernalia available to petitioners to help them pass the time.

4. Iraq Ba'th Party Congress, 1974. Quoted in Delwin Roy, "The Educational System of Iraq," *Middle Eastern Studies*, 29, no. 2 (1993): 168. For a more recent effort to assess the Iraqi educational system based largely on interviews with refugees, see Lene Kofoed Rasmussen, *The System of Education in Iraq* (Copenhagen: The Danish Refugee Council, 1999).

5. Interview with an Iraqi man residing in Cleveland who left Baghdad in 1998. The interview was conducted in December 2002.

6. Ibid.

7. Saddam Hussein, *al-Dimuqratiyya Masdar Quwwah li 'l-Fard wa al-Mujtama* (Baghdad: al-Thawra, 1977), pp. 14–15, 19–21. The quote and source are translated and cited in Kanan Makiya, *Republic of Fear*, p. 78.

8. *al-Jama'ah*.

9. Interview with a Baghdadi scholar who now resides in Amman and works for a Jordanian prince, September 2002.

10. S. H. Amin, *The Legal System of Iraq* (Glasgow, Scotland: Royston, 1989), pp. 47, 73, 76.

11. Interview with Chibli Mallat, November 2002.

12. Amin, *The Legal System of Iraq*, p. 101. The Egyptian jurist was 'Abd al-Razzaq al-Sanhuri.

13. Anthony Cordesman, *Iraq: Sanctions and Beyond*, ed. Ahmed Hashim (Boulder: Westview, 1997), p. 17.

14. See <http://www.jurist.law.pitt.edu/world/iraq.htm>. Accessed February 2003.

15. Telephone interview with Middle East commercial law expert, Howard Stovall, November 2002.

16. Telephone interview with Feisal Istrabadi, November 2002.

17. Telephone interview with Howard Stovall, November 2002.

18. Poonam Gupta, Rachel Kleinfeld, and Gonzalo Salinas, "Legal and Judicial Reform in Europe and Central Asia," World Bank 2002, pp. 13–19.

19. See <http://www1.worldbank.org/publicsector/legal/empirical research.htm>. Accessed February 2003.

20. Telephone interview with Rachel Belton, January 2002.

21. Ibid.

22. H. Faehendrich, "Al-Tanukhi," J. Sourdel Thomine, "Irak," both in *Encyclopedia of Islam*, vol. 10, electronic edition (Leiden: Brill,

2002), p. 192b. It bears noting that scholars do not agree unanimously on the details of Tanukhi's predicament in his final years. What is beyond doubt, however, is that he fell out of favor with the Abbasid court at some point late in life, and that his career as judge, like that of his colleagues, was always subject to the whims of the ruler.

Epilogue

1. *Ethics of the Fathers* (2:16). This saying is attributed to Rabbi Tarfon.
2. al-Kulayni, *al-Kafi*, v. 2, "Bab al-Sabr" ("Chapter on Patience"), Third Edition, Tehran, 1968.
3. Ecclesiastes 1:18.

Author's Biography

28-year-old Joseph Braude is a consultant to governments and corporations on Middle Eastern political, business, and cultural affairs. He is a fluent Arabic, Persian, and Hebrew speaker and a conversant German speaker. His broad network of friends and colleagues among the Arab world's young generation holds particular value in a region where more than 80% of the population is under the age of 30.

Joseph was born in the United States of scholarly and mercantile families. His paternal grandfather was one of the great translators of Babylonian and Palestinian rabbinic texts. His mother, born in Baghdad, hails from the Semah and Aslan families. The Semahs are an ancient seafaring merchant clan that lived in Mesopotamia for more than 2500 years and were one of Baghdad's leading electrical contractors into the early 1950s. The Aslans are a family of teachers and judges that resided in Baghdad for centuries. Joseph is a great-great grandson of Hakham Avraham Aslan, Baghdad's chief rabbi in the 1930s.

He majored in Near Eastern Languages and Civilizations at Yale University and went on to specialize in medieval Arabic and Islamic studies as a graduate student at Princeton. His studies afforded him the opportunity to learn and reside in several Middle Eastern capitals, including Amman, Cairo, Dubai, Riyadh, Tehran, Tel Aviv, and Tunis.

Since September of 2000, Joseph has resided in Cambridge, Massachusetts, where he works as Middle East and North Africa Senior Analyst for Pyramid Research, an advisory and consulting firm that specializes in the communications industry. His research has been quoted in *The New York Times*, *The Wall Street Journal*, and *USA Today*, as well as magazines such as

Talk. He has written many columns on communications technology and business in the Middle East in *Tradeline*, the
newsletter of the US-Arab Chamber of Commerce; *Arab American Business* magazine; and *SiliconIran* magazine. He has also
interviewed in Arabic on the Voice of America Arabic Service
and Radio Liberty / Radio Free Iraq, as well as in Persian on
Radio Liberty / Radio Free Iran. In 2002, he served on a panel of
expert listeners to evaluate the program content and broadcast
style of the daily US broadcast, Radio Free Iraq. He sits on the
board of advisors of the National Iranian American Council.

Joseph occasionally surfaces in Middle Eastern nightclubs
sitting in for the Oud player while singing an Iraqi song or two.
A classically trained jazz pianist, he is also a devotee of Arabic
music who has studied Oud at the Institute of the Musicians
Union in Cairo in 1995 and performed on Egyptian and Syrian
television.

The New Iraq is Joseph's first book.

Acknowledgments

This short book was made possible by many people and institutions. Some helped the project along at every phase, others were the sine qua non for a particular challenge, and the rest have advanced my broader effort to understand Iraq and the Middle East. First thanks go to those whose modesty and circumstances prevent them from accepting public acknowledgment.

Martin Peretz of *The New Republic* supported this project from its beginnings; his prescient comments and advice along the way were a source of constant strength. Vanessa Mobley at Basic Books believed in the book and worked tirelessly to edit and promote it. Her friendship, professionalism, and piercing critical eye have been an inspiration. James Levine was an outstanding literary agent whose diligence and support both reassured and sustained me.

Research assistants Brian Bender, Yoni Braude, Mose Isaac, Jesse Sage, Yusuf Tawfiq Shabot, Julie Tate, Frank Zaromb, and Tally Zingher worked meticulously with me to amass, read, summarize, and collate materials, as well as interview sources. Rachel Belton provided invaluable research and insights on all matters legal and judicial, and Abu 'l-Aynayn made a similar contribution to research on the Iraqi army. The manuscript was scrutinized and improved by all of them—in particular by my brother Yoni, whose attention to detail has always been my best defense—then read carefully by these trusted friends: my uncle Benjamin Braude, Ofra Bengio, Ahmed H. al-Rahim, Ted Rose, Emily Sadigh, Zachary Shrier, Zainab al-Suwaij, and my mother Rita Aslan Semah, a daughter of Baghdad. The book's errors are my own.

The following officials of the Iraqi government gave me the benefit of their perspectives: Sabah Yasin (ambassador of Iraq to Jordan, 2002), Jawad al-Ali (press attaché, Embassy of Iraq, Jordan, 2002), Hasan Abd al-Hamid (director of cultural programming, Iraqi Satellite Television, Baghdad, 2002), Abd al-Sattar al-Ma'ini (Ministry of Transport and Communications, Baghdad, 2002), and "Abu Abdullah" (cultural attaché, Embassy of Iraq, Tehran, 1998). Iraqi refugees and defectors who declined to be named in Saudi Arabia's Rafha camp, Iran, Jordan, Israel, London, and the United States spent long hours with me and my assistants, both in person and over the phone, to offer their perspectives and insights. Abd al-Karim Kazimi of the Islamic *Hawza* in Iran's religious capital, Qom, inspired me to think strategically about ways to break through the artificial barrier that has separated Americans from Iraqis in the interior of the country for so many years, and use the way station of Iraqi Kurdistan's communications network as a listening post. In Jordan, I especially thank Tammara Daghestani, Majdi Kohof, and Issa Matalka for their resourcefulness and diligence in introducing me to valuable Iraqi sources. In London, I thank Dhiya Kashi and Chibli Mallat for their guidance, as well as Rory MacMillan for sharing his experiences in the gritty mechanics of statebuilding. I am indebted to Namir al-Muzaffar at the Arab Thought Forum in Amman and his wife Khulud for their tireless efforts on my behalf and willingness to overlook the petulance of my youth. I also thank current and retired officials of the Jordanian government who have shared poignant insights and recollections over the years, and the Hashemite Kingdom of Jordan for its unflinching tolerance of my efforts. In Cleveland, I thank Ayad al-Rahim and his many friends in the Iraqi refugee community for their friendship and support. In New York, I thank Moctar Cheine for facilitating aspects of the research, Nana Asfour for her encouragement, and Gary Sick for inviting me to join his formidable online community, Gulf2000. In Washington, I thank the staff at Radio Free Iraq and Rend Franke at the Iraq Foundation for their kindness, encouragement, and assistance. In Cambridge, Jessica Gienow-Hecht and her student Harriet Greene shared valuable thoughts on the role of media and people traffic in the evolution of states, James R. Russell provided a brilliant tour of ancient Mesopotamia through history, and Omar Dewachi and Zainab al-Suwaij contributed enormously to my understanding of Iraq in the era of sanctions.

In the private sectors of Bahrain, Egypt, Jordan, Kuwait, Israel, Iran, Iraq, Palestine, Saudi Arabia, Turkey, and the UAE, the following businesspeople have provided valuable data and knowledge of the economics and entrepreneurship of the contemporary Middle East broadly speaking, and in several cases the particulars of the Iraqi economy and Iraqi business culture: Nuri al-Ani, Yusuf Bahlaq, Bilal Fayad, Gil Feiler, Adel Gammuh, Hani al-Jabsheh, Abd al-Rahman Janahi, Karim Kawar, Issa Matalka, Hossam Megahed, Ibrahim Muflih, Sa'd Naji, Hossam Nassar, Ibrahim al-Qadi, Phillip Rosenblatt, and Dina Samir.

At Yale University, Abbas Amanat, Fereshteh Amanat-Kowssar, Ahmed Dallal, Ayala Dvoretsky, Bassam Frangieh, Dimitri Gutas, and Tayyib al-Hibri inducted me into the field of Arabic and Islamic Studies as an undergraduate and provided superior instruction in Arabic, Persian, and Hebrew. In particular, Bassam Frangieh has been a trusted friend and mentor. At Princeton University's Department of Near Eastern Studies, Michael Cook trained me as a graduate student in the professional study of the Near East. Andras Hamori showed me the beauty of tenth- and eleventh-century Arabic prose from Baghdad. Hossein Modarressi instructed me in and embodied the majesty of Islamic law. Avrom Udovitch and Mark Cohen exposed the mystery of Geniza documents and Judeo-Arabic sources. And emeritus professor Bernard Lewis helped me attempt to formulate new hopes for the future of the Middle East through the prism of its rich history, literature, and cultures. This valuable base of enrichment was reinforced by outstanding instructors of language in Tehran, at the Deh Khoda Institute for Persian Language Study, and the Center for Arabic Study Abroad at the American University in Cairo.

The Jum'a 'l-Majid Center for Culture and Heritage in Dubai graciously and spontaneously hosted me as a fellow for the better part of a year in 1999, offering both the benefit of its scholars' erudition and the ideal springboard for a cultural and intellectual tour of the Gulf—and the interplay of Iraqis and locals

within it. I particularly wish to thank Dr. Jasim Muhammad
Jirjees and his family, Dr. Najib Abd al-Wahhab al-Fili, Jum'a
'l-Majid, and Seif al-Ghurair for their unending warmth and hos-
pitality throughout this period.

Teachers and students at the Institute of the Musicians
Union in Abdin, Cairo, in the summer of 1995 not only taught
me how to play the Oud; they also demonstrated through music
and storytelling the enduring legacy of premodern Near Eastern
artistic innovation. Oud virtuosos Yair Dalal and Yusef Ya'qub
Shem Tob, as well as the staff at the Babylonian Jewish Heritage
Center in Or Yehuda, Israel, helped me understand connections
between Iraqi music past and present and its many cultural
antecedents.

Pyramid Research, which employs me as its senior analyst for
the Middle East and North Africa, has provided the most collegial
corporate atmosphere I could wish for. Each in their own way,
Guy Engon Zibi, Denis McCauley, Catherine Forster Connolly,
and Giles Goodhead, have urged me to further my intellectual
interests while creating value for our clients, in effect rewarding
the perpetuation of my eccentricities. The intellectual value of
all my business and entrepreneurial experiences has been
enhanced by provocative conversations with Catholic University
of America scholar Jon Anderson, who leads the Arab Information Project at Georgetown University, and whose examination of
business and information technology in the Middle East through
the lens of cultural anthropology has been an epiphany for me.

Finally, I would like to acknowledge the living memory of
journalist Daniel Pearl, who was murdered in Pakistan in 2002
after a brief lifetime of bringing music, joy, and understanding to
the world. Although we never met, both of us are musicians and
both have maternal roots in Baghdad. I know somehow that he
would have enjoyed hearing about a new Iraq, and count myself
among the legions of young people who regard the infamous circumstances of his death as further motivation to struggle for a
better world.

Index